"Fascinating to read, very v   ..,
an intriguing plot and I enjoyed .. very much."
(Derek Jacobi, star of *I Claudius* and *Gladiator*)

"Vivid characters, devious plotting and buckets of gore
are enhanced by his unfamiliar choice of period.
Nasty, fun and educational."
(*The Daily Telegraph*)

"He knows how to deliver a fast-paced story and his grasp of the period
is impressively detailed."
(*The Mail on Sunday*)

"A rollicking and raunchy read . . . Anyone who enjoys their history with
large dollops of action, sex, intrigue and, above all, fun will absolutely
love this novel."
(*Historical Novels*)

"As always, [his] plotting is as brilliantly devious as the mind of his
sardonic and very earthy hero. This is a story of villainy that reels you in
from its prosaic opening through a series of death-defying thrills and
spills."
(*The Lancashire Evening Post*)

"It would be hard to over-praise this extraordinary series,
a near-perfect blend of historical detail and atmosphere
with the plot of a conspiracy thriller, vivid characters, high philosophy
and vulgar comedy."
(*The Morning Star*)

OTHER BOOKS BY SEAN GABB

Acts of the Apostles: A Parallel Text
Ars Grammatica
The Churchill Memorandum
The Column of Phocas
Cultural Revolution, Culture War
Dispatches from a Dying Country
Freedom of Speech in England
Literary Essays
Radical Coup
Return of the Skolli
Smoking, Class and the Legitimation of Power
Stories from Paul the Deacon
Stories from the Life of Christ
War and the National Interest
The York Deviation

WRITING AS RICHARD BLAKE

Conspiracies of Rome
Terror of Constantinople
Blood of Alexandria
Sword of Damascus
Ghosts of Athens
Curse of Babylon
Game of Empires
Death in Ravenna
Crown of Empire
Death of Rome I
Death of Rome II
The Devil's Treasure
The Boy from Aquileia
The Tyburn Guinea
The Break
How I Write Historical Fiction

Sean Gabb is a writer and teacher whose books have been translated into German, Italian, Spanish, Greek, Hungarian, Slovak and Chinese. He also directs the Centre for Ancient Studies.

VERGIL

THE AENEID

BOOK SIX

LATIN TEXT, WITH AN INTRODUCTION, NOTES, LATIN AND ENGLISH PROSE VERSIONS, AND VOCABULARIES

PREPARED BY SEAN GABB

sit mihi fas audita loqui, sit numine vestro
pandere res alta terra et caligine mersas.

For Radek & Katarina —

Best regards

Sean

CAS

CENTRE FOR ANCIENT STUDIES
DEAL
MMXIX

The Aeneid, Book Six: Latin Text, with an Introduction, Notes, Latin and English Prose Versions, and Vocabularies,
Prepared by Sean Gabb

First edition published in May 2019

© Sean Gabb, 2019

ISBN-13: 9781096888277

Published by:

The Centre for Ancient Studies
73 Middle Street
Deal, Kent CT14 6HN
England

Telephone: 07956 472 199
sean@seangabb.co.uk
www.seangabb.co.uk
www.classicstuition.co.uk

CONTENTS

DEDICATION

I dedicate this book to the memory
of my dear Mother
Hazel Anne Gabb (1937-2019)
Semper Memoranda

ADDRESS TO THE READER

Book VI of *The Aeneid* can be found in many other editions. The purpose of this edition is to make it as available as I can to the widest audience. I think of school students and undergraduate and graduate students throughout the English-speaking world. I think of young people in home education. I think of adults who are learning Latin by themselves, and who would like to read one of its greatest classics.

In this edition, therefore, I offer the following:

- The Latin text in a large and what I hope is an attractive format.
- A full set of notes to explain obscurities in the text.
- A list of all names and places mentioned in the text.
- A vocabulary that includes all the words found in the text.
- A separate vocabulary containing all the words that are used more than about eight times in the text.
- A rewriting of the text as Latin prose.
- A translation of the main text into English prose.

I also try to offer a reasonably full explanation of wider matters than those discussed in the notes. *The Aeneid* can be appreciated in itself as a most remarkable production. But appreciation of a work is always deepened by some knowledge of its context and of the difficulties overcome in its creation. More to the point, this edition of Book VI has been produced as a text for students. If you are one of these, you will be examined. How you will be examined I cannot say. If, though, you are sitting any examination similar to an A-Level in Latin, you will need to show awareness of the circumstances in which *The Aeneid* was written, and what influence these circumstances had on its writing. You will need to show an understanding of its technical underpinning as verse. You may also need to discuss its place in both Roman and then, after the end of Antiquity, in Latin literature.

All this being said, I pass to the main part of my Address.

The Life of Vergil

Publius Vergilius Maro, known interchangeably in English as Vergil or Virgil, was born on the 15th October 70 BC in Andes, a village about

28 miles from Mantua. Now in Northern Italy, Mantua at this time was a city in Cisalpine Gaul. This territory was incorporated into Italy only in 42 BC, though its free inhabitants had been granted full Roman citizenship in 49 BC. There is much doubt regarding Vergil's background. According to Macrobius, one of the ancient commentators, his father was in humble circumstances. This is unlikely, bearing in mind that Vergil received a long and elaborate education, and education was not free, and there is no evidence of the gratitude we might expect to see in his works had this been paid for by some wealthy patron. It is more likely that he was born into a minor landed family. This being so, he may have descended from Roman or Italian colonists. Little evidence for the Vergilius family, though, is attested in the surviving inscriptions.

He attended schools in Cremona, Milan, Rome and Naples. Here, he received the education standard among the higher classes in the Greek classics and in such Roman literature as had by this time been created. He particularly studied Rhetoric, Medicine and Astronomy. According to Servius, another of the commentators, he was notoriously shy, both among the other students and throughout his adult life. He is also said to have suffered consistently poor health, with pains in his head and stomach, and a tendency to spit blood. After briefly considering a career in the Law, he settled on poetry—some evidence here for shyness and ill-health, and much for a family of independent means.

He may have written his earliest works while a student in Naples, when he seems to have come under Epicurean influence. He may, in Rome, have fallen under the influence of the New Poetry Movement, which we know mainly in connection with Catullus, and which I will discuss later. But his first known and major work is *The Eclogues*, which he began in 42 BC and published three or four years later. This is a poem in ten books, or a group of ten poems, that comments on general issues under cover of praising a rural life. It is said to have been composed as a petition for the return of some family property confiscated to pay off the soldiers in the civil war that Octavian and Antony had fought against the assassins of Julius Caesar. But this is only an inference from the contents of the poem.

His next major work, *The Georgics*, Vergil composed under the patronage of Maecenas, who was effectively Minister of Culture in the new *régime* established by Octavian. The poem is, in its outward form, a treatise on farming. As with *The Eclogues*, though, it deals cautiously and by implication with many other issues. It was considered a great success in Latin poetry, and Vergil and Maecenas are said to have taken turns in reading it to Octavian on his return from defeating Antony in the last civil war.

The Aeneid: An Unrevised Draft

His last and greatest work, *The Aeneid*, he composed under a direct commission from Octavian, by now renamed Augustus. This is a long and elaborate epic in twelve books that tells the story of how, fleeing from the sack of Troy, Aeneas reached Italy, where he founded a new nation from which the Romans were descended. The poem is deliberately modelled on Homer, and part of its intention was to do for Latin what the Homeric Poems had done for Greek—this being to make it into a first class language of literature. Another part of its intention was to legitimise the rule of Augustus and the new order of things that he had created in the Mediterranean World.

Vergil worked slowly, composing, it is said, only three lines a day. After twelve years of labour, the poem was left unrevised. Some books appear to have been in a more complete state than others. We are told that Vergil read Book VI at a dinner party attended by Augustus and his family. Bearing in mind his shyness, and bearing in mind the great acclaim for the reading, we can assume that this book was at least substantially complete. But this is no more than an assumption, and we know little about the composition of the rest. We can agree that Vergil did not write his three lines a day, before moving to the next, and never going back. There is too much consistency in what we have. It is more likely that the completion in draft of one section inspired running changes in the earlier sections. Completion in whole of its draft, though, is not completion of a work. There are fifty-seven unfinished lines in *The Aeneid*. If some critics insist that these are short for dramatic effect, I am not convinced. Also, the last six books are of variable quality in terms of narrative and the drawing of character. Even the first six contain oddities that may be explained by clever interpretation—or can, more easily, be taken as evidence of first thoughts undeveloped or privately marked for replacement.

A Sudden Death

The story of his death indicates that what we have is an interrupted work in progress. In 20 BC, having completed the draft of *The Aeneid* more or less as we have it, Vergil travelled through Greece for a long holiday. He intended, after this, to spend three years on revising the

3

work. He met Augustus in Athens, where they spent time together. He then set out alone on the sea voyage home to Italy. His health finally broke down during a stay in Megara, and collapsed altogether on the last stretch of the voyage. He died on the 22nd September 19 BC, shortly after arriving at Brindisi. He was at the time forty-eight.

His last instructions were for the manuscript of *The Aeneid* to be destroyed. It may be that, shy to the end, he no longer believed he had produced the work of supreme genius that everyone else was expecting it to be. Or it may be that something in his last meeting with Augustus had brought a fundamental change of mind about the moral value of the work. Or it may simply be that, as the author, he was more sensible of its defects than anyone else has ever been. All we know is that, arriving in Brindisi shortly after the death, Augustus cancelled these instructions, and he ordered that the poem should be edited with minimal changes and published without delay. It was received at once, and ever after, as the greatest achievement in Roman poetry. It stands, with the Homeric Poems, with *The Divine Comedy*, and with *Paradise Lost*, as one of the greatest of all epic poems. Its influence on the Western mind has been great and profound.

The Circumstances of *The Aeneid*

Here, though, we move away from the scanty and unreliable details of biography to the wider circumstances of the text. Vergil wrote at a specific moment in Roman history; and he wrote, it is commonly agreed, for a specific purpose. One age had passed away—perhaps a series of ages had passed away—and a new was beginning. This new age needed to be explained and justified. If there is no book of *The Aeneid* from which *apologia* is absent, Book VI makes little sense without understanding the historical progress it explains and seeks to justify. We move, then, to an account of this progress.

Rome: From Republic to Empire

As it developed between the extinction of the Monarchy and the beginning, in 264 BC, of the wars with Carthage, Rome possessed a form of government that was both stable and perceived as legitimate. The Senate, its most powerful institution, was an assembly dominated by a landed nobility with strong military traditions. Executive power was in the hands of magistrates mainly drawn from senatorial families, though more or less chosen by the people. Much legislative power was directly in the hands of popular assemblies. Politics were not always a matter of consensus. There had been a long and bitter dispute between the nobility and the people. But this dispute was conducted within the bounds of the Constitution, and the Romans prided themselves on both their political moderation and their regard for the public good. Political authority derived immediately from fitness as shown by election and then by success. It derived ultimately from how its exercise accorded with a set of traditions that reached back to the divine origins of Rome itself.

Observing the Republic before its decay had visibly begun, Polybius contrasts its ruling class with the faithless, light-fingered counterparts in the Greek world. Indeed, where keeping faith and the public good are concerned, it stands comparison with the Greeks in the best ages of their history.

The wars with Carthage began a slow undermining of the Constitution. These wars lasted for decades at a time. They were expensive both in lives and in property. The second of them was fought mainly on Italian soil. But victory caused more damage than the wars. The first war ended in 241 BC, with Rome in possession of Sicily, and then of Sardinia. The second ended in 201 BC, with Rome dominant in the Western Mediterranean. By the end of the third, in 146 BC, Rome was supreme from one end of that sea to the other, and directly or indirectly in charge of its various hinterlands. The Roman Constitution worked well for an agricultural city-state. It worked for the head of a loose federation in Central Italy. It was as unsuited to the capital of a large and growing empire as it was to the empire as a whole.

The Poison of Unearned Wealth

Commercial wealth must be earned, and brings its own restraints. The enrichment that followed these conquests was based on plunder and then on tribute. Successful generals came back from the wars loaded with gold. Following earlier and less harmful precedents, City magistrates would complete their terms of office and then be sent out to govern the new territories. They also came back rich. Elective magistracies that offered little in themselves beyond prestige and a sense of duties performed became the key to riches beyond imagination. Bribery of electors became the rule. Competing embassies from the East were at all times in Rome, adding to the general corruption with lavish bribery of the powerful.

A gulf opened between the classes greater than had ever been known. Small farming, already hit by Hannibal's invasion of Italy, was now ruined by purchases and rentals of land that often amounted to theft, and its consolidation into immense plantations worked by slaves. Long military service overseas, plus the sale at cost price of food requisitioned from Sicily, disrupted the working of those smallholdings that were left untouched. The dispossessed poured into Rome, where they lived on a meagre public dole, or attached themselves as troublesome clients to the rich. The growing magnificence of the buildings in Rome was matched by the descent of its streets into a battleground of noble factions, all desperate for electoral success.

For the more civilised provinces outside Italy, things may have gone better than the history books often claim. There were acts of collective brutality—the sack of Corinth in 146 BC, for example. Gaius Verres was not the only rapacious governor. The Romans were seldom generous in the matter of assessing tribute. Beyond this, however, Rome offered solid benefits to its new subjects. The later successors of Alexander were sometimes insane and frequently incompetent. They had never lived at peace with each other. If Rome demanded tribute, it also gave peace for long periods, plus a reasonably honest administration, so that wealth could be created at least as fast as it was drained. But success only contributed to the growing problems in Rome. As with oil money in the Middle East, every fresh injection of non-commercial wealth was another dose of poison.

The Collapse of Order

After 133 BC, the noble brothers Gaius and Tiberius Gracchus tried to address these problems by constitutional means. Their project was to break up the larger plantations and recreate Italy as a land of yeoman farmers. The Empire would not be abandoned, nor its peoples raised to any equality of status. Instead its proceeds would be shared more evenly among the whole body of Roman citizens. If moderate by our own standards, the project of reform was resisted with such force by those who would lose from it that, for the first time, the Constitution broke down. The new oligarchs took up arms, and each brother was in turn killed or driven to suicide. Rome settled in to an uneasy peace lubricated by a more regular welfare to sedate the poor.

The next plan of reform came at the turn of the century with Gaius Marius, a successful general who had improved and enlarged the Army. This resulted in a formal civil war that was won by Lucius Cornelius Sulla, the military head of the wealthy. After 80 BC, he ruled as Dictator, killing and confiscating the property of his opponents. He also rolled back the surviving reforms of the Gracchi, strengthening the Senate at the expense of the popular assemblies. After his death in 78 BC, many of these changes were undone, and Rome went back to uneasy peace in which two semi-regular parties of populists and oligarchs competed for supremacy in the State.

It was now that Cicero rose to prominence. A weak and shifty politician, he sided with the oligarchs, while pleading for a "union of all good men" to settle their constitutional disputes by compromise. He had little influence on Pompey, who now took Sulla's place as the military defender of the rich, and none on Julius Caesar, who sided with the poor. His importance to later generations has lain in his status as perhaps the greatest writer of Latin prose, and in the survival of nearly all he wrote, and of little else by his contemporaries, so that we are forced to look at Roman politics through his eyes. His abilities as a writer almost blind us to his quasi-legal suppression of a populist revolt, and his possible commissioning of Milo to kill their populist opponent Clodius.

After an attempt at compromise, irreconcilable differences between Pompey and Caesar led to another civil war in 49-48 BC. Caesar won this and returned to Rome as sole ruler of the City and its empire. By now, the Constitution was a heap of rubble. Its only workable replacement was some species of absolute monarchy that would govern the Empire as a single unit, securing the rich, but treating them as one interest group among many.

The Failure of Caesarism

Though a very great man, Caesar lacked political imagination. He knew how to gain supreme power. He knew how to use it. He failed to see how power could be made into legitimate authority. No one could deny him the title of Dictator for Life. But he was now in advanced years as this was reckoned in all ages before our own. His relationship with Queen Cleopatra of Egypt, and the birth of their son, indicated a wish to found a ruling dynasty. If so, his personal collection of republican magistracies was no basis for a permanent scheme of rule. The only title he seems to have thought appropriate was that of King. If the Constitution was dead, the prejudice against undisguised monarchy was not. The oligarchs took their stand on constitutional propriety. Few populists appear to have been ready for so radical a break with tradition. Caesar also allowed the rumour to circulate that he saw Alexandria as a better capital than Rome of a Mediterranean empire with the balance of its wealth and population in the East. In March 44 BC, he was murdered in the Senate House.

After brief hopes of a restored Constitution, there was a new civil war. This time, Mark Antony, Caesar's main deputy, and Octavian—or Gaius Octavius Thurinus—Caesar's great-nephew and nominated heir, combined to defeat the assassins. Part of their agreement was a long death-list that included the elderly Cicero. He was hunted through Italy, and killed, and his head and hands were put on show in the Forum.

Since Octavian was only nineteen, and was without prior experience in political or military affairs, Antony assumed that he would be Caesar's true heir. Octavian, though, was a man of hidden talents. Once the civil war was won, the Empire was effectively divided between East and West, Antony ruling from Alexandria with Cleopatra as his wife, and Octavian from Rome. A decade of cold war ended in yet another civil war. Octavian won this at Actium in 31 BC, after which he was more supreme than Caesar had ever been—more supreme because the passing of time and the killing of opponents had blurred still further memory of a functioning republic.

The Augustan Settlement

It was now that Octavian showed an undeniable creative genius. Imagine a breakdown of our own constitution in England, and a series of civil wars. You win these and rule for a while as a military dictator. You then announce a return to constitutional government. You restore the old electoral machinery, and appoint ministers responsible to Parliament. The only change you make is that you are to be Prime Minister, Lord Chancellor, Speaker of the House of Commons, Archbishop of Canterbury, Director-General of the BBC, a non-executive director of every big company—oh, and commander in chief of the armed forces. You are all of these things for life. That is pretty well what Octavian did in Rome.

After a final purge of his opponents, he called a meeting of the Senate in January 27 BC. Here, he handed all his unusual powers back to "the Senate and People of Rome." In return, he was granted various civil and religious magistracies, or their equivalents, that raised him above the laws and gave him a formal veto over new laws. He also retained control of the armies, and the uncountable wealth of Egypt was confirmed as his personal estate. He then claimed to have restored the Ancient Constitution, with himself as nothing more than its temporary First Citizen, and with his new name of Augustus. There was no mention of kinship—no crown, or crowds of eunuch functionaries, or strip-searches of visitors; nor any suggestion of moving the capital to some other place, where the traditions of the Republic could be openly or insensibly retired.

Of course, the restoration was a fraud. The Empire was ruled by Augustus and a small cabinet of his wife and a few friends, its administration conducted through a growing bureaucracy of freed slaves. All this was underwritten by command of the armies. So long as he kept these on side, he was as absolute a ruler as any Greek tyrant. He could do anything he liked to anyone. If he chose not to continue behaving as he had, that was purely his choice based on good sense. There was no other restraint on his power. The Senate was a rubber stamp. The traditional magistracies were filled by his nominees. Because the one formal change made by Augustus was to raise the status of his rubber-stamp Senate, by transferring legislative power to it from the popular assemblies, the people at large had no authoritative voice. He died in advanced old age, in 14 AD. All his "temporary" powers were then granted to his chosen successor. Rome had passed, without any hope of reaction, from a Republic with provinces attached to an Empire ruled by an Emperor.

But there are frauds that no one cares to believe. Such was the settlement attempted by Caesar. And there are frauds that most people want to believe, and almost everyone agrees to believe. Such was the Augustan Settlement. Everyone got something. The surviving rich kept their property. The Roman poor got bread and circuses. The provincials got a return to peace and honest government. Conservatives could believe that everything was back as it had been, or was going there. Given their bread and circuses, the Roman poor gave up on populist radicalism. Nostalgia for the Republic was tolerated as a purely literary device. But most people appear to have looked at the chaos of the previous generations, and thanked whatever higher power they worshipped for the peace and modest economic expansion of the present.

Augustus went out of his way to make the new order of things acceptable. At nineteen, he was quite as ruthless as Antony and their minor partner Lepidus in drawing up that death-list. After winning at Actium, he arrived in Alexandria to finish with Antony and Cleopatra. Finding them dead by suicide, he finished the work by having Caesarion, Cleopatra's son by Caesar, hunted down and put to death. Though the boy was only thirteen, there was room in the New Order of

Things for one Caesar only. Once firmly in charge, Augustus spent the last forty years of his life playing Jolly Uncle to everyone in sight. Out of sight, in the Eastern Provinces, he was worshipped as a god.

The Return of Legitimacy

So far as it is based on force and fraud, every government has need of what the Marxist Louis Althusser called a *repressive state apparatus* and an *ideological state apparatus*. It needs both a mailed fist to keep control, and a velvet glove to hide the mailed fist and to make its use a less immediate option. Augustus had his legions. He had his armed guard inside Rome. He was also, working with Maecenas, a master of legitimisation. He would not be another Gracchus or Marius, trying to pull down the Old Order. He would not be another Sulla, forcing the poor back into their slums at spear point. He would not be another Caesar, trying to build a New Order that had no Roman precedent. He would not be a strong man, holding irreconcilable forces in a temporary balance. He was instead Augustus—the New Romulus, the Second Founder, The Restorer. He probably believed it. The best lies are uttered by those who believe them.

Self-consciously, he clothed himself in the Roman past. He revived the Secular Games in 17 BC, celebrating them for the first time in more than a century. He built new temples. He venerated the Gods. He consulted the Sibylline Books on all the proper occasions. He paid careful respect to the traditional magistrates and to the Senate. He discouraged public immorality, even exiling his own daughter for adultery. He showed his wife working at a loom—when she was not running his empire for him, or poisoning his friends and relatives. He welcomed Livy's immense *History*, which revived public interest in the past. He presided over a golden age of Roman literature—Livy, Horace, Ovid, Propertius, Tibullus, and, above all, Vergil.

The Aeneid as Legitimising Propaganda

The best legitimising ideology is one that not only shows the present as better than the past, but shows the present happy state as having grown inevitably out of the past. This is the overarching theme of *The Aeneid*. So far as he revived awareness in the Roman past, and showed the rewards of traditional virtue and the punishments of vice, Livy was useful to Augustus. But he takes an entirely conventional view of the past as better than the present, which is an age of moral decay—a time "when we can bear neither our vices nor their remedy." Vergil takes

10

the revolutionary step of locating the Golden Age in the present. For him, the Roman past is not a story of growth followed by decline, but a steady upward climb. It is an upward climb to the reign of Augustus.

A crude propagandist would have composed or commissioned an *Augustiad*, in which its hero was placed inescapably at the centre and continuously heaped with lavish praise. *The Aeneid* is set in the distant past. In his first book, Livy tells the story of Aeneas, but passes rapidly to what he sees as the more important and interesting Romulus, who had founded the City and given it his name. Vergil instead focusses wholly on Aeneas, placing Romulus in the crowd of other worthies.

Aeneas is a man who faces a total collapse of order. Troy has been taken and burned by the Greeks, its people killed or led off into slavery. On the direct order of Venus, his mother, he flees the disaster, holding his son by the hand and carrying his aged father on his back. Leading a small band of other survivors, he sets out by ship in search of a place where he can found a new city. He is not an obvious or an attractive hero. Compared with Achilles or Odysseus, or even the minor characters in Homer, he is a shadowy figure. But he is the embodiment of every Roman virtue. He is brave and loyal. He is carefully obedient to every command of the Gods. He obeys Venus in Book II, when his ordinary duty is to stay in Troy and fight to the end. He obeys Mercury in Book IV, when both interest and secular duty tell him to stay with Dido in Carthage. In Book VI, he follows the command of his father's ghost, and visits the Underworld—a place of horrors from which few have returned. In Italy, he must unite with the Arcadians. He must fight with Mezentius and Turnus before he can unite with the Latins. At all times, he faces overpowering odds or an easier alternative. At all times, he presses forward with the duty placed on him by the Gods. His efforts culminate in victory and the origin of the Roman People.

Augustus is Aeneas. He too has faced the dissolution of an established order. He too, through Caesar, his adopted and deified father, is the son of a god. He too, through an unwavering belief in what is right, and by duty to and help from the Gods, has struggled forward to victory and established a new order of things.

Augustus: Imperator Deorum Gratia

The catalogue of heroes given in Book VI has its immediate purpose for Aeneas to show the long race he is to beget and their glories. For its earliest audience, the purpose was to emphasise the connections of past and present. Augustus is not only Aeneas in some poetic and

11

metaphorical sense. It is not enough that they both show devotion to the Gods and to their country. They are also connected by lines of descent—lines of descent that reach further back and wider. Aeneas is the son of Venus. He is the ancestor of Romulus, who is a son of Mars. Romulus is the ancestor of Julius Caesar, who is also a god. Augustus, by the rite of adoption, is the son of Caesar. As such, he is the descendant of Aeneas and the Gods. By the fact of his reign, the past and present are tightly bound together.

In the first and most obvious sense, Augustus owed his power to victory in the last civil war. His moderation as supreme ruler then conferred working legitimacy. The effect of *The Aeneid*, and particularly of Book VI, made power and working legitimacy into long-term authority. Before the founding of the City—before even the arrival of Aeneas in Latium—that authority had been decreed by the Gods.

Though present by implication in many places, Augustus is mentioned by name three times in *The Aeneid*. In Book I, Jupiter prophesies that Aeneas will triumph over his enemies, and establish a line that will found Rome, which in turn will enjoy dominion unlimited by place or time. See lines 278-79:

> his ego nec metas rerum nec tempora pono
> imperium sine fine dedi....

At last, in lines 286-88:

> nascetur pulchra Troianus origine Caesar,
> imperium Oceano, famam qui terminet astris

The name is *Caesar*, not *Augustus*. But the following lines make it clear which member of the family is intended. Caesar never established peace in the Empire and closed the doors of the Temple of Janus. He never ended the years of bitterness.

In Book VIII, the description of the Shield of Aeneas explains the Battle of Actium and the divinely-ordained victory of Rome over the East. This is not only a military victory. The gods of both sides take part. The Roman gods prevail. They wanted Augustus to win. They want him to reign as a new kind of monarch.

At last, we have Book VI. At the end of his catalogue of Roman heroes, Anchises comes to its highest point—lines 791-98:

> hic vir, hic est, tibi quem promitti saepius audis,
> Augustus Caesar, divi genus, aurea condet

12

saecula qui rursus Latio regnata per arva
Saturno quondam, super et Garamantas et Indos
proferet imperium; iacet extra sidera tellus, 795
extra anni solisque vias, ubi caelifer Atlas
axem umero torquet stellis ardentibus aptum.

Augustus is the son of a god. He is another Saturn, who will restore the Golden Age. He will carry the bounds of empire to the edges of the world. His reign was decreed at the beginning. All else in Roman history has been directed towards it. He has not overthrown tradition, but completed it. To oppose him is not foolish, bearing in mind his command of the armies. It is not wrong, bearing in mind his settlement of all disputes. It would be a treason against the whole march of Roman history—a kind of sacrilege.

The Two Gates of Sleep

Against this interpretation, we have a troubling alternative. I have described Aeneas as shadowy and unattractive. He is very often the latter. He is not always brave, nor brave, nor determined, nor chaste, nor loyal, His treatment of Dido is hard to justify. He effectively seduces here in Book IV. He moves in with her. Then then dumps her without bothering to explain himself in terms other than a divorce lawyer might use. His killing of Turnus in Book XII is also hard to justify. He has beaten down the proud—but there is no sparing of the beaten. Here is not *pietas*, but only *furor*. Is it possible that Vergil is showing Aeneas as corrupted by power? He could find many instances in his own memory of Augustus as other than Jolly Uncle.

Perhaps this interpretation fails to take account of the large differences between us and the Ancients of what was expcted of a hero. On the other hand, a certain regard for the suffering of others is hardly lacking from *The Aeneid*. Beyong a few occasional and conventional expressions of pity, it does seem lacking in Aeneas.

Or we have the Two Gates of Sleep—one of ivory, one of horn. Through the horn true dreams come into the world. Through the ivory come false dreams. Right at the end of Book VI, with all the stirring predictions of future greatness still echoing, Anchises and the Sibyl take Aeneas through the Gate of Ivory. Is this a lapse in the narrative? As said, *The Aeneid* was left unfinished, and there are oddities. Or is Vergil dismissing the Augustan Settlement as yet another false hope?

His general view of the human state is bleak. We all end on the outer bank of the River Styx, begging to be ferried across. You can be a great hero, or in the prime of life. You can be a little girl or boy. Called away from life, you join the democracy of those holding out their hands for love of the farther bank. Those not given the proper funeral rites flitter about as ghosts of a hundred years. Those who do get across face an eternity of regret. A lucky few make it to the Elysian Fields. There, they are stripped of personal identity and made ready for another life that will end on that same outer bank. The exceptionally wicked are allowed to keep their personal identity, so they can be tortured for ever.

The Gods are not just or merciful. The world they rule is a place of violence and betrayal. Goodness has no automatic reward. Divine promises may be kept, or may be kept in ways that amount to deception. Palinurus was assured by Apollo he would not drown on the voyage to Sicily. Instead, he was suffered to be swept overboard and killed after he swam ashore. He complains. He begs to be taken from the Underworld. The Sibyl tells him in line 376:

> desine fata deum flecti sperare precando

Why should we suppose that a few military victories and an apparent tranquillity in the present will amount to any sort of Golden Age? Vergil knew Augustus. He had seen the purges. He was clever enough to see through the sham of the Augustan Settlement. Only his own usefulness as a propagandist had saved him from being kicked penniless off whatever property he had inherited. Sooner or later, Augustus would die. Then the civil wars might begin again. Just as easily, there would be a new Emperor. No one could predict in detail the tyranny of Caligula and Nero. It would take much more than a century for the Empire to complete its transformation into the union of a bureaucratic state and a class of landed parasites, both sucking wealth from a hundred million disarmed serfs. But Vergil could read the past, and it took no genius to think the future, though with a varied mix of horrors, would be the same as the past. Out goes Aeneas through the ivory gate. *Imperium sine fine* there might be. There was and would be no Golden Age.

A Reservation

This is a possible interpretation. Given a relevant question, it is something that needs to be raised in an examination essay. But it stands against the whole weight of *The Aeneid* as we have it and the circumstances of its writing. The poem is notable not only for its glorying of Augustus mostly by implication, but also for the gentleness of its nationalism and its lack of party spirit. Livy can often find something to admire in the enemies of Rome—see his portrait of Hannibal near the beginning of Book XXXI. But he admires them only to show how great the Romans were in defeating them. This is a device that Vergil never uses.

Of course, the Romans are the Lords of Creation. The Gods have decreed for them Empire without End, and Augustus as their ruler. But other peoples are not denigrated. The Greeks have taken and burned Troy. It is right that they should later be conquered by Rome. But they are not villains. They and the Trojans are part of the same civilisation, worshipping the same gods. In Book VIII, Aeneas makes a tight alliance with the Arcadians, a Greek people living on the site where Rome was later to be built. He makes this alliance by explaining how he and Evander, their King, share a common descent. In Book VI, Anchises goes out of his way to concede primacy to the Greeks in all the arts and sciences.

Vergil is even sympathetic to the Carthaginians. They are the greatest enemy Rome has ever faced. But they are shown as welcoming the Trojans. Dido takes Aeneas to her bed, and her later madness is entirely due to her being under a divine spell. We feel sorry for her in Book IV. We think little of Aeneas for what he fails to say to her in Book VI. This may be less a coded attack on Augustus than human sympathy.

Where party spirit is concerned, Antony cannot be treated sympathetically. The last civil war is too close in time. But the Roman kings and those who overthrew them stand peacefully together in the Catalogue of Heroes. So too the Scipios and the Gracchus brothers. So too Pompey and Caesar. If Sulla is missing, that is probably because of his bloody purge.

The past in *The Aeneid* is seen as a continuous chain, every link in which is essential to the present happy state of affairs. Because Augustus has reconciled every people and every interest, all that happened then was really for the best. Alive, they took different sides in the dispute that ended the Republic. Seen from the present, Caesar and Pompey had been working towards the same end.

Because all is now reconciled, the Romans are able to bring their main contribution to humanity—this being, in line 853,

parcere subiectis et debellare superbos

The Romans have been given Empire without End, and Augustus to Rule it. The Gods have given these things in order to bring on a universal rule of peace and justice. It is arguable that Vergil had been commissioned to produce a work of propaganda, and that he made his own views clear in subtextual asides and apparent oddities. Even so, the propaganda is of a quality that compels attention in its own right.

A Guide to Latin Scansion

The Aeneid is a poem. It is composed in a form that was originally alien to Latin, and which places strict limits on how Latin can be written. Vergil's achievement was to move these limits into the background. Part of the reason we admire a tightrope dancer is that he can move at all without falling off. Much earlier Latin verse is to be admired for the same reason. Vergil allows us to forget the rope and focus on the movements of the dancer. To see this, we need to discuss the rules of Latin scansion and what may have been their desired effect.

Perhaps the shortest and the clearest way to explain how Latin verse works is to begin with English. It allows us to move from something that everyone already understands, or can understand, to something that is not understood. The poetic rules of each language are radically different. For English verse, though, the tradition has long been to use terms of description borrowed from Latin. Since we are fully at home with our own language, and can directly hear its poetic rules in action, these terms of analysis will be less abstract than they might be if applied straight to Latin.

The Nature of English Verse

Let us take these lines by A.E. Housman:

> From Clee to heaven the beacon burns,
>   The shires have seen it plain,
> From north and south the sign returns
>   And beacons burn again.
>
> Look left, look right, the hills are bright,
>   The dales are light between,
> Because 'tis fifty years to-night
>   That God has saved the Queen.
>
> Now, when the flame they watch not towers
>   About the soil they trod,
> Lads, we'll remember friends of ours
>   Who shared the work with God....

The lines are of eight and six syllables, alternating. Each line can be broken down into groups of syllables, or *feet*. The nature of its feet determines its sound, or *metre*. In these lines, the feet are generally iambic—that is, a foot contains two syllables, the second of which is stressed. By stress I mean that a syllable is spoken with greater force. See, for example:

> The shíres | have séen | it pláin

Note how the accented vowels mark the stress of their syllables. In the whole of this discussion acute accents mark stress only, not any other quality a vowel or syllable may have.

Note how the accented syllables are not only stressed, but often contain longer vowels than those in the other syllables. In English, there is a tendency for stress and length to coincide. But this is only a tendency. There are many exceptions—*however*, for example, where the first vowel is long, but the second vowel, though short, carries the stress. See also line 7 above—*they tród*—where *trod* is stressed, but shorter than *they*. Length, or *quantity*, is something taken into account by a competent poet in English. But the main organising principle is stress. Accent in English is primarily one of stress.

Note how the feet given above are marked by dividing lines. If we are to mark feet in a line containing words of more than one syllable, the clearest method is to put the dividing lines above the line of verse. We may also choose to mark the accented syllables above the line. This gives us the following:

> x | x | x | x
> Lads, we'll remember friends of ours

Note how a single consonant at the end of a syllable is taken as the start of the next syllable, and how two consonants are split, so that the first is taken as closing the preceding syllable and the second as opening the next. Though mostly irrelevant in English, because generally not perceived, this rule is of great importance in Latin.

So they can fit into their iambic scheme, some liberty is allowed for the contraction of syllables. Thus, *heaven* in line 1 is contracted to *heav'n* and *towers* in line 9 is contracted to *tow'rs*. This gives the following rhythmic pattern:

> From Clée to héav'n the béacon búrns,
> The shíres have séen it pláin,

> From nórth and sóuth the sign réturns
> And béacons búrn agáin.

There are secondary patternings. The **first** is that a completely regular patterning, especially in a longer poem, produces a monotonous effect. This is countered by occasionally reversing the pattern. See how line 7 begins with a trochaic foot—that is, the first syllable is stressed and the second unstressed:

> Nów, when the fláme they wátch not tów'rs

The **second** is that lines are end-stopped—that is, the end of each line coincides with the end of a grammatical clause. The **third** is that lines are of differing length. This allows the second line in each group of two to continue whatever idea is contained in the first in a more compressed form. It also allows for more or less regular breaks, or audible pauses, within each line. In the eight-syllable lines, you will see that, because most English words are of not more than two syllables, there is a tendency for the line to break into separated groups of four syllables. Thus:

> From Clee to heaven ‖ the beacon burns

> From north and south ‖ the sign returns

> Look left, look right, ‖ the hills are bright

> Now, when the flame ‖ they watch not towers

Unvaried, this would again produce a monotonous effect. A competent poet, therefore, will insert occasional word bridges that tie these groups together:

> Because 'tis {fif ‖ ty} years to-night

> Lads, we'll {remem ‖ ber} friends of ours

There is then either no break, or the break will be shifted from after the fourth to after the third or fifth syllables. In the six-syllable lines, there is a tendency to a break after the fourth syllable. Given a competent handling, though, of the eight-syllable lines, this is not important; and the break can be moved back one or two syllables, or eliminated.

The last secondary patterning is the rhyme. Lines of equal length are tied together by rhyming ends. Rhyme is not a fixed requirement in English verse. Most of Milton and Shakespeare do not rhyme. It does, however, give a further recognisable shape to verse, and it often places a useful constraint on a writer to think about the words he is using.

The Nature of Quantitative Verse

This overview of English being given, we turn to Latin verse. As said, this operates on radically different principles. Feet are patterns not of stressed and unstressed, but of long and short syllables. Latin poetry is *quantitative*. Rhyme is of minor importance, and is usually seen within lines. There is much less tendency for lines to be end-stopped. Within a line, a break, or *caesura*, is much more likely to be seen inside a foot, rather than at its end. Unlike in English, there is a regular scheme of elision.

Unless otherwise stated, all words and lines given below in Latin are taken from Book VI of *The Aeneid*.

Long and Short Syllables

In Latin, all vowels are either long or short. Long vowels can be marked thus: $\bar{a}, \bar{e}, \bar{\imath}, \bar{o}, \bar{u}$. Short vowels can be marked thus: $\breve{a}, \breve{e}, \breve{\imath}, \breve{o}, \breve{u}$. An example of $\bar{a}$ in English is *father*, and of $\breve{a}$ is *cap*. An example of $\bar{e}$ is *bear*, and of $\breve{e}$ is *red*. Because they are always long, diphthongs—*æ, au, ei, eu, œ, ui*—are not marked. Long signs alone——are used in dictionaries to show the quantity of words. They are also used in basic texts, produced for learners, to show the correct pronunciation. Because all vowels not marked as long can be taken as short by default, short signs——are only used for the analysis of verse, or where some particular clarity is required.

Note that these marks indicate length, never stress. If there is a relationship in Latin between length and stress, it is not automatically the case that long vowels are stressed.

Syllables also are long or short. A syllable is *long by nature* if it contains a vowel that itself is long. Take the second word of line 1— *fātŭr*. The first syllable is long by nature, because its vowel, *a*, is long. The second is short by nature because the *u* is short.

A syllable is *long by position* if it contains a short vowel, but this is followed by two consonants. Thus, *fātŭr* becomes *fātūr* in line 1 because the syllable *u* is followed by the *l* of *lacrimans*. This not to say that the final vowel *u* is lengthened. The vowel itself remains short. It

19

is the syllable as a whole that is lengthened by position.

Two consonants do not need to be in the same word for a syllable to be lengthened. A syllable also becomes long by position if closed by a doubled consonant. This is not so in English, where the spelling of *tapper* shows that the first syllable is short, while the first syllable in *taper* is long. In Latin, doubled consonants are pronounced separately, and lengthen preceding syllables that are otherwise short. Thus, the *u* at the beginning of *suppostaque* in line 24 is short, but its syllable becomes long by position because of the doubled *p*.

There are apparent exceptions to this rule. Regardless of whether its vowel is long or short, a syllable followed by *x* or *z* is always long. Syllables followed by combinations, within the same word, of *ch*, *ph*, *th*, *qu*, and sometimes *gu* and *su*, are usually short. So are syllables followed—again within the same word—by combinations of *b*, *c*, *d*, *g*, *p*, *t* or *p* with *l* or *r*.

But these are not exceptions. *x* is a single letter for two sounds—*k* and *s*. *z* in Latin is also a single letter for the two sounds *d* and *s*, or *s* and *d*. *l* and *r*, are soft consonants, and are taken as binding so tightly to a preceding hard consonant that they can amount to single sounds.

Elision of Vowels

I turn to the rules of elision. Though exceptions are allowed, a vowel at the end of one word that is followed by a word beginning with another vowel is not sounded. Thus *classique inmittit* in line 1 becomes *classiqu' inmittit*. In line 7, *abstrusa in venis* becomes *abstrus' in venis*.

h at the beginning of a next word does not shield a preceding final vowel. Thus, in line 31, *Icare, haberes* becomes *Icar', haberes*. This is because h was often not sounded, and hardly ever taken as *having position*. It is the same with final *m*. Thus, in line 2, *tandem Euboicis* and *Cumarum adlabitur* become *tand' Euboicis* and *Cumar' adlabitur*.

See also line 93, where *iterum hospita* becomes *iter' hospita*. It seems that final *m* in Latin was sounded at best faintly. In earlier Latin verse—Lucretius, for example—final *s* had no position.

Where *est* is concerned, the rule is reversed, and the word loses its own vowel. Thus, in line 14, *ut fama est* becomes *ut fama 'st*. In line 50, *adflata est* becomes *adflata 'st*. This is the case even when a preceding word ends with *m*, which now keeps position. Thus, in line 173, *dignum est* becomes *dignum 'st*.

To put this together, see line 264:

Di, quibus imperium est animarum, umbraeque silentes

This becomes:

Di, quibus imperium 'st animar', umbraeque silentes

These rules do not apply at the ends and beginning of lines. In a line ending with a vowel, or *m* or *h*, there is no elision if the first word of the next line begins with a vowel. See lines 3-4:

obvertunt pelago proras; tum dente tenaci
ancora fundabat naves et litora curvae

Tenaci / ancora does not become tenac' / ancora

Feet as Basic Unit of Verse

I turn now to the matter of feet. Applied to English verse, these Latinate rules are often denounced as an imposition. The Housman poem given above might more accurately be described as a set of alternating lines of eight and six syllables, each with four or three stresses and various internal breaks. Certainly, most lines of English verse written before about 1920 tend to have a fixed numbers of syllables. If I do not think so, subdivision into feet may be superfluous. For Latin verse, the rules are essential to understanding its metre. There are metres—the various kinds of hendecasyllable, for example—where the number of syllables is fixed. But this is an effect of rules about the combining of feet. In other metres, syllabic length can vary from one line to the next. In all metres, the basic unit of Latin verse is the foot.

The metre of *The Aeneid* is dactylic hexameter. Each line contains six feet, each of which is by default a dactyl—or a long followed by two short syllables ($-\ \breve{}\ \breve{}$). Purely dactylic lines are unusual. They would be monotonous. They would constrain the choice of words. There is none in *Aeneid* VI. Therefore, any dactylic foot can be replaced by a spondee—or two longs ($-\ -$). This being said, the fifth foot is almost invariably a dactyl, and the last foot is almost never a dactyl—it can be either a spondee or a trochee ($-\ \breve{}$). From this, it follows that a hexameter has a theoretical minimum of twelve syllables and a theoretical maximum of eighteen.

Let us show this with the first two lines of *Aeneid* VI:

Sic fatur lacrimans, classique inmittit habenas
et tandem Euboicis Cumarum adlabitur oris

We can mark, or *scan*, these as follows:

$$— \ {-}{\mid}{-} \ \smallsmile \ \smallsmile \ {\mid}{-} \qquad {-}{\mid}{-} \qquad {-}{\mid}{-} \ \smallsmile \ \smallsmile \ {\mid}{-}{-}$$
Sic fatur lacrimans, classiqu', inmittit habenas

$$- \ — \ {\mid}{-} \ \smallsmile \ \smallsmile \ {\mid}{-}{-}{\mid}{-} \qquad {-}{\mid}{-} \ \smallsmile \ \smallsmile \ {\mid}{-} \ \smallsmile$$
et tand' Euboicis Cumar' adlabitur oris

Note again that, in these examples and those that follow, *syllables* are marked as long or short, not their *vowels*. Remember that, when *fătŭr* becomes *fātūr*, the vowel itself does not change its nature. It is the syllable as a whole that is changed.

In many examinations, students are required to scan a number of lines. After a while of practice, you can do this in your head. You can even see the pattern as you read the lines. In an examination, though, or if you are a beginner, the best way of scanning a line is to start at the end. The last two syllables are nearly always a spondee or a trochee. If you cannot tell the length of the last syllable, you will get away with marking the foot as | – x. You mark your break and move back. The next three syllables will nearly always be a dactyl. Once you have marked that break, you have only four feet left. You turn to the first syllable if the line. This must always be long. It should not be hard to say if it opens a dactyl or a spondee. That leaves you with two more feet. You will know you have gone wrong if you find yourself with three longs in a foot, or a long and one or three shorts.

The Caesura

Now to the caesura, which is the audible break within a line. As said, it mostly comes within a foot, and very rarely between feet. Hexameters have a primary caesura, which usually coincides with a break in sense. This comes at one of several normal positions. It can come after the first syllable of the second foot; after the first syllable in the third foot (the "masculine" caesura); after the second syllable in the third foot if that foot is a dactyl (the "feminine" caesura); after the first syllable of the fourth foot (the hephthemimeral caesura).

Here is an example of a masculine caesura—line 1:

Sic fatur lacrimans, ‖ classique inmittit habenas

Here is a feminine caesura—line 322:

Anchisa generate, ‖ deum certissima proles

22

Here is a hephthemimeral caesura—line 3:

> obvertunt pelago proras; ‖ tum dente tenaci

There can be a secondary caesura elsewhere in the line, or a primary caesura at any point. Or, when a particular effect is required, there can be lines without any identifiable caesura—see line 316:

> ast alios longe submotos arcet harena

These rules for the caesura sound highly abstract. But the break is always perceptible, and it always contributes to the overall sound of the line. More to the point, examinations in England hardly ever ask for the caesura to be marked when lines are to be scanned.

The Sound of Latin Verse

So far, I have discussed the rules of metre. Equally important, for anyone who wants to read Vergil as well as scan him, is how Latin poetry is supposed to sound. Every Classical Latin metre is borrowed from Greek, which was sometimes as different from Latin as Latin is from English. As spoken before about 100 AD, Greek appears to have had an accent that contained no perceptible stress. Words were instead patterned by variations of pitch. One reason why the Romans, and many other peoples, fell in love with Greek was that its ordinary speech sounded like song. But these variations of pitch had a limited use in the metres of their poetry, which were otherwise wholly quantitative.

Accent and Quantity Distinguished

As in English, though perhaps weaker, accent in Latin was primarily a matter of stress. For some of its early period, stress in Latin tended to fall on the first syllable of a word. By the classical period, this had shifted to the penultimate. A Latin word of more than two syllables is stressed on the next to last syllable—the *penultimate*—if this is long by nature or position. If it is not long, the stress moves back to the syllable before that—the *antepenultimate*—regardless of whether this is long or short. Thus, in *ănĭmārŭm*, the stress falls on the penultimate *ār*, because this is long—*ănĭmā́rŭm*. If the enclitic *–que* is added, the previously final short syllable is lengthened by position to become *ănĭmārŭmquĕ*; and, now that it is a long penultimate, *ŭm* carries the stress—*ănĭmārŭ́mquĕ*. Or, if *ănĭmārŭm* is elided to *ănĭmār'* the stress moves back to *ăn*, because Latin does not usually suffer a final stress, and because the new penultimate is short—*ắnĭmār'*.

23

Note again that, while it may once, or for special purposes, have had variations of pitch—as it does in English—accent in Latin was primarily one of stress. As with English, the words *accent* and *stress* are used interchangeably in this section.

Now, if we read Latin verse according to the spoken accent, there is a clash with its quantitative metre. There are hexameter lines in which accent and metre coincide. See, for example, *Aeneid* IV.486:

$$- \quad - \quad \vdash \quad \smile\smile \vdash \quad \smile \quad \| \smile \vdash \smile\smile \vdash \quad \smile \quad \smile \vdash \smile$$

spárgens úmida mélla sopóriferúmque papáver

In this line, you will see that there is a stress on the first syllable of every foot. But this kind of line is a rare exception. The general case in Latin verse is that a stress can fall on any syllable in a foot, and only by apparent chance on the dominant long foot. See again lines 1-2:

$$- \quad -\vdash \quad \smile \quad \smile | - \quad - | - \quad - | - \smile \quad \smile | - -$$

Síc fatur lácrimans, clássiqu', inmíttit habénas

$$- \quad - \quad | \quad - \quad \smile\smile \vdash - \vdash - \vdash \smile \quad \smile \vdash \smile$$

et tánd' Eubóicis Cúmar' adlábitur óris

A Conflict between Accent and Quantity?

This is a problem for anyone whose own language contains a powerful stress. In English, we are so used to patterns of stress that we barely perceive quantity. We can see it in Latin. Given a little practice in the rules explained above, we can mark the longs and shorts in any line, and group them into feet. We can even try to pronounce final vowels as long. But I have been reading Latin verse for a very long time. I am a reasonably decent poet in English. If I read Latin verse aloud as ordinary speech, or if I listen to other readings on the same scheme, quantity has at best a ghostly presence. I am overwhelming aware of the stresses. Following its own stated rules as quantitative verse, I am less aurally aware of *The Aeneid* as formal verse than I am of *A Shropshire Lad*. It sounds to me like rather sonorous free verse of the sort made popular by T.S. Eliot.

A Forcible Resolution

One possible solution is to regard Latin verse as a specialised dialect of the language and to read it aloud as such. In the past year, I have had two German students of A-Level Latin. Both of these have read Vergil by shifting the stresses to coincide with the first syllable of every foot. Therefore, a reading as ordinary speech of lines 3-4 gives:

> obvértunt pélago próras; tum dénte tenáci
> ancóra fundábat náves et lítora cúrvae

Shifting the stresses so they coincide with the first syllable in every foot gives:

> óbvertúnt pelagó prorás; tum dénte tenáci
> áncora fúndabát navés et lítora cúrvae

This appears to be the custom in Germany. I believe it is also the custom in America. I find it irritating. It reduces the most impressively grand lines in Vergil to something that borders on the incompetent— rather as we despise poets in English who make *buttresses* rhyme with *confesses*. I grant it brings out the quantitative rhythm, by overlaying a parallel set of stresses. It may be useful for seeing that students in a class are scanning the lines correctly. But I find it so unnatural that I am reluctant to believe that the Romans themselves could have recited their poetry in this manner. If there is evidence that they did, of course, every objection must fall to the ground. I must then make the same surrender as those scholars who were convinced that ancient statues were chastely white, until they were shown the remnants of the paint used to colour them. I do not think, however, that the evidence points in that direction. It does seem that the Romans recited their poetry as ordinary speech.

No Need for Resolution

The **first evidence** is in the hexameter line itself. The last two feet are almost invariably a dactyl and a spondee or trochee—an *adonic* (– ˇ ˇ |—x). Almost equally invariably, the stresses in these feet coincide with the first syllable of each foot. See lines 1-4:

> …míttit habénas

> …lábitur óris

> dénte tenáci

> lítora cúrvae

The main exceptions in *Aeneid* VI are when Greek words come at the end of a line—see 623, 895:

…tosqu' hýmenǽos

…ens élephánto

It seems in other lines that an effort is made to give a reader just enough coincidence of accent and quantity to make the hexameter aurally plain. The natural implication is that coincidence in other feet is not intended.

The **second evidence** comes from around the end of the classical period of Latin, when the heard distinction between long and short had faded, or was fading, and stress was becoming the dominant patterning of the spoken word. Commodian was a poet from the North African provinces who wrote in the middle of the third century. Africa seems to have been the first part of the Latin world where this distinction faded. The opening of his *Instructiones* reads:

> Praefatio nostra viam erranti demonstrat
> Respectumque bonum, cum venerit saeculi meta
> Aeternum fieri, quod discredunt inscia corda:
> Ego similiter erravi tempore multo.

I leave it to you to scan these lines. You will see that they do not scan as quantitative hexameters. It seems as if the poet has given up on recalling what is supposed to be long or short—distinctions that he and his readers do not hear—and intends instead to reproduce the *sound* of hexameters as read as ordinary speech. *Errántī dēmōnstrăt* is not an adonic, but it sounds like one if the stress alone is taken into account. The first four feet also do not scan, and the stresses here fall without any attempt at the kind of rhythm you would expect from a scanning pronunciation. It is a fair presumption that this is a reproduction of how real quantitative verse was read at least in the third century, and perhaps much earlier.

The **third evidence** is from the papyri. In 1937, a Greek lexicon of Vergil, produced around 500 AD, was found at Nessana in Egypt. This gives a number of lines that have been marked with acute accents to show where emphases should fall. They fall invariably on the syllables stressed in ordinary speech. See, for example, *Aeneid* II.39:

> scínditur incértum stúdia in contrária vúlgus

Why these marks were placed is open to doubt. Some believe they were to show foreign learners how Latin words should be pronounced in everyday speech. But they might have been placed to show how Vergil should be read. If so, we have further reason to believe that Latin verse was read as ordinary speech.

Accent and Quantity as Coordinate Rhythms

Now, for the avoidance of doubt, I do not in the least deny that quantity was heard by Vergil and his readers. Though their Latin had a stress accent, it also had a clear distinction of long and short syllables. This distinction seems to have been powerfully audible in Latin until at least the second century. I am sure it was more powerfully audible than it is to me. Again for the avoidance of doubt, I do not mean that the "ordinary speech" in which the Romans recited their verse was identical to ordinary conversation. I think it reasonable to believe that special effort was made to ensure that longs and shorts were clearly heard, and that special care was taken with enunciation—much as we see when English verse is recited. Even after the loss of quantity in Latin, poets and their readers were expected either to sound longs and shorts against the nature of their own spoken language, or to see them on the page.

We have a clear duty, if we are to appreciate the whole effect of Latin verse, to put aside the habits of our own language and to make as clear a distinction as we can between longs and shorts.

At the same time, it may be that Latin verse had a double rhythm. There was the quantitative rhythm. This could be heard by everyone, though understood only by those educated in the Greek classics. There was also an accentual rhythm. This was not wholly independent. Stress in Latin is a function of quantity, and particular quantitative metres will give rise to particular accentual rhythms. But each rhythm produced its own effect.

Indeed, though I may have implied that there is something contemptible about the lines by Commodian given above, that is not my intention. They have a fine accentual rhythm that supports their direct message. They can be seen as an interesting experiment, or as one example of an established form that was lost in the shipwreck of Roman literature in the two centuries after 500 AD. If there were two coordinate rhythms in Latin verse, why not detach them? Why not liberate verse from a set of rules that amounted to a straitjacket, now they were no longer heard, and focus on what could be heard?

There are examples from the Middle Ages of this "liberation." In 814,

Louis the Pious visited Orleans. The local Bishop welcomed him with an ode in quantitative Sapphics. This is an eleven-syllable metre, comprising five feet, which are usually a trochee, a spondee, a dactyl, a trochee and either a trochee or a spondee. After every three lines, there is a single adonic. The ode begins:

> ēn ădēst Caēsār pĭŭs ēt bĕnīgnŭs,
> ōrbĕ quī tōtō rŭtŭlāt cŏrūscŭs,
> ātquĕ praē cūnctīs bŏnĭtātĕ pōllēt
>   mūnĕrĕ Chrīstī.

A few years later, perhaps the same Bishop wrote another ode to Louis:

> térra maríque víctor hónoránde
> Caésar Augúste Hlúdowíce, Chrísti
> dógmate clárus, décus aévi nóstri,
>   spés quoque régni.

These lines do not scan as Sapphics. They do, however, reproduce the same accentual rhythm as a quantitative Sapphic produces when there is a caesura after the long in the third foot. Why the same writer produced different kinds of Sapphic on each occasion is less important than that he did. The ninth century is a long time after the third, but not so very long after the end of Antiquity. We have some evidence, then, of two traditions. Quantitative verse was perhaps considered more elegant. But accentual was not an insult to its recipient.

Assuming the foregoing to be correct, Vergil's metrical genius has normally been discussed in terms of how he fully adapted the rules of the Greek quantitative hexameter to Latin, so that he could write without the frequent clumsiness of earlier poets. It may be that part of his genius lay in producing a wholly satisfying and harmonious effect at the same time in both schemes of rhythmical arrangement. If this is the case, the shifting of stresses I mention above is not merely without authority, but even harms the intended effect.

In support of this hypothesis, I will return to the matter of Greek verse. The Greek accent was primarily one of varied pitch. If this had a limited influence on the formal quantitative metre of Greek verse, it was heard and appreciated. There would, then, have been the same double rhythm—though the different nature of accent and the different connection between quantity and accent in the two languages would have produced a different kind of rhythmical interplay.

We see this principle of double effect more clearly in the later history of Greek literature. By the sixth century, the Greek accent had shifted to one primarily of stress. As in Latin, the distinction between longs and shorts had faded. Read as ordinary speech, therefore, quantitative verse had no heard metrical shape. The immense authority of the ancient classics meant that they had to be read; and there was a small but continuing production of verses written according to the ancient rules. For general consumption, though, verse was written according to a new double scheme. A poet would write lines that scanned as quantitative iambic trimeter, but with an arrangement of words that produced an audible rhythm in the spoken language. It gave people a sense of continuity with the past, yet also gave a poetry that was not metrical chaos when read aloud, or when read to the uneducated. Because this double effect was too hard to achieve with the old dactylic metres, the hexameter gave way, in the Greek middle ages, to iambic trimeter as the verse form for epic poetry. The quantitative rules were insensibly retired, until a new metre based on accent had emerged. Such was the origin of the πολιτικός στίχος, a verse form used to this day.

If therefore, you would understand Vergil as a poet, you should learn the rules of Latin scansion, and then read the lines as ordinary speech— that is, according to the spoken accent. Effort should be made to sound the unaccented long syllables—but quantitative patterns and the spoken accent should be taken as coordinate elements in the overall effect.

Vergil as Roman Poet

In most editions of Roman poetry, these rules of scansion are relegated to an appendix, or given in some other way as an afterthought. I suggest they are essential to understanding Vergil as a Roman poet. A discussion of them belongs in any main introduction. You should now realise what I mean above when I speak of dancing on a tightrope. If writing good English verse is not easy, writing fair English verse is not that hard. Our metres are natural to our language, and writing verse needs some practice, but little education. Writing Latin verse is impossible without first learning a number of complex rules—rules that evolved for a different language, and that place limits on the choice and arrangement of words. In making these rules work so well that they seem native to Latin, Vergil stands at the end of a long development. Most earlier attempts have been lost. Enough remains, though, for us to trace the main lines of development.

The Hellenising of Rome

Every nation has its poetry, and the Romans are no exception. Unfortunately, we have almost nothing that they wrote in their own metres. We know of a Saturnian metre that was used in the early days of Latin. Barely a hundred lines have survived. Here is one of the longer connected examples, an epitaph of one of the Scipios, written around 150 BC:

> Gnaevō patre prōgnātus, fortis uir sapiēnsque
> cuius fōrma virtūtī parissuma fuit
> cōnsul, cēnsor, aedīlis quī fuit apud vōs
> Taurāsiam, Cisaunam, Samnium cēpit
> subigit omnem Lūcānam, opsidēsque abdūcit.

I have marked the syllables long by nature, but cannot say what use these are to a reading. Is the metre quantitative or accentual? Is it a mix of both? I have said there was a time when Latin was stressed on the first syllable of a word. Are these lines to be stressed there? Or is this rather late example to be stressed according to the penultimate rule? Should the syllables *nam* and *que* in the last line be elided? Given another few hundred lines, we could answer these questions. Given what we have, there are theories but no agreement.

Moving from north to south, Italy before the dominion of Rome was divided between peoples who spoke four different languages, or groups of languages. There were the Celts, a barbarous and frequently troublesome race. There were the Etruscans, of whose ways and language we know much less than we wish we did. There were speakers of the various Italic languages, or which Latin was one. There were the Greeks, who had colonised Sicily and Southern Italy in waves of settlement that continued into the Classical period. The Romans, then, were aware of the Greeks from the beginnings of their own history. They knew the Greeks as traders and as rivals or allies. Because they were the special people of Antiquity, it was impossible to know about the Greeks without coming under their influence. We can be sure there was much indirect influence. The Etruscans had a deep and continuing influence on the Romans, and these had been deeply influenced by the Greeks. From the Etruscans the Romans took an adapted version of the Greek alphabet. They seem also to have taken some of their mythology and religion, and some political institutions. Certainly, on the eve of the first war with Carthage, in 264 BC, the Romans had finished the conquest of Southern Italy. All the Greek colonies in that region were now subject to Rome, and Rome was open to their cultural influence.

These wars with Carthage made Rome a great power in the Mediterranean world. The Ancients did not specialise in diplomatic history, but we can be sure they engaged in diplomacy as involved as our own. Because of their trading interests and their conflicts with each other, the Greek states of the East must have taken a keen interest in the unfolding events in the Western Mediterranean. We know that, towards the end of the first war, Carthage approached Ptolemy II of Egypt for an emergency loan of two thousand talents. Though he politely refused, we can take this as evidence for much diplomatic intrigue. Both Roman and Carthaginian envoys would have been at work in all the Eastern capitals. The Romans would have seen at first-hand what Greek civilisation had to offer in its main centres.

Its costs already mentioned, one of the benefits of unearned wealth is that it allows the emergence of a cultivated leisure class. This emerged in Rome during the third century BC. There was a new taste for the arts, and the vast mass of Greek civilisation flattened anything the Romans had for themselves. After fighting in it, Gnaeus Naevius wrote an epic on the first war with Carthage. He wrote this in Saturnian verses. Around the same time, Livius Andronicus translated *The Odyssey* into the same metre. But these works come at the end of a native tradition. They gave no new life to it. The emerging consensus in Rome was that Greek quantitative metres should be adapted to Latin—or Latin to Greek metres.

In deciding this, the Romans determined for themselves a unique relationship with Greece. Unlike the Macedonians and the higher classes in Egypt and Syria, they would not forget or hide their own language and make themselves into Greeks. Unlike the Jews and Carthaginians, they would not use Greek for certain limited purposes, but keep otherwise to their own ways. Instead, they would embrace the whole of Greek civilisation, but add to it a second language and a second literature. Their future epic poetry would be in Latin hexameters.

Adapting Quantitative Metres to Latin

However, while in its classical period a quantitative language, Latin does not easily fit into Greek metres. It has more syllables long by nature. Because more of its words end in consonants, it has more syllables long by position. Its words tend to be shorter. It has fewer open vowels within words. It prefers *m* to *n*, and uses fewer liquid consonants. Adding the differences of accent already mentioned, Latin sounds different. These difficulties can be solved by a careful arrangement of words. The resulting difficulty is that sense may be sacrificed to sound. In Latin prose, as it developed, there are conflicts to be resolved that do not arise in Greek. For verse, even a natural flexibility of word order must be stretched towards breaking point.

In principle, the main difficulties were solved almost at once. Around the beginning of the second century BC, Quintus Ennius wrote his *Annales*, an epic on the history of Rome. Most of it is now lost, but enough remains to see the approach he took. Many of his lines are remarkable for so early an effort. See:

Musae quae pedibus magnum pulsatis Olympum

The line scans. It has a strong masculine caesura. Except in the two last feet, there is no attempt at correspondence between accent and quantity. There is an alternating and not obtrusive alliteration of *m* and *p*. The accentual rhythm gives the line a suitably confident, peremptory sound. If all the lines had been of this nature, the Romans might have pulled off an achievement as remarkable as when, starting form nothing, they built a fleet and took mastery of the sea from Carthage. Sadly, the surviving lines are not all of this quality. See these:

Assaraco natus Capys optimus isque pium ex se

est locus, Hesperiam quam mortales perhibebant

occiduntur ubi potitur ratus Romulus praedam

avium, praepetibus sese pulchrisque locis dant

O Tite, tute, Tati, tibi tanta, tyranne, tulisti!

These lines scan, or can be made to scan. But they are at least experimental. The third is lumbering. The last is staccato, and has a comical effect probably not intended. The overall arrangement of the poem seems to lack invention. *The Annales* remained popular for many centuries—long enough for Hadrian to admire them as the greatest Latin epic. They do not compare with their Greek models.

So it continued for the next century. The *De Rerum Natura* of Lucretius is as great a poem as we have from Antiquity. It has passages of great power and beauty. It shows how Latin is, at an early age, capable of expressing difficult philosophical arguments. It outclasses anything comparable we still have in Greek. But the lines often have what may have become a deliberate roughness. See, from Book II:

> nam vel uti pueri trepidant atque omnia caecis
> in tenebris metuunt, sic nos in luce timemus
> inter dum, nihilo quae sunt metuenda magis quam
> quae pueri in tenebris pavitant finguntque futura.
> hunc igitur terrorem animi tenebrasque necessest
> non radii solis neque lucida tela diei
> discutiant, sed naturae species ratioque.

Lucretius is a poet of supreme greatness. But it is as if, starting with imitations from the Greek, Roman poetry is moving in a different line of development. It might eventually have produced a more substantial body of great work. If so, this would have been as different from its original inspiration as was the rhymed and accentual Latin verse of the later Middle Ages.

We see a second start with Catullus and the other—now lost—poets of his generation. They take as their starting point the basic fact of the previous century, that quantitative verse can be written in Latin. Where they depart from the line of development I mention is their insistence of a return to the Greek originals, with a focus on the Alexandrian School. Their bias is away from grand themes, in favour of the personal and the subjective. The poetry has a gloss and smoothness not so far seen in Latin—a confident use of allusion; an emphasis on the sound of words, as well as their sense. If I ignore his hendecasyllables, the Catullan hexameter has a new confidence and perfection:

> multas per gentes et multa per aequora vectus

The line opens an elegy on a dead brother. Its objects are grouped symmetrically, their consonants flowing into each other. Driven by the placing of accents, they move with a quietly sad rise and fall towards the subject participle. Here, a slight pause is required, both by sense and by the joining of two hard consonants. Everything is under control and in place. Change the position of a single word—*per multas gentes*, perhaps—and the line still scans, but its effect is ruined. Cicero disliked the New Poets. He mocked their poetry as trivial and self-indulgent. It was an event in Roman literature as significant as his prose—and far more of one than his own attempts at verse.

The Vergilian Synthesis

The poets of the Augustan Golden Age take both lines of development—the earnestness and force of the older poets, and the focus on beauty of the newer school—and they combine them into a body of work that, for the first time, allows Latin to stand beside Greek as one of the two classical languages of Antiquity. Vergil, in particular, breaks through every natural limitation of his language. He can be grand. He can be personal. He can speak in epigrams confined to a single line, or in sentences drawn out over a long block of lines. His invention never fails. His imagination is always lively. Above all, what had, just a few generations earlier, had been the blunt and unexpressive language of a race of farmers and soldiers is made to sing.

This is what makes Vergil important not simply in terms of when he lived, and what influences shaped his poetry. He is also a very great poet. He takes the entire legacy of Roman poetry, plus its Greek models, and adds something wonderful of his own. See, for example, lines 83-87:

> o tandem magnis pelagi defuncte periclis
> (sed terrae graviora manent), in regna Lavini
> Dardanidae venient (mitte hanc de pectore curam),
> sed non et venisse volent. bella, horrida bella,
> et Thybrim multo spumantem sanguine cerno.

As ever, the lines break down into patterns of long and short syllables. Each has its caesuara. Each has its different though related accentual pattern. Then we have the choice and arrangement of words. See how the *nd* in *tandem* help the word stand out, before it flows into *magnis*. This word in turn stands out slightly, because of the clash of *s* and *p* from different words. See how the penultimate in *graviora* has a drawling, ominous sound. See the sudden choppiness of *mitte hanc de pectore curam*. Look at the alliterative patterns, and how, in the fourth line, the tension is heightened by the sudden change of *n* and *v* alternating to *b*; or at the contrast of short and long words; or at the sudden and memorable epigram that pulls everything together. See, in short, how the hexameters flow with mournful grandeur, and how perfect is the match of form with content. I could do much more. The problem with genius is that it can be dissected, but never fully understood. If it could be reduced to a formula, there would be more of it—or it might be levelled into democratic flatness.

34

The Reception of The Aeneid

Even before it was published, Propertius believed *The Aeneid* would eclipse Homer. It became an instant classic in Rome and in all the provinces where Latin was the educated language. It was taken as the model of all language and poetry. It became a common authority on style and grammar. Schoolboys were made to learn it by heart. Ovid parodies it. Pliny quotes from it repeatedly without needing to say what it is. There are Vergilian tags among the graffiti in Pompeii.

The Christians admired it no less than the Pagans. Some thought Vergil had, in the fourth book of his *Eclogues*, predicted the birth of Christ. In any event, he had celebrated the reign of Augustus, in which Christ was born, and which had created the borderless world in which St Paul moved with so little hindrance. In the fourth century, Proba, an aristocratic convert, wrote her *De Laudibus Christi*, a rearrangement of Vergilian lines into a retelling of the Gospels.

His fame continued undiminished in the Middle Ages. He is quoted by Bede, by Paul the Deacon, and by Liutprand, among others. He remained a figure in popular culture, the subject of legends about his wisdom, and even his powers as a sorcerer. Even before the end of Antiquity, his works were used for divination. You consulted the *Sortes Vergilianae* by asking a question, then opening his works at random, and finding an answer in the first line clearly read.

His fame rose higher still in the Renaissance. He is Dante's guide in *The Divine Comedy*, and the inspiration of poets and sculptors. He was the model for unlimited imitation in Latin verse. The first printed edition of his works was in 1469, with another 750 to the end of the sixteenth century. His influence pervades the birth of English and French literature. To write even superficially of this influence would contain a history of our own literature. Until the twentieth century, everyone in the higher classes was expected to have some acquaintance with his works in Latin. Today, he remains popular in translation. His alleged tomb outside Naples is a frequented place of pilgrimage.

A negative consequence of his fame is that he reduced Latin verse to a scheme that could be applied without the slightest inspiration. His genius could not be copied. His formulae could be, and were. Starting with Silius Italicus, there must be hundreds of thousands of extant hexameters, all scanning and harmonious, all variously unreadable. This derives from the choice made during the Augustan Golden Age, to refine Latin as a language of literature without reference to the language of the people. So far as it was made into a counterpart of

Greek, Latin was detached from its spoken root. The decay of genius after the second century turned allowed composition to become a mechanical exercise. The insistence of fixed rules of composition then contributed further to the decay of genius. Latin verse has an interesting birth and a glorious noon, and an unending and sclerotic afternoon. The supreme perfection of Vergil has much to be blamed for this. Had Roman poetry followed Lucretius more than Vergil, its course would have been different. It might have been less sclerotic. The Lucretian hexameter is an open arc, the Vergilian a closed circle. The only escape it allows is from perfection.

But this is a problem for discussion elsewhere. For the moment, we have a study text of *Aeneid* Book VI. More than two thousand years after its author's death, I am producing this with technology that Vergil himself would have thought supernatural. So far as it is read and used, I stand as one humble link in the chain of transmission that begins at a dinner party attended by Augustus, and continues into an unlimited future:

et quasi cursores vitai lampada tradunt

The Texts

Like everything else we have from the Ancient World, *The Aeneid* was transmitted, until the invention of printing, in handwritten copies. Errors are inevitable to such a process over so long a period. However, because it is in a metre that allows few variations, and because it was transmitted in many copies, there are few problems with this text, and these exist mainly for those whose job it is to look for them.

I downloaded the text I am using from the Internet. I have added quotation marks. These are almost as useful as full stops, and may be more useful than commas. Because it has been the fashion since about 1850, I have put the text all in lowercase, except for names. I have kept *v* for consonantal *u*. This may not have been used by Vergil, but seems to have been general within a century of his death. It is also a permitted derogation for us from the demands of the reformed pronunciation. How you sound these is your business. I have added the archaic spellings of some words that have come to us in one branch of the manuscript tradition. I think these were intended by Vergil.

To avoid ambiguity, I have standardised the *is* endings in plural nominative and accusative nouns of the third declension to *es*. My guiding principle throughout has not been to make any contribution to the critical scholarship—a contribution I am not in the least qualified to make—but to produce a text convenient for students.

With convenience still in mind, I have added a rewriting of the text as Latin prose. Much of Vergil's difficulty as an author comes from his taste for mentioning people or things by allusion, and by implying meanings rather than stating them. He is a poet, not a newspaper writer who expects to be read once and thrown aside. As I have argued already, he is also constrained in his choice and arrangement of words by a set of rules that are not native to his language. I cannot say how often I have helped students in class, not by explaining a difficult passage in English, but by reordering its words, and sometimes by substituting more common words.

The prose version I give is by Charles de La Rue, commonly known as Ruaeus, a French Jesuit of the seventeenth century. He produced it so that students with a moderate understanding of Latin could follow the main text. He reorders the text, changing words here and there, adding in italics words missed out by Vergil, replacing allusions with direct mentions, and generally turning a most elaborate work of art into clear prose. The advantage his version has over a translation into French—or English—is that it corresponds far better with the original. If you read a modern translation, you are reading what is effectively an original work. With Ruaeus, you are engaging with a simplified but still recognisable Vergil.

There are many photographed copies on the Internet of editions from the eighteenth and nineteenth centuries that include this prose version. It used to be a favourite of editors, and of students. John Dryden relied much on it for his translation into English verse. I did hope to find one that I could scan. Sadly, the original text was always printed in a small font, and all the copies I could find were too degraded to be of use. I have therefore retyped it, changing a few spellings—chiefly of consonantal *j* to *i*—adding speech marks, and breaking it into sections that correspond to the divisions in the main text. I could have done more to standardise with the main text. But this would have involved too many changes to what is itself a classic.

After some thought, I have added a translation of the main text into English prose. There is no shame in using this, though I do suggest its use as a last resort—only if Vergil himself cannot be made to give up his meaning, or if Ruaeus fails to help in Latin. I did think of using the Dryden translation into heroic couplets. Considered as poetry, this is the best version I know. But I eventually settled on the prose translation made by Joseph Davidson in 1723. I have not been able to find who Davidson was, or if this was his real name. But his was, I believe, the first translation into English prose. As with Ruaeus, it used to be a favourite of editors and students, enoying or suffering many changes until the end of the nineteenth century. If it sometimes owes more to Ruaeus than to Vergil, it is a very good translation. I do not think anyone will have trouble with reading English from three hundred years ago. But, though similar, Davidson's English is just sufficiently removed from our own to create a sense of distance that I find satisfying, and that I do not see in newer and perhaps more accurate translations.

I give thanks here to Mario Huet, who has retyped Davidson from an edition of 1725, complete with original spellings and punctuation, and with italicised words, as in Ruaeus, to mark what has been inserted. Again, I have added quotation marks and broken it into paragraphs that allow it to stand as a parallel text with Ruaeus.

I also give thanks to Lewis Collard and Colum Dread, who proofed the English text of this book. I am dreadful at proofing my own work, and such freedom from typing mistakes as the English text displays is due for them them than to any diligence of my own.

Bibliography

Colt Archaeological Institute, 1950. *Excavations at Nessana: Literary Papyri.* Princeton: Princeton University Press.

Connington, J., 1876. *P. Vergili Maronis Opera.* London: Whittaker.

Davidson, J., 1723. *The Works of Virgil Translated into English Prose As Near the Original as the Different Idioms of the Latin and English Languages will Allow.* London: Longman et al..

Page, T. E., 1888. *P. Vergili Maronis Aeneidos Liber VI: Edited with Notes and Vocabulary for the Use of Schools.* London: Macmillan & Co. Ltd.

Rose, H., 1936. *A Handbook of Latin Literature from the Earliest Times to the Death of St Augustine.* London: Methuen & Co. Ltd.

Sigwick, A., 1899. *P. Vergili Maronis Opera, with Introduction and English Notes.* Cambridge: Cambridge University Press.

Staughton, W., 1813. *The Works of Virgil with the Latin Interpretation of Ruaeus.* Philadelphia: Philip H. Nicklin.

Wilkinson, L., 1963. *Golden Latin Artisty.* Cambridge: Cambridge University Press.

Select Vocabulary

Here follows a separate vocabulary containing all the words that are used more than about eight times in the text. I place this before the text, and I advise intermediate readers to study it before starting on the text. A knowledge in advance of the most frequent words will minimise the amount of searching for definitions. It may also allow other words to be guessed from their context.

a, ab, *prep abl* by (agent), from (departure, cause, remote origin, time); after (reference);

accipio, accipere, accepi, acceptus *v* **(3rd)** *trans* take, grasp, receive, accept, undertake; admit, let in, hear, learn; obey;

ad *prep acc* to, up to, towards; near, at; until, on, by; almost; according to; about w, num;

addo, addere, addidi, additus *v* **(3rd)** *trans* add, insert, bring, attach to, say in addition; increase; impart; associate;

adeo *adv* to such a degree, pass, point; precisely, exactly; thus far; indeed, truly, even;

aequor, aequoris *n* **(3rd)** *n* level, smooth surface, plain; surface of the sea; sea, ocean;

aeternus, aeterna -um, aeternior -or - us, aeternissimus -a -um *adj* eternal, everlasting, imperishable;

aetherius, aetheria, aetherium *adj* ethereal, heavenly, divine, celestial; of the upper atmosphere; aloft; lofty;

agmen, agminis *n* **(3rd)** *n* stream; herd, flock, troop, crowd; marching army, column, line; procession;

agnosco, agnoscere, agnovi, agnitus *v* **(3rd)** recognise, realise, discern; acknowledge, claim, admit to, responsibility;

ago, agere, egi, actus *v* **(3rd)** drive, urge, conduct, act; spend (time w, cum); thank (w, gratias); deliver (speech);

aio (defective), assert; say yes, so, affirm, assent; prescribe, lay down;

alter *conj* the one ... the other (alter ... alter); otherwise;

amnis, amnis *n* **(3rd)** *m* river (real, personified), stream; current; (running) water; the river Ocean;

amo, amare, amavi, amatus *v* **(1st)** love, like; fall in love with; be fond of; have a tendency to;

amor, amoris *n* **(3rd)** *m* love; affection; affair; illicit passion;

anima, animae *n* **(1st)** *f* soul, spirit, vital principle; life; breathing; wind, breeze; air (element);

annus, anni *n* **(2nd)** *m* year (astronomical, civil); age, time of life; year's produce; circuit, course;

ante *adv* before, previously, first, before this, earlier; in front, advance of; forwards;

aperio, aperire, aperui, apertus *v* **(4th)** *trans* uncover, open, disclose; explain, recount; reveal; found; excavate; spread out;

aqua, aquae *n* **(1st)** *f* water; sea, lake; river, stream; rain, rainfall (pl.), rainwater; spa; urine;

arbor, arboris *n* **(3rd)** *f* tree; tree trunk; mast; oar; ship; gallows; spearshaft; beam; squid?;

ardeo, ardere, arsi, arsus *v* **(2nd)** be on fire; burn, blaze; flash; glow, sparkle; rage; be in a turmoil, love;

armo, armare, armavi, armatus *v* **(1st)** *trans* equip, fit with armour; arm; strengthen; rouse, stir; incite war; rig (ship);

aspicio, aspicere, aspexi, aspectus *v* **(3rd)** *trans* look, gaze on, at, see, observe, behold, regard; face; consider, contemplate;

at *conj* but, but on the other hand; on the contrary; while, whereas; but yet; at least;

ater, atra -um, atrior -or -us, aterrimus -a -um *adj* black, dark; dark-coloured (hair, skin); gloomy, murky; unlucky; sordid, squalid; deadly, terrible, grisly (esp. connected with underworld); poisonous; spiteful;

atque *conj* and, as well, soon as; together with; and moreover, even; and too, also, now; yet;

audio, audire, audivi, auditus *v* **(4th)** hear, listen, accept, agree with; obey; harken, pay attention; be able to hear;

aura, aurae *n* **(1st)** *f* breeze, breath (of air), wind; gleam; odor, stench; vapor; air (pl.), heaven;

aureus, aurea, aureum *adj* of gold, golden; gilded; gold bearing; gleaming like gold; beautiful, splendid;

auris, auris *n* **(3rd)** *f* ear; hearing; a discriminating sense of hearing, "ear" (for); pin on plow;

aurum, auri *n* **(2nd)** *n* gold (metal, colour), gold money, riches;

aut *conj* or, or rather, else; either...or (aut...aut) (emphasizing one);

autem *conj* but (postpositive), on the other hand, contrary; while, however;

moreover, also;

bellum, belli *n* **(2nd)** *n* war, warfare; battle, combat, fight; (at, in) (the) war(s); military force, arms;

bellus, bella -um, bellior -or -us, bellissimus -a -um *adj* pretty, handsome, charming, pleasant, agreeable, polite; nice, fine, excellent;

cado, cadere, cecidi, casus *v* **(3rd)** *intrans* fall, sink, drop, plummet, topple; be slain, die; end, cease, abate; decay;

causa, causae *n* **(1st)** *f* cause, reason, motive; origin, source, derivation; responsibility, blame; symptom; occasion, subject; plea, position; lawsuit, case, trial; proviso, stipulation; thing(s);

celer, celeris -e, celerior -or -us, celerrimus -a -um *adj* swift, quick, agile, rapid, speedy, fast; rash, hasty, hurried; lively; early;

cerno, cernere, crevi, cretus *v* **(3rd)** *trans* sift, separate, distinguish, discern, resolve, determine; see; examine; decide;

classis, classis *n* **(3rd)** *f* class, division of Romans; grade (pupils); levy, draft; fleet, navy; group, band;

coniunx, coniugis *n* **(3rd)** *c* spouse, mate, consort; husband, wife, bride, fiancee, intended; concubine; yokemate;

contra *prep* *acc* against, facing, opposite; weighed against; as against; in resistance, reply to; contrary to, not in conformance with; the reverse of; otherwise than; towards, up to, in direction of; directly over, level with; to detriment of;

corpus, corporis *n* **(3rd)** *n* body; person, self; virility; flesh; corpse; trunk; frame(work); collection, sum; substantial, material, concrete object, body; particle, atom; corporation, guild;

credo, credere, credidi, creditus *v*

(3rd) trust, entrust; commit, consign; believe, trust in, rely on, confide; suppose; lend (money) to, make loans, give credit; believe, think, accept as true, be sure;

crudelis, crudele, crudelior -or -us, crudelissimus -a -um *adj* cruel, hardhearted, unmerciful, severe, bloodthirsty, savage, inhuman; harsh, bitter;

cura, curae *n* **(1st)** *f* concern, worry, anxiety, trouble; attention, care, pains, zeal; cure, treatment; office, task, responsibility, post; administration, supervision; command (army);

currus, currus *n* **(4th)** *m* chariot, light horse vehicle; triumphal chariot; triumph; wheels on plough; cart;

de *prep abl* down, away from, from, off; about, of, concerning; according to; with regard to;

deinde *adv* then, next, afterward; thereon, henceforth, from there, then; in next position, place;

deus, dei *n* **(2nd)** *m* god; divine essence, being, supreme being; statue of god;

dico, dicere, dixi, dictus *v* **(3rd)** say, declare, state; allege, declare positively; assert; plead (case); talk, speak; make speech; play (instrument); pronounce, articulate; utter; mean; name, call; appoint, fix, set (date); designate, declare intention of giving;

dies, diei *n* **(5th)** *c* day; daylight; (sunlit hours); (24 hours from midnight); open sky; weather; specific day; day in question; date of letter; festival; lifetime, age; time;

disco, discere, didici, discitus *v* **(3rd)** *trans* learn; hear, get to know, become acquainted with; acquire knowledge, skill of, in;

do, dare, dedi, datus *v* **(1st)** *trans* give; dedicate; sell; pay; grant, bestow, impart, offer, lend; devote; allow; make; surrender, give over; send to die;

ascribe, attribute; give birth, produce; utter;

doceo, docere, docui, doctus *v* **(2nd)** teach, show, point out;

domus, domus *n* **(4th)** *f* house, building; home, household;

duco, ducere, duxi, ductus *v* **(3rd)** lead, command; think, consider, regard; prolong;

durus, dura -um, durior -or -us, durissimus -a -um *adj* hard, stern; harsh, rough, vigourous; cruel, unfeeling, inflexible; durable;

dux, ducis *n* **(3rd)** *m* leader, guide; commander, general; Duke (mediaeval, Bee);

ecce *interi* behold! see! look! there! here!

edo, edare, edidi, editus *v* **(1st)** *trans* eject, emit; put, give forth (buds); beget; bear (fruit); display, evince, exhibit; utter solemnly; pronounce, decree (oracle); deliver (message); issue (command); publish; disclose, tell, relate, make known; declare, make formal statement; cause; see birth of;;

effundo, effundere, effudi, effusus *v* **(3rd)** *trans* pour out, away, off; allow to drain; shower; volley (missiles); send, stream forth; shed (blood, tears); discharge (vomit, urine), debouch, emit; flow out, overflow; break out; bear, yield, bring forth; expend, use up; unseat, eject, drop, discard; stretch, spread out, extend; spread (sail); loosen, slacken, fling, give rein;

ego, mei *pron pers* I, me;

enim *conj* namely (postpos.); indeed; in fact; for; I mean, for instance, that is to say;

eo, ire, ivi(ii), itus *v* go, walk; march, advance; pass; flow; pass (time); ride; sail;

equus, equi *n* **(2nd)** *m* horse; steed;

ergo *adv* therefore; well, then, now;

eripio, eripere, eripui, ereptus *v* (3rd) snatch away, take by force; rescue;

et *conj* and, and even; also, even; (et ... et = both ... and);

ex *prep abl* out of, from; by reason of; according to; because of, as a result of;

facilis, facile, facilior -or -us, facillimus -a -um *adj* easy, easy to do, without difficulty, ready, quick, good natured, courteous;

fallo, fallere, fefelli, falsus *v* (3rd) deceive; slip by; disappoint; be mistaken, beguile, drive away; fail; cheat;

fama, famae *n* (1st) *f* rumour; reputation; tradition; fame, public opinion, ill repute; report, news;

fatum, fati *n* (2nd) *n* utterance, oracle; fate, destiny; natural term of life; doom, death, calamity;

fero, ferre, tuli, latus *v* bring, bear; tell, speak of; consider; carry off, win, receive, produce; get;

ferrum, ferri *n* (2nd) *n* iron; any tool of iron; weapon, sword;

figo, figere, fixi, fixus *v* (3rd) fasten, fix; pierce, transfix; establish;

flamma, flammae *n* (1st) *f* flame, blaze; ardor, fire of love; object of love;

fleo, flere, flevi, fletus *v* (2nd) cry for; cry, weep;

flumen, fluminis *n* (3rd) *n* river, stream; any flowing fluid; flood;

for, fari, fatus sum *v* (1st) *dep* speak, talk; say;

fulgeo, fulgere, fulsi, – *v* (2nd) flash, shine; glow, gleam, glitter, shine forth, be bright;

funus, funeris *n* (3rd) *n* burial, funeral; funeral rites; ruin; corpse; death;

genitor, genitoris *n* (3rd) *m* father; creator; originator;

gens, gentis *n* (3rd) *f* tribe, clan; nation, people; Gentiles;

genus, generis *n* (3rd) *n* birth, descent, origin; race, family, house, stock, ancestry; offspring, descent; noble birth; kind, sort, variety; class, rank; mode, method, style, fashion, way;

habeo, habere, habui, habitus *v* (2nd) have, hold, consider, think, reason; manage, keep; spend, pass (time);

haud *adv* not, not at all, by no means; not (as a particle);

hic *adv* here, in this place; in the present circumstances;

hinc *adv* from here, from this source, cause; hence, henceforth;

horreo, horrere, horrui, – *v* (2nd) dread, shrink from, shudder at; stand on end, bristle; have rough appearance;

huc *adv* here, to this place; to this point;

iaceo, iacere, iacui, iacitus *v* (2nd) *intrans* lie; lie down; lie ill, in ruins, prostrate, dead; sleep; be situated;

iam *adv* now, already, by, even now; besides;

ille, illa, illud *pron* that; those (pl.); also *demonstrative*; that person, thing; the well known; the former;

imago, imaginis *n* (3rd) *f* likeness, image, appearance; statue; idea; echo; ghost, phantom;

impono, imponere, imposui, impositus *v* (3rd) impose, put upon; establish; inflict; assign, place in command; set;

imus, ima, imum *adj* inmost, deepest, bottommost, last; (inferus);

ingens, ingentis (gen.), ingentior -or -us, ingentissimus -a -um *adj* not natural, immoderate; huge, vast, enormous; mighty; remarkable, momentous;

inter *prep acc* between, among; during;

ipse, ipsa, ipsum *pron* himself, herself, itself; the very, real, actual one; in person; themselves (pl.);

is, ea, id *pron* he, she, it, they (by gender number); *demonstrative*: that, he, she, it, they, them;

iter, itineris *n* **(3rd)** *n* journey; road; passage, path; march;

iuvenis, iuvenis *n* **(3rd)** *c* youth, young man, woman;

iuxta *adv* nearly; near, close to, near by, hard by, by the side of; just as, equally;

labor, labi, lapsus sum *v* **(3rd)** *dep* slip, slip and fall; slide, glide, drop; perish, go wrong;

lacrima, lacrimae *n* **(1st)** *f* tear; exuded gum, sap; bit of lead; quicksilver from ore; weeping (pl.); dirge;

limen, liminis *n* **(3rd)** *n* threshold, entrance; lintel; house;

litus, litoris *n* **(3rd)** *n* shore, seashore, coast, strand; river bank; beach, landing place;

locus, loci *n* **(2nd)** *m* place, territory, locality, neighbourhood, region; position, point; aim point; site;

loquor, loqui, locutus sum *v* **(3rd)** *dep* speak, tell; talk; mention; say, utter; phrase;

lumen, luminis *n* **(3rd)** *n* light; lamp, torch; eye (of a person); life; day, daylight;

maestus, maesta -um, maestior -or - us, maestissimus -a -um *adj* sad, unhappy; mournful, gloomy; mourning; stern, grim; ill-omened, inauspicious;

magnus, magna -um, maior -or -us, maximus -a -um *adj* large, great, big, vast, huge; much; powerful; tall, long, broad; extensive, spacious; great (achievement); mighty; distinguished; skilled; bold, confident; proud; full, complete, utter, pure; intense; loud; at

high price; notable, famous; old;

maneo, manere, mansi, mansus *v* **(2nd)** remain, stay, abide; wait for; continue, endure, last; spend the night (sexual);

manus, manus *n* **(4th)** *f* hand, fist; team; gang, band of soldiers; handwriting; (elephant's) trunk;

memoro, memorare, memoravi, memoratus *v* **(1st)** remember; be mindful of (w, gen, acc); mention, recount, relate, remind, speak of;

meus, mea, meum *adj* my (personal possession); mine, of me, belonging to me; my own; to me;

miser, misera -um, miserior -or -us, miserrimus -a -um *adj* poor, miserable, wretched, unfortunate, unhappy, distressing;

mitto, mittere, misi, missus *v* **(3rd)** send, throw, hurl, cast; let out, release, dismiss; disregard;

monstro, monstrare, monstravi, monstratus *v* **(1st)** show; point out, reveal; advise, teach;

mors, mortis *n* **(3rd)** *f* death; corpse; annihilation;

moveo, movere, movi, motus *v* **(2nd)** move, stir, agitate, affect, provoke, disturb;

multus, multa -um, -, plurimus -a -um *adj* much, many, great, many a; large, intense, assiduous; tedious;

munus, muneris *n* **(3rd)** *n* service; duty, office, function; gift; tribute, offering; bribes (pl.);

nam *conj* for, on the other hand; for instance;

nepos, nepotis *n* **(3rd)** *c* grandson, daughter; descendant; spendthrift, prodigal, playboy; secondary shoot;

neque *adv* nor; and not, not, neither;

nomen, nominis *n* **(3rd)** *n* name, family

name; noun; account, entry in debt ledger; sake; title, heading;

noster, nostra, nostrum *adj* our;

nox, noctis *n* **(3rd)** *f* night [prima nocte => early in the night; multa nocte => late at night];

nullus, nulla, nullum (gen -ius) *adj* no; none, not any; (pronominal adj)

numen, numinis *n* **(3rd)** *n* divine will, divinity; god;

nunc *adv* now, today, at present;

oculus, oculi *n* **(2nd)** *m* eye;

omnis, omnis *n* **(3rd)** *c* all men (pl.), all persons;

oro, orare, oravi, oratus *v* **(1st)** beg, ask for, pray; beseech, plead, entreat; worship, adore;

os, oris *n* **(3rd)** *n* mouth, speech, expression; face; pronunciation;

ostendo, ostendere, ostendi, ostensus *v* **(3rd)** show; reveal; make clear, point out, display, exhibit;

palus, pali *n* **(2nd)** *m* stake, pile, pole, unsplit wood; peg, pin; execution stake; wood sword; fence (pl.);

pars, partis *n* **(3rd)** *f* part, region; share; direction; portion, piece; party, faction, side; role (of actor); office, function, duty (usu. pl.);

pater, patris *n* **(3rd)** *m* father; [pater familias, patris familias => head of family, household];

pectus, pectoris *n* **(3rd)** *n* breast, heart; feeling, soul, mind;

per *prep* *acc* through (space); during (time); by, by means of;

peto, petere, petivi, petitus *v* **(3rd)** attack; aim at; desire; beg, entreat, ask (for); reach towards, make for;

poena, poenae *n* **(1st)** *f* penalty, punishment; revenge, retribution; [poena dare => to pay the penalty];

pono, ponere, posui, positus *v* **(3rd)** *trans* put, place, set; station, post (troops); pitch (camp); situate; set up; erect; specify, put down; cite, quote; locate; depict; classify; assume, suppose; bury; lay (foundation, keel); found (town), build; plant (trees); provide, serve; ut, lay down (load, arms), take off (clothes); shed (leaves); cut (nails); esteem, value, count; impose; ordain; lend, put out, offer, wager; rid, drop;

posco, poscere, poposci, – *v* **(3rd)** ask, demand;

possum, posse, potui, – *v* be able, can;

premo, premere, pressi, pressus *v* **(3rd)** press, press hard, pursue; oppress; overwhelm;

primus, prima, primum *adj* first, foremost, best, chief, principal; nearest, next; [in primis => especially];

prior, prior, prius *adj* ahead, in front, leading; previous, earlier, preceding, prior; former; basic;

procul *adv* away; at distance, far off;

proles, prolis *n* **(3rd)** *f* offspring, descendant; that springs by birth, descent; generation; race, breed;

puer, pueri *n* **(2nd)** *m* boy, lad, young man; servant; (male) child;

puppis, puppis *n* **(3rd)** *f* stern, aft (of ship); poop; ship; back;

puto, putare, putavi, putatus *v* **(1st)** *trans* think, believe, suppose, hold; reckon, estimate, value; clear up, settle;

quantus, quanta, quantum *adj* how great; how much, many; of what size, amount, degree, number, worth, price;

qui *adv* how?; how so; in what way; by what, which means; whereby; at whatever price;

quin *conj* so that not, without; that not; but that; that; [quin etiam => moreover];

quis, quis, quid *pron* anyone, anybody,

anything; someone, something; one or another;

quisque, quaeque, quodque *pack* (w, -que) each, each one; every, everybody, everything (more than 2); whatever;

quondam *adv* formerly, once, at one time; some day, hereafter;

ramus, rami *n* **(2nd)** *m* branch, bough;

reddo, reddere, reddidi, redditus *v* **(3rd)** return; restore; deliver; hand over, pay back, render, give back; translate;

regno, regnare, regnavi, regnatus *v* **(1st)** reign, rule; be king; play the lord, be master;

regnum, regni *n* **(2nd)** *n* royal power; power; control; kingdom;

relinquo, relinquere, reliqui, relictus *v* **(3rd)** leave behind, abandon; (pass.) be left, remain; bequeath;

ripa, ripae *n* **(1st)** *f* bank;

ruo, ruere, rui, rutus *v* **(3rd)** destroy, ruin, overthrow; rush on, run; fall; charge (in + acc); be ruined;

sacer, sacra, sacrum *adj* sacred, holy, consecrated; accursed, horrible, detestable;

sacerdos, sacerdotis *n* **(3rd)** *c* priest, priestess;

saevus, saeva -um, saevior -or -us, saevissimus -a -um *adj* savage; fierce, ferocious; violent, wild, raging; cruel, harsh, severe; vehement;

sanguis, sanguinis *n* **(3rd)** *m* blood; family;

sed *conj* but, but also; yet; however, but in fact, truth; not to mention;

sedeo, sedere, sedi, sessus *v* **(2nd)** sit, remain; settle; encamp;

sedes, sedis *n* **(3rd)** *f* seat; home, residence; settlement, habitation; chair;

sequor, sequi, secutus sum *v* **(3rd)** *dep* follow; escort, attend, accompany; aim at, reach after, strive for, make for, seek; support, back, side with; obey, observe; pursue, chase; range, spread over; attain;

servo, servare, additional, forms *v* watch over; protect, store, keep, guard, preserve, save;

sic *adv* thus, so; as follows; in another way; in such a way;

silva, silvae *n* **(1st)** *f* wood, forest;

sino, sinere, sivi, situs *v* **(3rd)** allow, permit;

sono, sonare, sonavi, sonatus *v* **(1st)** make a noise, sound; speak, utter, emit sound; be spoken of (as); express, denote; echo, resound; be heard, sound; be spoken of (as);

sors, sortis *n* **(3rd)** *f* lot, fate; oracular response;

sto, stare, steti, status *v* **(1st)** stand, stand still, stand firm; remain, rest;

sub *prep abl* under, beneath, behind, at the foot of (rest); within; during, about (time);

subeo, subire, subivi(ii), subitus *v* **intrans** go, move, pass, sink, extend underneath, into; climb, come, go up, ascend; steal in on; lace, be placed under, in support; come up w, aid; assume a form; undergo, endure

sui (gen) *pron* reflex. him, her, it, oneself; him, her, it; them (selves) (pl.); each other, one another;

summum, summi *n* **(2nd)** *n* top; summit, end, last; highest place; top surface; (voice) highest, loudest;

surgo, surgere, surrexi, surrectus *v* **(3rd)** rise, lift; grow;

suus, sua, suum *adj* his, one's (own), her (own), hers, its (own); (pl.) their (own), theirs;

talis, talis, tale *adj* such; so great; so excellent; of such kind;

tandem *adv* finally; at last, in the end;

45

after some time, eventually; at length;

tantus, tanta, tantum *adj* of such size; so great, so much;

tego, tegere, texi, tectus *v* **(3rd)** cover, protect; defend; hide;

templum, templi *n* **(2nd)** *n* temple, church; shrine; holy place;

teneo, tenere, tenui, tentus *v* **(2nd)** hold, keep; comprehend; possess; master; preserve;]; represent; support;

terra, terrae *n* **(1st)** *f* earth, land, ground; country, region;

thalamus, thalami *n* **(2nd)** *m* bedroom; marriage;

tollo, tollere, sustuli, sublatus *v* **(3rd)** *trans* lift, raise; destroy; remove, steal; take, lift up, away;

traho, trahere, traxi, tractus *v* **(3rd)** draw, drag, haul; derive, get;

tu, tui *pron pers* you, thee;

tum *adv* then, next; besides; at that time;

turbo, turbare, turbavi, turbatus *v* **(1st)** disturb, agitate, throw into confusion;

tuus, tua, tuum *adj* your (*sing.*);

ubi *adv* where; in what place; (time) when, whenever; as soon as; in which; with whom;

ullus, ulla, ullum (gen -ius) *adj* any;

umbra, umbrae *n* **(1st)** *f* shade; ghost; shadow;

umbro, umbrare, umbravi, umbratus *v* **(1st)** cast a shadow on, shade;

unda, undae *n* **(1st)** *f* wave;

unde *adv* from where, whence, from what or which place; from which; from whom;

urbs, urbis *n* **(3rd)** *f* city; City of Rome;

ut *conj* to (+ subjunctive), in order that, to; how, as, when, while; even if;

vates, vatis *n* **(3rd)** *m* prophet, seer, mouthpiece of deity; oracle, soothsayer; poet (divinely inspired);

veho, vehere, vexi, vectus *v* **(3rd)** bear, carry, convey; pass, ride, sail;

venio, venire, veni, ventus *v* **(4th)** come;

verus, vera -um, verior -or -us, verissimus -a -um *adj* true, real, genuine, actual; properly named; well founded; right, fair, proper;

vestis, vestis *n* **(3rd)** *f* garment, clothing, blanket; clothes; robe;

via, viae *n* **(1st)** *f* way, road, street; journey;

video, videre, vidi, visus *v* **(2nd)** see, look at; consider; (*passive*) seem, seem good, appear, be seen;

virgo, virginis *n* **(3rd)** *f* maiden, young woman, girl of marriageable age; virgin, woman sexually intact;

virus, viri *n* **(2nd)** *n* venom (sg.), poisonous secretion of snakes, creatures, plants; acrid element;

vis, viris *n* **(3rd)** *f* strength (bodily) (pl.), force, power, might, violence; resources; large body;

vita, vitae *n* **(1st)** *f* life, career, livelihood; mode of life;

vivus, viva, vivum *adj* alive, fresh; living;

voco, vocare, vocavi, vocatus *v* **(1st)** call, summon; name; call upon;

**volo, velle, volui, – ** *v* wish, want, prefer; be willing, will;

vox, vocis *n* **(3rd)** *f* voice, tone, expression;

vultus, vultus *n* **(4th)** *m* face, expression; looks;

P. VERGILI MARONIS
AENEIDOS LIBER SEXTVS

*The Sibyl foretells Aeneas the adventures he should meet
with in Italy. She attends him to hell; describing to him the
various scenes of that place, and conducting him to his
father Anchises, who instructs him in those sublime
mysteries, of the soul of the world, and the transmigration;
and shows him that glorious race of heroes, which was to
descend from him and his posterity.*

Sic fatur lacrimans, classique inmittit habenas
et tandem Euboicis Cumarum adlabitur oris.
obvertunt pelago proras; tum dente tenaci
ancora fundabat naves et litora curvae
5   praetexunt puppes. iuvenum manus emicat ardens
litus in Hesperium; quaerit pars semina flammae
abstrusa in venis silicis, pars densa ferarum
tecta rapit silvas inventaque flumina monstrat.

**Lines 1–13: Aeneas travels to Italy and lands there, and goes to the Temple of
Apollo at Cumae to consult the Sibyl.**

Line 1: **Sic fatur lacrimans**—At the end of Book V, Aeneas has lamented the death
of Palinurus, his helmsman. Book VI leads directly on. Also, see Homer, *Iliad*, I.357:
ὡς φάτο δάκρυχέων. Homer is Vergil's main influence.

Line 1: **Inmittit habenas**—A metaphor taken from the management of horses; loosing
the sails so they might be filled by the wind.

Line 2: **Tandem**—At last; after such long wanderings.

Euboicis Cumarum—Cumae Κύμαι, was a town north of the Bay of Naples. It was
said to be the oldest Greek settlement in Italy, and to have been founded by men from
both Cyme in Asia Minor and from Chalcis in Euboea.

Line 3: **Obvertunt pelago**—Turned towards the sea for ease of getting away.

Line 6: **Hesperium**—From Ἕσπερος, "the evening star," sometimes meaning
"western." Also an occasional Greek name for Italy. The word is used as an adjective
to govern *litus*.

Semina flammae—From Homer, Odyssey, V.490: σπέρμα πυρός, "seeds of fire." The
Ancients believed that sparks were already present in flint, and only needed to be
struck out of it.

at pius Aeneas arces quibus altus Apollo
10   praesidet horrendaeque procul secreta Sibyllae,
antrum inmane, petit, magnam cui mentem animumque
Delius inspirat vates aperitque futura.
iam subeunt Triviae lucos atque aurea tecta.

Daedalus, ut fama est, fugiens Minoia regna

Line 9: **At pius Aeneas**—*Pius* (good to the Gods and his own) is a common title given to and used by Aeneas throughout the Poem.

Arces—The hill where stood the Temple of Apollo, with the cave of the Sibyl close by. The temple is said to have been hollowed out of rock, so that the whole resembled a cave. If so, the Sibyl may have had her retreat in the innermost part of the temple.

Line 10: **Secreta**—"The secret place," used as a noun.

Line 10: **Sibyllae**—The Sibyl of Cumae, Σίβυλλᾰ; the priestess in charge of the Oracle of Apollo. Deiphobe, daughter of Glaucus, is said to have been a most beautiful woman. She was propositioned by Apollo and promised, in return for her favours, whatever she might ask. She asked to live as many years as the grains of the sand she was holding in her hand. He granted her wish, and she still refused to sleep with him. Therefore, he construed her wish strictly, allowing her almost unending life, but not health or beauty. By the time Aeneas meets her, she has already lived seven hundred years, and has become the God's oracle.

Do not confuse Deiphobe the Sibyl with Deiphobus the third husband of Helen. Both appear in this Book.

Line 11: **Mentem animumque**—By *animus* Vergil means the soul in general, and by *mens* the intellectual faculties. This is a common distinction in Latin.

Line 12: **Delius**—Apollo, "the Delian One" was born on Delos.

Line 13: **Triviae**—*Trivia* is another name for Diana.

Lines 14–41: The Temple described, together with the carvings on its gates. The Sibyl calls everyone inside.

Line 14: **Daedalus**—Δαίδαλος, was a craftsman of genius. He was commisioned by King Minos to Crete, to build the Labyrinth where the Minotaur could be hidden. This was the hybrid monster—*biformis*—born of his wife's passion for a bull—*veneris monimenta nefandae*. Minos fed the Minotaur with a yearly tribute from Athens of seven boys and girls chosen by lot.

At last, Theseus, son of Aegeus, the King of Athens, went to Crete. There, helped by Ariadne, the daughter of Minos, he killed the Minotaur and freed the Athenians.

Daedalus and his son, Icarus, were forbidden to leave Crete. Some say this was to keep the Royal Secret safe. Vergil takes the alternative view, that he had angered Minos by assisting Pasiphae in her unorthodox romance. He and Icarus were shut away in a tower. However, see Ovid, *Metamorphoses*, VIII.185-87:

15   praepetibus pennis ausus se credere caelo
     insuetum per iter gelidas enavit ad Arctos,
     Chalcidicaque levis tandem super astitit arce.
     redditus his primum terris tibi, Phoebe, sacravit
     remigium alarum posuitque inmania templa.
20   in foribus letum Androgeo; tum pendere poenas
     Cecropidae iussi (miserum!) septena quotannis
     corpora natorum; stat ductis sortibus urna.
     contra elata mari respondet Cnosia tellus:
     hic crudelis amor tauri suppostaque furto
25   Pasiphae mixtumque genus prolesque biformis
     Minotaurus inest, Veneris monimenta nefandae,
     hic labor ille domus et inextricabilis error;
     magnum reginae sed enim miseratus amorem
     Daedalus ipse dolos tecti ambagesque resolvit,
30   caeca regens filo vestigia. tu quoque magnam

"terras licet" inquit "et undas
obstruat: et cælum certe patet; ibimus illac:
omnia possideat, non possidet aera Minos."

So, making wings from feathers held with wax, they flew from the island. Icarus, however, flying too close to the sun, lost his wings, and fell into the sea close by the island of Samos. Daedalus arrived safe in Italy. There he built a temple for Apollo and dedicated his wings—*remigium alarum posuit*.

Line 17: **Chalcidica**—"Of Cumae." See above.

Line 18: **Phoebe**—From Φοῖβος, meaning "bright." One of the main epithets applied to Apollo.

Line 20: **Androgeo**—Greek genitive of Androgeus, Ἀνδρόγεως; a son of King Minos. He was killed by the Athenians, and the yearly tribute of Athenian youth was their punishment.

Line 21: **Cecropidae**—"Athenians." From Cecrops, Κέρκωψ, founder of Athens.

Line 23: **Respondet**—Refers to the carvings on the opposite panel.

Cnosia—Adjective from Cnossos, Κνωσός; the ancient capital of Crete, and taken as referring to the whole island. Close by the modern city of Heracleion.

Line 24: **Supposta**—Poetic form of *supposita*; shortened to fit the metre. Vergil often changes words and grammar for metrical puroses. See my comments on this in the relevant part of my Address to the Reader.

Line 30: **Vestigia**—A reference to Theseus. Vergil has both a taste and a talent for deliberate ambiguity. The expression may be from Catullus 5.113

49

partem opere in tanto, sineret dolor, Icare, haberes.
bis conatus erat casus effingere in auro,
bis patriae cecidere manus. quin protinus omnia
perlegerent oculis, ni iam praemissus Achates

35   adforet atque una Phoebi Triviaeque sacerdos,
Deiphobe Glauci, fatur quae talia regi:
"non hoc ista sibi tempus spectacula poscit;
nunc grege de intacto septem mactare iuvencos
praestiterit, totidem lectas ex more bidentis."

40   talibus adfata Aenean (nec sacra morantur
iussa viri) Teucros vocat alta in templa sacerdos.

excisum Euboicae latus ingens rupis in antrum,
quo lati ducunt aditus centum, ostia centum,
unde ruunt totidem voces, responsa Sibyllae.

45   ventum erat ad limen, cum virgo "poscere fata
tempus" ait; "deus ecce deus!" cui talia fanti

Errabunda regens tenui vestigia filo
where Theseus is the subject of the sentence.

Line 31: **Sineret dolor**—Should be *si sinesset dolor*. To fit the metre, the particle is suppressed, and the pluperfect becomes an imperfect subjunctive.

Line 32: **Conatus erat**—Daedalus, though his name needs to be inferred from the context.

Line 33: **Omnia**—To be scanned as a trochee: *omnya*.

Line 34: **Achates**—A follower of Aeneas, sent ahead—*praemissus*—to give notice of the visit.

Line 36: **Deiphobe Glauci**—see note to line 10.

Line 36: **Regi**—"To the King (Aeneas)."

Line 38: **Grege intacto**—That is, oxen never been set to work, and therefore fit for sacrifice.

Line 39: **Praestiterit**—Subjunctive of wish.

Lines 42–76: The Sibyl commands Aeneas to pray. He prays for a happy end to his wanderings, with a home in Italy for himself and his people.

Line 44: **Unde ruunt... response Sibyllae**—Through these doors are communicated the responses of the Sibyl.

Line 45: **Fata**—"Oracles."

ante fores subito non vultus, non color unus,
non comptae mansere comae; sed pectus anhelum,
et rabie fera corda tument, maiorque videri
50 nec mortale sonans, adflata est numine quando
iam propiore dei. "cessas in vota precesque,
Tros" ait "Aenea? cessas? neque enim ante dehiscent
attonitae magna ora domus." et talia fata
conticuit. gelidus Teucris per dura cucurrit
55 ossa tremor, funditque preces rex pectore ab imo:
"Phoebe, graves Troiae semper miserate labores,
Dardana qui Paridis derexti tela manusque
corpus in Aeacidae, magnas obeuntia terras
tot maria intravi duce te penitusque repostas
60 Massylum gentes praetentaque Syrtibus arva:
iam tandem Italiae fugientes prendimus oras.
hac Troiana tenus fuerit fortuna secuta;
vos quoque Pergameae iam fas est parcere genti,

Line 50: **Nec mortale**—Read *nec fortior mortale.*

Line 52: **Aenea**—Greek vocative of Aeneas.

Line 54: **Teucris**—"Trojans." From Teucer, the first king of Troy and son of the river-god Scamander and the nymph Idaea. Before the arrival of Dardanus, the land eventually called Dardania (and later still the Troad) was known as Teucria and the inhabitants as Teucrians.

Line 57: **Dardana**—"Trojans." Adjective drawn from Dardanus, a son of Zeus who settled the area that eventually became Troy.

Paridis—Paris, Πάρις, also known as Alexander, Ἀλέξανδρος; a son of King Priam and Queen Hecuba of Troy. Best known for his elopement with Helen, Queen of Sparta, which was the immediate cause of the Trojan War. Later in the war, he fatally wounds Achilles in the heel. The name Paris is probably Luwian and comparable to *Pari-zitis,* attested as a Hittite scribe's name.

Line 58: **Aeacidae**—Achilles; from Aeacus, a grandfather of Achilles.

Line 60: **Massylum**—A North African race who lived to the west of Carthage. The usual genitive plural is *Massylorum.*

Line 62: **Hac... tenus**—*Hactenus*

Line 63: **Pergameae**—Pergama was the citadel of Troy, and is used in place of "Trojans."

Fas est—Can mean "it is permitted," or "it is just." Here, it means the first of these.

dique deaeque omnes, quibus obstitit Ilium et ingens
65   gloria Dardaniae. tuque, o sanctissima vates,
praescia venturi, da (non indebita posco
regna meis fatis) Latio considere Teucros
errantesque deos agitataque numina Troiae.
tum Phoebo et Triviae solido de marmore templum
70   instituam festosque dies de nomine Phoebi.
te quoque magna manent regnis penetralia nostris:
hic ego namque tuas sortes arcanaque fata
dicta meae genti ponam, lectosque sacrabo,
alma, viros. foliis tantum ne carmina manda,
75   ne turbata volent rapidis ludibria ventis;
ipsa canas oro." finem dedit ore loquendi.

at Phoebi nondum patiens inmanis in antro
bacchatur vates, magnum si pectore possit
excussisse deum; tanto magis ille fatigat
80   os rabidum, fera corda domans, fingitque premendo.
ostia iamque domus patuere ingentia centum

Line 70: **Festos... dies**—The *ludi Appolinares* begun in 212 BC.

Line 71: **Penetralia**—The Sibylline Books. The Sibyl offered nine of these to King Tarquin the Proud. When he refused to pay what was asked, she burnt three and offered the remainder at the same price. When he again refused, she burnt another three, again offering the remainder at the same price. He then bought them, and had them placed in the Temple of Jupiter on the Capitoline Hill, where they were consulted at times of national emergency. They were lost in a fire in 82 BC, but reconstructed.

Lines 73-74: **Lectosque sacrabo...viros**—The *Viri Electi* were the body of offficials charged with managing and consulting the Sibylline Books. These officials were always drawn from the nobility, and their consultations of the Books generally fitted a political agenda.

Line 74: **Foliis ne carmina manda**—Before papyrus came into general use among the Greeks, dried leaves of the palm tree were used for writing.

Line 76: **Finem dedit ore loquendi**—may be an editorial completion that has crept from the marginal comment on an early manuscript.

Lines 77–97: Inspired by Apollo, the Sibyl promises Aeneas every success in Italy, but only after wars as long and terrible as that of Troy.

Lines 78-79: **Possit excussisse deum**—The perfect infinitive is used as a counterpart here to the Greek aorist. The present would be more usual.

sponte sua vatisque ferunt responsa per auras:
"o tandem magnis pelagi defuncte periclis
(sed terrae graviora manent), in regna Lavini
85 Dardanidae venient (mitte hanc de pectore curam),
sed non et venisse volent. bella, horrida bella,
et Thybrim multo spumantem sanguine cerno.
non Simois tibi nec Xanthus nec Dorica castra
defuerint; alius Latio iam partus Achilles,
90 natus et ipse dea; nec Teucris addita Iuno
usquam aberit, cum tu supplex in rebus egenis
quas gentes Italum aut quas non oraveris urbes!
causa mali tanti coniunx iterum hospita Teucris
externique iterum thalami.
95 tu ne cede malis, sed contra audentior ito,
qua tua te Fortuna sinet. via prima salutis
(quod minime reris) Graia pandetur ab urbe."

talibus ex adyto dictis Cumaea Sibylla
horrendas canit ambages antroque remugit,

Line 84: **Terrae**—Possibly a locative case.

Line 87: **Et Thybrim** *etc*—"Like the Roman, I seem to see the River Tiber foaming with much blood." (Enoch Powell, 20th April 1968)

Line 88: **Simois... Xanthus**—The two rivers close by Troy. They are likened to the Tiber and the Numicius. The Sibyl is emphasising the similarity of the Italian Promised Land to the former home of the Trojans.

Line 90: **Natus... ipse dea**—Another similarity. Both Turnus, son of the Rutiluan King, and Achilles were the sons of minor divinities.

Line 94: **Externique iterum thalami**—*The Aeneid* was left unfinished. Here is one of the fifty-seven lines throughout the whole work that Vergil intended to revisit.

Line 95: **Tu ne cede** *etc*—This line is the motto of the Ludwig von Mises Institute.

Line 97: **Graia... ab urbe**—The city of Pallanteum, capital of Arcadia. For the dealings of Aeneas with King Evander and the Arcadians, see Book VIII.

Lines 98–123: Aeneas accepts the hard fate laid out for him by the Sibyl. He asks only that he should first be allowed to visit the Underworld to converse with Anchises, his late father.

Line 98: **Ex adyto**—The innermost retreat of the Sibyl, where only she and her priestess were allowed to go.

100   obscuris vera involvens: ea frena furenti
           concutit et stimulos sub pectore vertit Apollo.
           ut primum cessit furor et rabida ora quierunt,
           incipit Aeneas heros: "non ulla laborum,
           o virgo, nova mi facies inopinave surgit;
105   omnia praecepi atque animo mecum ante peregi.
           unum oro: quando hic inferni ianua regis
           dicitur et tenebrosa palus Acheronte refuso,
           ire ad conspectum cari genitoris et ora
           contingat; doceas iter et sacra ostia pandas.
110   illum ego per flammas et mille sequentia tela
           eripui his umeris medioque ex hoste recepi;
           ille meum comitatus iter maria omnia mecum
           atque omnes pelagique minas caelique ferebat,
           inualidus, vires ultra sortemque senectae.
115   quin, ut te supplex peterem et tua limina adirem,
           idem orans mandata dabat. gnatique patrisque,
           alma, precor, miserere (potes namque omnia, nec te
           nequiquam lucis Hecate praefecit Avernis),

Line 100: **Obscuris vera involvens**—It was the nature of oracles to wrap truths in mystery. None of the Greek oracles ever gave a straight answer to any question.

Line 107: **Acheronte**—Acheron, Ἀχέρων; uncertain etymology. A river of the Underworld. Both Cocytus and Phlegethon flow into it.

Line 108: **Cari genitoris**—That is, Anchises, the father whom Aeneas carried on his shoulders from burning Troy, and who died on their subsequent wanderings at Drepanum in Sicily.

Line 109: **Contingat... doceas**—Both subjunctives are dependent on *oro*.

Line 116: **Mandata dabat**—See Book V.731, in which Anchises appears to Aeneas and instructs him to make a visit to Elysium, the Sibyl as his guide.

Line 118: **Avernis**—Avernus is a volcanic lake near to Cumae. Because of its sulphurous fumes, it was believed to have a connection with the Underworld. As an aside, Vergil and other poets frequently use proper names as adjectives. Though convenient, this can involve much obscurity—often with intent, as when, for example, a lesser-known ancestor is used as an adjective to describe an unnamed person of considerable fame.

si potuit manes accersere coniugis Orpheus
120 Threicia fretus cithara fidibusque canoris,
si fratrem Pollux alterna morte redemit
itque reditque viam totiens. quid Thesea, magnum
quid memorem Alciden? et mi genus ab Iove summo."

talibus orabat dictis arasque tenebat,
125 cum sic orsa loqui vates: "sate sanguine divom,
Tros Anchisiade, facilis descensus Averno:
noctes atque dies patet atri ianua Ditis;

Line 119: **Si potuit**—If the following persons visited the Underworld, and were able to return, why not Aeneas?

Line 120: **Threicia**—Refers to the story of Orpheus, born in Thrace, who visited the Underworld to claim back his wife Eurydice.

Line 121: **Fratrem Pollux alterna morte redemit**—Castor and Pollux were half-brothers. Pollux, being a son of Jupiter, was immortal, but Castor was mortal. When Castor was killed in a fight, the best Pollux could arrange was for each to pass half a year forever in the Underworld.

Line 122: **Thesea**—Theseus and his friend Pirithous tried to carry off Proserpina from the Underworld. They were caught and detained there, until Hercules was able to set only Theseus free. Note the Greek accusative.

Line 123: **Alciden**—Hercules, though a son of Jupiter, was often called Alcides on account of his mother's husband Alcaeus. The name Hercules does not fit into an hexameter, and so this alternative or some other must be used.

Quid Memorem—"What more need I say?" A favourite device for cutting short a list of examples.

Mi genus ab Iove—For *mi* read *mihi*. Hercules was a son of Jupiter. Aeneas, because a son of Venus, was a grandson of Jupiter. He was descended from Jupiter also on his father's side, though Dardanus.

Lines 124–155: The Sibyl commands Aeneas to find the Golden Bough, which, like a cross against vampires, will let him pass unharmed through the Underworld. Before then, he must give proper burial to Misenus, one of his fellows who has drowned.

Line 124: **Aras tenebat**—To set hands on an altar is a universal gesture of supplication.

Line 125: **Divom**—Archaism for the genitive plural *divum*. Vergil is fond of these archaisms. Their purpose is to reinforce the setting of his story in the distant past.

Line 126: **Averno**—The Sibyl here uses Avernus as a general name for the Underworld. Note the dative of place.

Line 127: **Ditis**—Dis was the God of the Underworld; also called Hades and Pluto.

sed revocare gradum superasque evadere ad auras,
hoc opus, hic labor est. pauci, quos aequus amavit

130 Iuppiter aut ardens evexit ad aethera virtus,
dis geniti potuere. tenent media omnia silvae,
Cocytusque sinu labens circumvenit atro.
quod si tantus amor menti, si tanta cupido est
bis Stygios innare lacus, bis nigra videre

135 Tartara, et insano iuvat indulgere labori,
accipe quae peragenda prius. latet arbore opaca
aureus et foliis et lento vimine ramus,
Iunoni infernae dictus sacer; hunc tegit omnis
lucus et obscuris claudunt convallibus umbrae.

Line 132: **Cocytus**—*Κωκυτός* "lamentation," another river of the Underworld. For a general view of these rivers, see *Paradise Lost*, II.576 *et seq.*:

> four infernal Rivers that disgorge
> Into the burning Lake thir baleful streams;
> Abhorred *Styx* the flood of deadly hate,
> Sad *Acheron* of sorrow, black and deep;
> *Cocytus*, nam'd of lamentation loud
> Heard on the ruful stream; fierce *Phlegeton*
> Whose waves of torrent fire inflame with rage.
> Farr off from these a slow and silent stream,
> *Lethe* the River of Oblivion roules
> Her watrie Labyrinth, whereof who drinks,
> Forthwith his former state and being forgets,
> Forgets both joy and grief, pleasure and pain.

Line 134: **Stygios... lacus**—Adjective from Styx, *Στύξ*, "hate," another river of the Underworld. Here the adjective describes the central marsh where all the rivers meet.

Bis...bis—He would do these things twice: now, and when he finally died.

Line 137: *Aureus...ramus*—Mistletoe growing on an oak tree. According to J.G. Frazer, in *The Golden* Bough, the oak tree was worshipped by "all the branches of the Aryan stock in Europe.... To the savage the world in general is animate, and trees and plants are no exception to the rule. He thinks that they have souls like his own, and he treats them accordingly." Thus, many trees or groves of trees were considered sacred, with the oak being the most important tree for many cultures. Oak trees were seen as protective and were themselves guarded from harm.

Line 138: **Iunoni infernae**—Prosperpina, the Queen of the Underworld. Daughter of the Goddess Ceres; stolen by Pluto and carried as his wife into the Underworld. Released by the mediation of Jupiter for only six months of the year, during which Ceres blesses the Earth with heat and plenty.

140 sed non ante datur telluris operta subire
    auricomos quam quis decerpserit arbore fetus.
    hoc sibi pulchra suum ferri Proserpina munus
    instituit. primo avulso non deficit alter
    aureus, et simili frondescit virga metallo.
145 ergo alte vestiga oculis et rite repertum
    carpe manu; namque ipse volens facilisque sequetur,
    si te fata vocant; aliter non viribus ullis
    vincere nec duro poteris convellere ferro.
    praeterea iacet exanimum tibi corpus amici
150 (heu nescis) totamque incestat funere classem,
    dum consulta petis nostroque in limine pendes.
    sedibus hunc refer ante suis et conde sepulcro.
    duc nigras pecudes; ea prima piacula sunto.
    sic demum lucos Stygis et regna invia vivis
155 aspicies." dixit, pressoque obmutuit ore.

    Aeneas maesto defixus lumina vultu
    ingreditur linquens antrum, caecosque volutat
    eventus animo secum. cui fidus Achates
    it comes et paribus curis vestigia figit.
160 multa inter sese vario sermone serebant,
    quem socium exanimum vates, quod corpus humandum

Line 142: **Sibi pulchra suum**—For the beauty of Properpina, see *Paradise Lost*, V.268-70:

> Proserpin gathering flours
> Her self a fairer Floure by gloomie Dis
> Was gatherd.

Line 150: **Incestat funere**—"Pollutes with death."

Line 151: **Consulta**—Decrees (of the Gods).

Lines 156–211: The body of Misenus is found. While preparing wood for the funeral pyre, Aeneas is led by two doves, sacred to his mother, Venus. They lead him to the Golden Bough.

Line 156: **Defixus lumina**—This would normally be an ablative absolute. That, however, would not fit the metre.

Line 157: **Caecos volutat**—"He turns over in his mind the blind or unknown things."

diceret. atque illi Misenum in litore sicco,
ut venere, vident indigna morte peremptum,
Misenum Aeoliden, quo non praestantior alter
165 aere ciere viros Martemque accendere cantu.
Hectoris hic magni fuerat comes, Hectora circum
et lituo pugnas insignis obibat et hasta.
postquam illum vita victor spoliavit Achilles,
Dardanio Aeneae sese fortissimus heros
170 addiderat socium, non inferiora secutus.
sed tum, forte cava dum personat aequora concha,
demens, et cantu vocat in certamina divos,
aemulus exceptum Triton, si credere dignum est,
inter saxa virum spumosa inmerserat unda.
175 ergo omnes magno circum clamore fremebant,
praecipue pius Aeneas. tum iussa Sibyllae,
haud mora, festinant flentes aramque sepulcri
congerere arboribus caeloque educere certant.
itur in antiquam silvam, stabula alta ferarum;
180 procumbunt piceae, sonat icta securibus ilex
fraxineaeque trabes cuneis et fissile robur
scinditur, advolvunt ingentes montibus ornos.
Nec non Aeneas opera inter talia primus
hortatur socios paribusque accingitur armis.
185 atque haec ipse suo tristi cum corde volutat
aspectans silvam inmensam, et sic forte precatur:
"si nunc se nobis ille aureus arbore ramus
ostendat nemore in tanto! quando omnia vere

Line 162: **Misenum**—Misenus, *Μισηνός*, was trumpeter to Aeneas. In Book IV, we learn that he had challenged the gods to a musical contest on the conch shell, and for his impudence was drowned by Triton. His being called *Aeolides* arose from the legendary connection between the Aeolian and Campanian Cumae.

Line 166: **Hectoris**—Hector, *Ἕκτωρ*; first-born son of King Priam and Queen Hecuba, who was a descendant of Dardanus and Tros, the founder of Troy. Married to Andromache, with whom he had an infant son, Scamandrius (whom the people of Troy called Astyanax). He acted as leader of the Trojans and their allies in the defence of Troy, and was killed by Achilles.

heu nimium de te vates, Misene, locuta est."
190   vix ea fatus erat, geminae cum forte columbae
ipsa sub ora viri caelo venere volantes,
et viridi sedere solo. tum maximus heros
maternas agnovit aves laetusque precatur:
"este duces, o, si qua via est, cursumque per auras
195   derigite in lucos ubi pinguem dives opacat
ramus humum. tuque, o, dubiis ne defice rebus,
diva parens." sic effatus vestigia pressit
observans quae signa ferant, quo tendere pergant.
pascentes illae tantum prodire volando
200   quantum acie possent oculi servare sequentum.
inde ubi venere ad fauces grave olentis Averni,
tollunt se celeres liquidumque per aera lapsae
sedibus optatis gemina super arbore sidunt,
discolor unde auri per ramos aura refulsit.
205   quale solet silvis brumali frigore viscum
fronde virere nova, quod non sua seminat arbos,
et croceo fetu teretes circumdare truncos,
talis erat species auri frondentis opaca
ilice, sic leni crepitabat brattea vento.
210   corripit Aeneas extemplo avidusque refringit
cunctantem, et vatis portat sub tecta Sibyllae.

Line 193: **Maternas...aves**—Doves were sacred to Venus, the mother of Aeneas, on account of their fecundity. No one cursed with an infestation of pigeons will take so romantic a view of this matter.

Line 205: **Brumali frigore**—The mistletoe flourishes in the winter, and this time is chosen to contrast its leaves and the bareness of the tree on which it grows.

Line 206: **Quod non sua seminat arbos**—may refer to the growth of the mistletoe from a tree which is not really its parent. Or it may allude to the belief of the Ancients that it was really the excrement of birds. We nowadays know that it is a parasitic growth, the seeds of which are deposited by birds on other trees.

Nec minus interea Misenum in litore Teucri
flebant et cineri ingrato suprema ferebant.
principio pinguem taedis et robore secto
215   ingentem struxere pyram, cui frondibus atris
intexunt latera et ferales ante cupressos
constituunt, decorantque super fulgentibus armis.
pars calidos latices et aena undantia flammis
expediunt, corpusque lavant frigentis et unguunt.
220   fit gemitus. tum membra toro defleta reponunt
purpureasque super vestis, velamina nota,
coniciunt. pars ingenti subiere feretro,
triste ministerium, et subiectam more parentum
aversi tenuere facem. congesta cremantur
225   turea dona, dapes, fuso crateres olivo.
postquam conlapsi cineres et flamma quievit,
reliquias vino et bibulam lavere favillam,
ossaque lecta cado texit Corynaeus aeno.
idem ter socios pura circumtulit unda
230   spargens rore levi et ramo felicis olivae,
lustravitque viros dixitque novissima verba.
at pius Aeneas ingenti mole sepulcrum
imponit suaque arma viro remumque tubamque
monte sub aerio, qui nunc Misenus ab illo
235   dicitur aeternumque tenet per saecula nomen.

Lines 212–235: Meanwhile, the Trojans were conducting the funeral of Misenus in all its details. Aeneas raises a tomb over his remains.

Line 212: **Nec minus interea**—A common means of expressing transition in Vergil.

Line 219: **Expediunt**—The meaning is that they boiled water. The rest of the line is from Ennius:

Tarcuini corpus bona femina lavit et unxit

Line 221: **Purpureas super vestis**—In the better class of Roman funerals, the dead were wrapped in purple robes prior to burning.

Line 234: **Monte...Misenus**—Monte Miseno is a mountain close by Naples.

his actis propere exsequitur praecepta Sibyllae.
spelunca alta fuit vastoque inmanis hiatu,
scrupea, tuta lacu nigro nemorumque tenebris,
quam super haud ullae poterant impune volantes
240 tendere iter pennis: talis sese halitus atris
faucibus effundens supera ad convexa ferebat.
[unde locum Grai dixerunt nomine Aornon.]
quattuor hic primum nigrantes terga iuvencos
constituit frontique invergit vina sacerdos,
245 et summas carpens media inter cornua saetas
ignibus imponit sacris, libamina prima,
voce vocans Hecaten caeloque Ereboque potentem.
supponunt alii cultros tepidumque cruorem
succipiunt pateris. ipse atri velleris agnam
250 Aeneas matri Eumenidum magnaeque sorori
ense ferit, sterilemque tibi, Proserpina, vaccam;
tum Stygio regi nocturnas incohat aras
et solida imponit taurorum viscera flammis,

Lines 236–263: Aeneas begins the preliminaries of his descent. Black cattle are sacrificed to the infernal powers at the mouth of a cave. As dawn comes, the approach of Hecate is perceived, and Aeneas and the Sibyl descend into the Underworld.

Line 242: **Unde... Aornon**—This line may be spurious. It is missing in several manuscripts, and may have crept in from a marginal note. There is no consensus.

Line 245: **Summas... saetas**—Those parts of a sacrifice first cut off and cast into the fire.

Line 247: **Voce vocans Hecaten**—Hecate was invoked not by words, but by sounds to represent the howling of dogs or the hissing of snakes.

Erebo—*Erebus*, Ἔρεβος, "darkness." One of the names of the Underworld. Also the name of one of the first five beings in existence, born of Chaos.

Line 248: **Supponunt...cultros**—Harsh words at a sacrifice were taken as a bad omen, and were carefully avoided.

Line 250: **Matri Eumenidum**—The Eumenides, Εὐμενίδες; three evil divinities, called "The Kindly Ones" by the Greeks out of fear and respect.

pingue super oleum fundens ardentibus extis.
255 ecce autem primi sub limina solis et ortus
sub pedibus mugire solum et iuga coepta moveri
silvarum, visaeque canes ululare per umbram
adventante dea. "procul, o procul este, profani,"
conclamat vates, "totoque absistite luco;
260 tuque invade viam vaginaque eripe ferrum:
nunc animis opus, Aenea, nunc pectore firmo."
tantum effata furens antro se inmisit aperto;
ille ducem haud timidis vadentem passibus aequat.

Di, quibus imperium est animarum, umbraeque silentes
265 et Chaos et Phlegethon, loca nocte tacentia late,
sit mihi fas audita loqui, sit numine vestro
pandere res alta terra et caligine mersas.

ibant obscuri sola sub nocte per umbram
perque domos Ditis vacuas et inania regna:
270 quale per incertam lunam sub luce maligna

Line 254: **Super**—The final syllable of *super* is made long to fit the metre. The Roman poets took fewer liberties than the Greek, Homer being especially free in his disregard of quantity when it suited him. See Martial, IX.11:

> sed Graeci quibus est nihil negatum
> et quos Ἄρες Ἄρες decet sonare:
> nobis non licet esse tam disertis
> qui Musas colimus seueriores.

Line 257: **Visae canes ululare**—The baying dogs here are supernatural. They accompany Hecate.

Line 258: **Procul, o procul este, profane**—Most religions have a rule against the presence of the impure or uninitiated at their ceremonies. The injunction is to the companions of Aeneas, who are not to go with him on his journey to the Underworld.

Lines 264–267: Vergil himself prays to the Powers of Darkness for inspiration to describe what follows.

Line 265: **Chaos**—χάος, the empty state preceding the creation of the universe.

Phlegethon—Φλεγέθων, "Burning," another river of the Underworld.

Lines 268—94: Description of the Entrance to the Underworld.

Line 270: **Luce maligna**—A light that shines so faintly, it may resent any taking of pleasure in seeing it.

est iter in silvis, ubi caelum condidit umbra
Iuppiter, et rebus nox abstulit atra colorem.
vestibulum ante ipsum primisque in faucibus Orci
Luctus et ultrices posuere cubilia Curae,
pallentesque habitant Morbi tristisque Senectus,
et Metus et malesuada Fames ac turpis Egestas,
terribiles visu formae, Letumque Labosque;
tum consanguineus Leti Sopor et mala mentis
Gaudia, mortiferumque adverso in limine Bellum,
ferreique Eumenidum thalami et Discordia demens
vipereum crinem vittis innexa cruentis.
in medio ramos annosaque bracchia pandit
ulmus opaca, ingens, quam sedem Somnia vulgo
vana tenere ferunt, foliisque sub omnibus haerent.
multaque praeterea variarum monstra ferarum,
Centauri in foribus stabulant Scyllaeque biformes
et centumgeminus Briareus ac belua Lernae
horrendum stridens, flammisque armata Chimaera,

Line 273: **Orci**—Orcus; a Roman god of the Underworld. The word may be cognate with "ogre."

Line 274: **Ultrices... Curae**—Troubles that are the punishment for sin.

Line 278: **Consanguineus Leti Sopor**—Death and Sleep are often stand as brothers.

Line 280: **Ferrei**—To be read here as two syllables.

Line 286: **Centauri**—Combined men and horses, said to live in Thessaly.

Scyllae—Scylla, Σκύλλα, a monster living on one side of a narrow channel, opposite her counterpart Charybdis. The two sides of the strait were within an arrow's range of each other—so close that sailors attempting to avoid Charybdis would pass dangerously close to Scylla and *vice versa*.

Line 287: **Briareus**—Βριάρεως, "Strong," one of the three Hecatoncheires, or hundred-handed giants, who helped overthrow the Titans.

Belua Lernae—The Lernaean Hydra; a beast with nine heads that lived in Lerna, a marsh close to Argos.

Line 288: **Chimaera**—Χίμαιρα, a fire-breathing hybrid monster of Lycia in Asia Minor, composed of the parts of more than one animal. It is usually depicted as a lion, with the head of a goat arising from its back, and a tail that might end with a snake's head.

Gorgones Harpyiaeque et forma tricorporis umbrae.
290 corripit hic subita trepidus formidine ferrum
Aeneas strictamque aciem venientibus offert,
et ni docta comes tenuis sine corpore vitas
admoneatvolitare cava sub imagine formae,
inruat et frustra ferro diverberet umbras.

295 hinc via Tartarei quae fert Acherontis ad undas.
turbidus hic caeno vastaque voragine gurges
aestuat atque omnem Cocyto eructat harenam.
portitor has horrendus aquas et flumina servat
terribili squalore Charon, cui plurima mento
300 canities inculta iacet, stant lumina flamma,
sordidus ex umeris nodo dependet amictus.
ipse ratem conto subigit velisque ministrat
et ferruginea subvectat corpora cumba,
iam senior, sed cruda deo viridisque senectus.
305 huc omnis turba ad ripas effusa ruebat,
matres atque viri defunctaque corpora vita
magnanimum heroum, pueri innuptaeque puellae,
impositique rogis iuvenes ante ora parentum:
quam multa in silvis autumni frigore primo
310 lapsa cadunt folia, aut ad terram gurgite ab alto

Line 289: **Gorgones**—Winged she-monsters with sharp teeth and claws. Only Medusa had the power to turn men into stone.

Line 294: **Admoneat... inruat**—This would normally be an imperfect or pluperfect subjunctive. Various reasons are given for the irregularity. The most obvious is that only the present subjunctive fits the metre.

Lines 295–336: They approach the ferry that will carry them across the Styx. The Sibyl explains that the ghosts eager but unable to cross are of the unburied, and that they must wait a hundred years. Aeneas grieves over the fate of the unburied, seeing among them his fellow lost in the wreck between Sicily and Africa.

Line 297: **Cocyto**—Cocytus, Κωκυτός, "Lamentation," another river of the Underworld.

Line 298: **Portitor**—In the time of Vergil meant a customs officer; only later a porter.

Line 299: **Charon**—Χάρων; the Ferryman of the Dead; a silent and terrifying figure, who would row those souls given the right burial across the Styx.

quam multae glomerantur aves, ubi frigidus annus
trans pontum fugat et terris inmittit apricis.
stabant orantes primi transmittere cursum
tendebantque manus ripae ulterioris amore.

315   navita sed tristis nunc hos nunc accipit illos,
ast alios longe summotos arcet harena.
Aeneas miratus enim motusque tumultu
"dic," ait, "o virgo, quid volt concursus ad amnem?
quidve petunt animae? vel quo discrimine ripas

320   hae linquunt, illae remis vada livida verrunt?"
olli sic breviter fata est longaeva sacerdos:
"Anchisa generate, deum certissima proles,
Cocyti stagna alta vides Stygiamque paludem,
di cuius iurare timent et fallere numen.

325   haec omnis, quam cernis, inops inhumataque turba est;
portitor ille Charon; hi, quos vehit unda, sepulti.
nec ripas datur horrendas et rauca fluenta
transportare prius quam sedibus ossa quierunt.

Lines 305-12: **Huc omnis... apricis**—For an earlier working of these lines by Vergil, see his account of Orpheus in *Georgics*, IV.471-80:

> At cantu commotae Erebi de sedibus imis
> umbrae ibant tenues simulacraque luce carentum,
> quam multa in foliis avium se milia condunt
> vesper ubi aut hibernus agit de montibus imber,
> matres atque viri defunctaque corpora vita
> magnanimum heroum, pueri innuptaeque puellae,
> impositique rogis iuvenes ante ora parentum,
> quos circum limus niger et deformis harundo
> Cocyti tardaque palus inamabilis unda
> alligat et noviens Styx interfusa coercet.

Lines 313-14 : **Orantes... transmittere**—Note here the use of the infinitive after *oro* rather than the usual *ut* and subjunctive. On the one hand, this may be a Greek influence. On the other, it may be a requirement of the metre. Producing an effect so grand and striking as this, and keeping to the normal conventions of the language, may have been beyond even Vergil's power.

Line 318: **Volt**—*vult*; another archaism.

Line 321: **Olli**—*illi*; another archaism.

Longaeva—See the note to line 36. The Sibyl is very old.

centum errant annos volitantque haec litora circum;
330   tum demum admissi stagna exoptata revisunt."
constitit Anchisa satus et vestigia pressit
multa putans sortemque animo miseratus iniquam.
cernit ibi maestos et mortis honore carentis
Leucaspim et Lyciae ductorem classis Oronten,
335   quos simul a Troia ventosa per aequora vectos
obruit Auster, aqua involvens navemque virosque.

Ecce gubernator sese Palinurus agebat,
qui Libyco nuper cursu, dum sidera servat,
exciderat puppi mediis effusus in undis.
340   hunc ubi vix multa maestum cognovit in umbra,
sic prior adloquitur: "quis te, Palinure, deorum
eripuit nobis medioque sub aequore mersit?
dic age. namque mihi, fallax haud ante repertus,
hoc uno responso animum delusit Apollo,
345   qui fore te ponto incolumem finesque canebat
venturum Ausonios. en haec promissa fides est?"

Line 330: **Exooptata revisunt**—The Underworld is divided into five regions: the Entrance, populated by allegorical and imaginary creatures; The Styx, where Charon humiliates the dead; the far bank of the Styx, where suicides and children and so forth spent eternity; Tartarus, or the Pagan Hell; Elysium, or the Place of the Blessed.

Line 332: **Animo**—A variant here in the manuscripts is *animi*. If *animi*, it might be "pondering much the unfair lot *of* the soul." Or it might be an archaic use of the locative. But I choose to follow the majority tradition.

Lines 337–383: Aeneas meets Palinurus, and asks how he was lost at sea, despite an apparent promise by Apollo that he would survive the voyage. Palinurus explains that he fell overboard by accident, and begs that he may either be buried or taken with Aeneas across the Styx. The Sibyl refuses him, but says he shall have a funeral, and that the place where he was killed shall bear his name.

Line 338: **Libyco nuper cursu**—Referring to the voyage from Libya, though they had stopped in Sicily. Remember that the poem was left unfinished.

Dum sidera servat—Though a present tense here, the main verb is pluperfect. Another fitting of grammar to the metre.

ille autem: "neque te Phoebi cortina fefellit,
dux Anchisiade, nec me deus aequore mersit.
namque gubernaclum multa vi forte revulsum,
350   cui datus haerebam custos cursusque regebam,
praecipitans traxi mecum. maria aspera iuro
non ullum pro me tantum cepisse timorem,
quam tua ne spoliata armis, excussa magistro,
deficeret tantis navis surgentibus undis.
355   tris Notus hibernas immensa per aequora noctes
vexit me violentus aqua; vix lumine quarto
prospexi Italiam summa sublimis ab unda.
paulatim adnabam terrae; iam tuta tenebam,
ni gens crudelis madida cum veste gravatum
360   prensantemque uncis manibus capita aspera montis
ferro invasisset praedamque ignara putasset.
nunc me fluctus habet versantque in litore venti.
quod te per caeli iucundum lumen et auras,
per genitorem oro, per spes surgentis Iuli,
365   eripe me his, invicte, malis: aut tu mihi terram
inice, namque potes, portusque require Velinos;
aut tu, si qua via est, si quam tibi diva creatrix
ostendit (neque enim, credo, sine numine divom
flumina tanta paras Stygiamque innare paludem),
370   da dextram misero et tecum me tolle per undas,

Line 347: **Phoebi cortina**—The Oracle at Delphi included a cauldron supported by a tripod. Apollo had apparently promised that Palinurus would survive the voyage. Palinurus explains that he did survive the voyage, but fell overboard, and swam to shore, where he was killed by the natives. The Ancients enjoyed putting ambiguities into the mouths of their gods. See, for example, the story of Croesus and the Oracle of Delphi, given in Herodotus, A.85-89.

Line 358: **Tuta**—*Loca* or *litora* is to be understood from the adjective.

Lines 365-66: **Terram inice**—The Ancients thought it an act of terrible disrespect not to throw at least a dusting of earth on a dead body. See the main premise of *Antigone*, where Creon has decreed that the fallen traitors are to be left unburied, and Antigone disobeys by dusting her brother's body. When they found a body, the Greeks and Romans did not dig a grave for it, but raised a mound over it.

Line 366: **Velinos**—Velia, Ἐλέα, a town on the west coast of Lucania.

sedibus ut saltem placidis in morte quiescam."
talia fatus erat coepit cum talia vates:
"unde haec, o Palinure, tibi tam dira cupido?
tu Stygias inhumatus aquas amnemque severum
375   Eumenidum aspicies, ripamve iniussus adibis?
desine fata deum flecti sperare precando,
sed cape dicta memor, duri solacia casus.
nam tua finitimi, longe lateque per urbes
prodigiis acti caelestibus, ossa piabunt
380   et statuent tumulum et tumulo sollemnia mittent,
aeternumque locus Palinuri nomen habebit."
his dictis curae emotae pulsusque parumper
corde dolor tristi; gaudet cognomine terra.

ergo iter inceptum peragunt fluvioque propinquant.
385   navita quos iam inde ut Stygia prospexit ab unda
per tacitum nemus ire pedemque advertere ripae,
sic prior adgreditur dictis atque increpat ultro:
"quisquis es, armatus qui nostra ad flumina tendis,
fare age, quid venias, iam istinc et comprime gressum.
390   umbrarum hic locus est, somni noctisque soporae:

Line 376: **Desine fata deum,** *etc*—A fair summary of how the Ancients regarded their gods. See, for a parallel comment, *King Lear*, IV.1.36-38:

> As flies to wanton boys are we to th' gods,
> They kill us for their sport.

Line 383: **Gaudet cognomina terra**—The killers of Palinurus were later afflicted by plague. An oracle told them their inhumanity had brought this on them as punishment. They attoned by building him a cenotaph and giving his name to the place where they had killed him.

Lines 384–416: As Aeneas and the Sibyl approach the Styx they are stopped by Charon, who says that living persons may not pass, and that much harm has already resulted from the breach of the rule. The Sibyl insists that Aeneas comes with good intentions, and shows the Golden Bough. Charon gives way, and carries them across the dark water.

Line 384: **Ergo iter inceptum celerant**—Here, *ergo* denotes not a consequence from what has been said, but a return to the main subject

corpora viva nefas Stygia vectare carina.
nec vero Alciden me sum laetatus euntem
accepisse lacu, nec Thesea Pirithoumque,
dis quamquam geniti atque invicti viribus essent.
395   Tartareum ille manu custodem in vincla petivit
ipsius a solio regis traxitque trementem;
hi dominam Ditis thalamo deducere adorti."
quae contra breviter fata est Amphrysia vates:
"nullae hic insidiae tales (absiste moveri),
400   nec vim tela ferunt; licet ingens ianitor antro
aeternum latrans exsangues terreat umbras,
casta licet patrui servet Proserpina limen.
Troius Aeneas, pietate insignis et armis,
ad genitorem imas Erebi descendit ad umbras.
405   si te nulla movet tantae pietatis imago,
at ramum hunc" (aperit ramum qui veste latebat)
"agnoscas." tumida ex ira tum corda residunt;
nec plura his. ille admirans venerabile donum
fatalis virgae longo post tempore visum
410   caeruleam advertit puppim ripaeque propinquat.
inde alias animas, quae per iuga longa sedebant,
deturbat laxatque foros; simul accipit alveo
ingentem Aenean. gemuit sub pondere cumba

Line 391: **Corpora viva**—The ghosts are sometimes called *corpora*; see Book V.303 etc.

Line 394: **Dis... geniti**—Neptune was the ancestor of Theseus, Jupiter of Pirithous.

Line 398: **Amphrysia vates**—Adjective describing the Sibyl, because Apollo once fed the flocks of Admetus close by the River Amphresus.

Line 402: **Patrui**—Pluto is both husband and uncle of Prosperine.

Line 404: **Erebi**—Erebus, Ἔρεβος, "deep shadow." Often conceived as a primordial deity, representing the personification of darkness. Hesiod identifies him as one of the first five beings in existence, born of Chaos.

Line 407: **Agnoscas**—probably a jussive subjunctive.

Line 413: **Ingentem Aenean**—Heroes in ancient epic poetry are generally big. Since there is little in the character's actions and speech to suggest size, Vergil seems to recognise the need to bring this every so often to our attention.

sutilis et multam accepit rimosa paludem.
415 tandem trans fluvium incolumes vatemque virumque
informi limo glaucaque exponit in ulua.

Cerberus haec ingens latratu regna trifauci
personat adverso recubans inmanis in antro.
cui vates horrere videns iam colla colubris
420 melle soporatam et medicatis frugibus offam
obicit. ille fame rabida tria guttura pandens
corripit obiectam, atque inmania terga resolvit
fusus humi totoque ingens extenditur antro.
occupat Aeneas aditum custode sepulto
425 evaditque celer ripam inremeabilis undae.

continuo auditae voces vagitus et ingens
infantumque animae flentes, in limine primo
quos dulcis vitae exsortes et ab ubere raptos
abstulit atra dies et funere mersit acerbo;
430 hos iuxta falso damnati crimine mortis.

Line 414: **Sutilis**—"Sewn." The vessel is covered with stiched leather. It is intended for carrying passengers who weigh nothing.

Paludem—"Water."

Lines 417—425: They next see Cerberus, who barks furiously. The Sibyl throws him a drugged cake, which he eats, and he falls asleep.

Line 417: **Cerberus**—The guard dog of the Underworld, keeping the dead inside and the living out. Unauthorised visitors needed to placate or drug him.

Line 424: **Sepulto**—That is, asleep.

Lines 426–439: They come to the ghosts of those who died before their time— infants, executed criminals, suicides.

Line 426: **Vagitus**—The wail of infants. See Lucretius, II.576-77:

> miscetur funere vagor
> quem pueri tollunt visentes luminis oras.

Line 429: **Funere mersit acerbo**—This line may refer to the custom of burying those who had died prematurely before daybreak, the calamity being thought too great for the sun to behold.

nec vero hae sine sorte datae, sine iudice, sedes:
quaesitor Minos urnam movet; ille silentum
consiliumque vocat vitasque et crimina discit.
proxima deinde tenent maesti loca, qui sibi letum
435   insontes peperere manu lucemque perosi
proiecere animas. quam vellent aethere in alto
nunc et pauperiem et duros perferre labores!
fas obstat, tristisque palus inamabilis undae
alligat et novies Styx interfusa coercet.

440   nec procul hinc partem fusi monstrantur in omnem
Lugentes campi; sic illos nomine dicunt.
hic quos durus amor crudeli tabe peredit
secreti celant calles et myrtea circum
silva tegit; curae non ipsa in morte relinquunt.
445   his Phaedram Procrinque locis maestamque Eriphylen

Line 431: **Sine sorte... sine iudice**—In some ancient trials, not only jurors but also judges were chosen by lot. The phrase means without due process of law. Rather tough on the victims of injustice to be punished in the Underworld.

Hae... sedes—seems to be a generic term for the Underworld.

Line 432: **Quaesitor Minos**—A title given to the presiding judge in certain trials. Minos was the grandfather of the Minos why built the Labyrinth. He was also Chief Judge of the Underworld. He shakes the urn that contains the sentence for every soul passing before him.

Line 435: **Insontes**—Because they had done nothing to deserve death, which was therefore gratuitous.

Line 436: **Proiecere animas**—In John Dryden's translation: "prodigally throw their lives away."

Lines 440–476: They come to the Fields of Mourning, where live those who died for love. Here Aeneas sees Dido, whom he tries to soothe, telling her that he knew not what would be the consequences to her of his departure, and that he went away most unwillingly, because the gods had ordered it. She maintains sullen silence, and at last breaks away, leaving him in sorrow.

Line 443: **Myrtea**—The myrtle was sacred to Venus.

Line 445: **Phaedram**—Phaedra, Φαίδρα, was the wife of Theseus, who, rejected by her step-son Hyppolytus, hanged herself.

Procrin—Procris was accidentally killed by her husband, Cephalus, while she was spying on him to see if he had a mistress. The case is a Greek accusative.

crudelis nati monstrantem vulnera cernit,
Evadnenque et Pasiphaen; his Laodamia
it comes et iuvenis quondam, nunc femina, Caeneus
rursus et in veterem fato revoluta figuram.
450   inter quas Phoenissa recens a vulnere Dido
errabat silva in magna; quam Troius heros
ut primum iuxta stetit agnovitque per umbras
obscuram, qualem primo qui surgere mense
aut videt aut vidisse putat per nubila lunam,
455   demisit lacrimas dulcique adfatus amore est:
"infelix Dido, verus mihi nuntius ergo
venerat exstinctam ferroque extrema secutam?
funeris heu tibi causa fui? per sidera iuro,
per superos et si qua fides tellure sub ima est,
460   inuitus, regina, tuo de litore cessi.

Eriphylen—Eriphyle, Ἐριφύλη, was the wife of Amphiaraus. Bribed with a fine necklace, she persuaded him into the mission of the Seven against Thebes. When he found what she had done, he asked his sons to kill her when they grew up. One of them, Alcmaeon, did so. Another Greek accusative.

Line 447: **Evadnen**—Evadne was the wife of Capaneus, another of the Seven against Thebes. She threw herself into her husband's funeral pyre. Yet another Greek accusative.

Pasiphaen—Pasiphae, Πασιφάη, the wife of King Minos of Crete. See above.

Laodamia—Wife of Protisilaus, the first man ashore when Troy was invaded, and killed with a spear wound in his armpit. Laodamia begged the Gods to restore him for a short while, at the end of which she died with him.

Line 448: **Caeneus**—Caenis was a young woman changed by Jupiter into a man. After his death as *Caeneus*, his sex was changed again.

Line 450: **Phoenissa... Dido**—A Greek adjective applied to Carthage, of which Dido had been the Queen. Her marriage to Aeneas, and the circumstances of his departure from Carthage, are narrated in Book IV.

Recens a vulnere—Refers to her suicide, which is described in Book IV.

Line 456: **Verus... nuntius**—refers to the blaze of the funeral pyre, from which Aeneas discovered Dido's fate.

Line 460: **Inuitus, regina, *etc*.**—Imitated from Catullus. 64.39-40:

> inuita, O regina tuo de vertice cessi,
> inuita: adiuro teque tuumque caput.

sed me iussa deum, quae nunc has ire per umbras,
per loca senta situ cogunt noctemque profundam,
imperiis egere suis; nec credere quivi
hunc tantum tibi me discessu ferre dolorem.
465   siste gradum teque aspectu ne subtrahe nostro.
quem fugis? extremum fato quod te adloquor hoc est."
talibus Aeneas ardentem et torva tuentem
lenibat dictis animum lacrimasque ciebat.
illa solo fixos oculos aversa tenebat
470   nec magis incepto voltum sermone movetur
quam si dura silex aut stet Marpesia cautes.
tandem corripuit sese atque inimica refugit
in nemus umbriferum, coniunx ubi pristinus illi
respondet curis aequatque Sychaeus amorem.
475   nec minus Aeneas casu percussus iniquo
prosequitur lacrimis longe et miseratur euntem.

inde datum molitur iter. iamque arva tenebant
ultima, quae bello clari secreta frequentant.
hic illi occurrit Tydeus, hic inclutus armis
480   Parthenopaeus et Adrasti pallentis imago,
hic multum fleti ad superos belloque caduci

Aeneas here admits more than he admitted when speaking to Dido in life (IV. 333 foll.), where all that he said was that he was going to Italy because the gods ordered him, his real will being to remain with her in Carthage.

Line 470: **Voltum**—Archaic accusative of *vultus*.

Line 471: **Marpesia**—Marpessa was a mountain on Paros from which a very hard marble was quarried. Dido is hard of heart.

Line 474: **Sychaeus**—the husband of Dido; murdered by her brother.

Lines 477–493: They come to the place of dead heroes. The Trojans who fell at Troy crowd about Aeneas. The Greeks are scared.

Line 478: **Ultima**—The last part of the region occupied by those who are neither in Tartarus nor in Elysium

Lines 479-80: **Tydeus… Parthenopaeus… Adrasti**—Tydeus, Parthenoaeus and Adrastus were three others of the Seven against Thebes. This was fought about thrity years before the Trojan War began.

Dardanidae, quos ille omnes longo ordine cernens
ingemuit, Glaucumque Medontaque Thersilochumque,
tris Antenoridas Cererique sacrum Polyboeten,
485 Idaeumque etiam currus, etiam arma tenentem.
circumstant animae dextra laevaque frequentes,
nec vidisse semel satis est; iuvat usque morari
et conferre gradum et veniendi discere causas.
at Danaum proceres Agamemnoniaeque phalanges
490 ut videre virum fulgentiaque arma per umbras,
ingenti trepidare metu; pars vertere terga,
ceu quondam petiere rates, pars tollere vocem
exiguam: inceptus clamor frustratur hiantis.

atque hic Priamiden laniatum corpore toto
495 Deiphobum videt et lacerum crudeliter ora,
ora manusque ambas, populataque tempora raptis
auribus et truncas inhonesto vulnere naris.
vix adeo agnovit pavitantem ac dira tegentem
supplicia, et notis compellat vocibus ultro:
500 "Deiphobe armipotens, genus alto a sanguine Teucri,
quis tam crudeles optavit sumere poenas?
cui tantum de te licuit? mihi fama suprema

Line 485: **Idaeum**—Idaeus was King Priam's charioteer.

Line 489: **Danaum**—*Danai, Δαναοί*, a noun used by Homer for "Greeks." It derives from Danaus, a mythical king of Argos. *Danaum* is gentive plural.

 Agamemnoniae—Agamemnon was the Great King who led the Greek attack on Troy.

Lines 492-93: **Vocem exiguam** –The shrill, piping voice which is often supposed of the dead

Lines 494–547: Aeneas sees Deiphobus, cruelly mangled, and is told the story of his death. The Sibyl reminds him that they must hurry about the main business of their visit to the Underworld.

Line 495: **Deiphobum**—Deiphobus, *Δηίφοβος*, not to be confused with the Sibyl. He was, with Hector and Paris, one of the sons of King Priam. After the death of Paris, he was given Helen for his wife. He was killed with horrible mutilations during the sack of Troy.

nocte tulit fessum vasta te caede Pelasgum
procubuisse super confusae stragis acervum.
505   tunc egomet tumulum Rhoeteo in litore inanem
constitui et magna manis ter voce vocavi.
nomen et arma locum servant; te, amice, nequivi
conspicere et patria decedens ponere terra."
ad quae Priamides: "nihil o tibi, amice, relictum;
510   omnia Deiphobo solvisti et funeris umbris.
sed me fata mea et scelus exitiale Lacaenae
his mersere malis; illa haec monimenta reliquit.
namque ut supremam falsa inter gaudia noctem
egerimus, nosti: et nimium meminisse necesse est.
515   cum fatalis equus saltu super ardua venit
Pergama et armatum peditem gravis attulit aluo,
illa chorum simulans euhantis orgia circum
ducebat Phrygias; flammam media ipsa tenebat
ingentem et summa Danaos ex arce vocabat.
520   tum me confectum curis somnoque gravatum
infelix habuit thalamus, pressitque iacentem
dulcis et alta quies placidaeque simillima morti.
egregia interea coniunx arma omnia tectis
emovet, et fidum capiti subduxerat ensem:
525   intra tecta vocat Menelaum et limina pandit,
scilicet id magnum sperans fore munus amanti,
et famam exstingui veterum sic posse malorum.

Line 503: **Pelasgum**—The Pelasgians were said to have been the original inhabitants of Greece, conquered and displaced by the Greeks at the end of the Bronze Age. Some traces of their language—Θάλασσα, Κόρινθος, *etc.*—may survive in Greek. Here, the word is used to mean "Greeks."

Line 505: **Rhoeteo... litore**—The place where Deiphobus was buried.

Line 507: **Locum servant**—Preserve the memory of the place.

Line 511: **Lacaenae**—*Lacaeana*, Λάκαινα, a Spartan woman; applied to Helen.

Line 523: **Coniunx**—His wife, Helen.

Line 525: **Menelaum**—Menelaus, Μενέλαος, "Wrath of the People." King of Sparta, was Helen's first and fourth husband.

quid moror? inrumpunt thalamo, comes additus una
hortator scelerum Aeolides. di, talia Grais
530 instaurate, pio si poenas ore reposco.
sed te qui vivum casus, age fare vicissim,
attulerint. pelagine venis erroribus actus
an monitu divom? an quae te fortuna fatigat,
ut tristes sine sole domos, loca turbida, adires?"
535 Hac vice sermonum roseis Aurora quadrigis
iam medium aetherio cursu traiecerat axem;
et fors omne datum traherent per talia tempus,
sed comes admonuit breviterque adfata Sibylla est:
"nox ruit, Aenea; nos flendo ducimus horas.
540 hic locus est, partes ubi se via findit in ambas:
dextera quae Ditis magni sub moenia tendit,
hac iter Elysium nobis; at laeva malorum
exercet poenas et ad impia Tartara mittit."
Deiphobus contra: "ne saevi, magna sacerdos;
545 discedam, explebo numerum reddarque tenebris.
i decus, i, nostrum; melioribus utere fatis."
tantum effatus, et in verbo vestigia torsit.

respicit Aeneas subito et sub rupe sinistra

Line 529: **Aeolides**—Sisyphus, son of Aolus, is said to have been the true father of Ulysses. Therefore the adjective.

Line 535: **Aurora**—Goddess of the Dawn; continuation in Latin of the Indo-European name *Housos*.

Line 542: **Elysium**—The Elysian Fields, Ἠλύσιον πεδίον, a place in the Underworld reserved for mortals related to the Gods or other heroes, or those chosen by the Gods to be saved from the common fate of mortals. A place somewhat more exclusive— and more obviously enjoyable—than the Calvinist Heaven.

Line 543: **Tartara**—Tartarus. The Underworld was generally a place of negative evils. Tartarus was a kind of Hell, in which the exceptionally wicked or unfortunate were positively tormented for eternity.

Lines 548–627: Looking round, Aeneas sees a great and terrible fortress, groans and cries of horror coming from it. The Sibyl explains that this is the place of torment for the truly wicked. She alone of the undamned has ever gone inside. She describes the horrors within.

moenia lata videt triplici circumdata muro,
550   quae rapidus flammis ambit torrentibus amnis,
Tartareus Phlegethon, torquetque sonantia saxa.
porta adversa ingens solidoque adamante columnae,
vis ut nulla virum, non ipsi exscindere bello
caelicolae valeant; stat ferrea turris ad auras,
555   Tisiphoneque sedens palla succincta cruenta
vestibulum exsomnis servat noctesque diesque.
hinc exaudiri gemitus et saeva sonare
verbera, tum stridor ferri tractaeque catenae.
constitit Aeneas strepitumque exterritus hausit.
560   "quae scelerum facies? o virgo, effare; quibusue
urgentur poenis? quis tantus plangor ad auras?"
tum vates sic orsa loqui: "dux inclute Teucrum,
nulli fas casto sceleratum insistere limen;
sed me cum lucis Hecate praefecit Avernis,
565   ipsa deum poenas docuit perque omnia duxit.
Cnosius haec Rhadamanthus habet durissima regna
castigatque auditque dolos subigitque fateri
quae quis apud superos furto laetatus inani

Line 549: **Moenia**—"Fortress."

Line 551: **Tartareus Phlegethon**—Acts as a moat, presumably outside the walls.

Line 542: **Adamante**—From ἀδάμας, "unconquerable." A substance of total hardness. "Adamantine" is an adjective used by Milton in *Paradise Lost*—*eg* I.44-49:

> Him the Almighty Power
> Hurld headlong flaming from th' Ethereal Skie
> With hideous ruine and combustion down
> To bottomless perdition, there to dwell
> In Adamantine Chains and penal Fire,
> Who durst defie th' Omnipotent to Arms.

Once closed, neither gods nor men can open the gates of Tartarus.

Line 555: **Tisiphone**—Τισιφόνη, "Avenger of Murder," or Tilphousia, was one of the three Furies. Her sisters were Alecto and Megaera. She was the one who punished crimes of murder: parricide, fratricide and homicide. Here, she guards Tartarus, a function given in *Paradise Lost* to a personification of Sin.

Line 566: **Rhadamanthus**—Ῥαδάμανθυς; A brother of Minos and a fellow Judge of the Underworld.

distulit in seram commissa piacula mortem.
570 continuo sontes ultrix accincta flagello
Tisiphone quatit insultans, torvosque sinistra
intentans anguis vocat agmina saeva sororum.
tum demum horrisono stridentes cardine sacrae
panduntur portae. cernis custodia qualis
575 vestibulo sedeat, facies quae limina servet?
quinquaginta atris inmanis hiatibus Hydra
saevior intus habet sedem. tum Tartarus ipse
bis patet in praeceps tantum tenditque sub umbras
quantus ad aetherium caeli suspectus Olympum.
580 hic genus antiquum Terrae, Titania pubes,
fulmine deiecti fundo volvuntur in imo.
hic et Aloidas geminos inmania vidi
corpora, qui manibus magnum rescindere caelum
adgressi superisque Iovem detrudere regnis.
585 vidi et crudeles dantem Salmonea poenas,
dum flammas Iovis et sonitus imitatur Olympi.
quattuor hic invectus equis et lampada quassans
per Graium populos mediaeque per Elidis urbem
ibat ovans, divomque sibi poscebat honorem,

See Milton's imitation in *Paradise Lost*, II.879-83:

> on a sudden op'n flie
> With impetuous recoile and jarring sound
> Th' infernal dores, and on thir hinges grate
> Harsh Thunder, that the lowest bottom shook
> Of Erebus.

Line 577: **Saevior**—More savage than Tisiphone.

Line 579: **Ad aetherium Olympum**—"To the high point of Heaven."

Line 580: **Titania pubes**—The Titans were giants who supported Saturn against Jupiter, but were eventually consigned to the Underworld.

Line 582: **Aloidas**—Otus and Ephialtes, supposed sons of Aloeus, but really of Neptune, who tried to overthrow the Gods by heaping the moutains Ossa on Olympus and Pelion on Ossa. They were killed by Apollo.

Line 585: **Salmonea**—Salmoneus of Elis, who claimed divine honours without right.

Line 587: **Lampada quassans**—brandishing his torches before hurling them, so as to give force to the blow and make the blaze brighter.

590   demens, qui nimbos et non imitabile fulmen
          aere et cornipedum pulsu simularet equorum.
          at pater omnipotens densa inter nubila telum
          contorsit, non ille faces nec fumea taedis
          lumina, praecipitemque inmani turbine adegit.
595   nec non et Tityon, Terrae omniparentis alumnum,
          cernere erat, per tota novem cui iugera corpus
          porrigitur, rostroque inmanis vultur obunco
          immortale iecur tondens fecundaque poenis
          viscera rimaturque epulis habitatque sub alto
600   pectore, nec fibris requies datur ulla renatis.
          quid memorem Lapithas, Ixiona Pirithoumque?
          quos super atra silex iam iam lapsura cadentique
          inminet adsimilis; lucent genialibus altis
          aurea fulcra toris, epulaeque ante ora paratae
605   regifico luxu; Furiarum maxima iuxta
          accubat et manibus prohibet contingere mensas,
          exsurgitque facem attollens atque intonat ore.
          hic, quibus invisi fratres, dum vita manebat,
          pulsatusve parens et fraus innexa clienti,
610   aut qui divitiis soli incubuere repertis
          nec partem posuere suis (quae maxima turba est),
          quique ob adulterium caesi, quique arma secuti
          impia nec veriti dominorum fallere dextras,
          inclusi poenam exspectant. ne quaere doceri
615   quam poenam, aut quae forma viros fortunave mersit.

Line 595: **Tityon**—Tityos, Τιτυός; a monster who threatened Latona, the mother of Apollo and Diana.

Line 599: **Epulis**—Dative plural of *epulum*.

Line 601: **Lapithas**—The Lapiths were a people who lived in the mountains of Thessaly. Their king, Ixion, was taken by Jupiter on a visit to Olympus, where he tried to seduce June. His punishment was to be fixed to a wheel that revolved forever. Pirithous—see above—was his son.

saxum ingens volvunt alii, radiisque rotarum
districti pendent; sedet aeternumque sedebit
infelix Theseus, Phlegyasque miserrimus omnis
admonet et magna testatur voce per umbras:
620 *'discite iustitiam moniti et non temnere divos.'*
vendidit hic auro patriam dominumque potentem
imposuit; fixit leges pretio atque refixit;
hic thalamum invasit natae vetitosque hymenaeos:
ausi omnes inmane nefas ausoque potiti.
625 non, mihi si linguae centum sint oraque centum,
ferrea vox, omnes scelerum comprendere formas,
omnia poenarum percurrere nomina possim."

haec ubi dicta dedit Phoebi longaeva sacerdos,
"sed iam age, carpe viam et susceptum perfice munus;
630 acceleremus" ait; "Cyclopum educta caminis
moenia conspicio atque adverso fornice portas,
haec ubi nos praecepta iubent deponere dona."
dixerat et pariter gressi per opaca viarum
corripiunt spatium medium foribusque propinquant.

Line 616: **Saxum ingens**—Sisyphus, Σίσυφος, was the king of Ephyra—later known as Corinth—punished for his general wickedness by being made to roll an immense boulder up a hill, only for it to roll down when it nears the top, repeating this action for eternity. Through the classical influence on modern culture, tasks that are both laborious and futile are therefore described as Sisyphean.

Line 618: **Phlegyas**—Φλεγύας; the father of Ixion, and also of a daughter, Coronis. When Apollo seduced Coronis, Ixion was so angry, he set fire to a temple of the God, and his punishment was to be bound to a winged and fiery wheel that was always spinning. None of this is mentioned by Vergil, who leaves it to the knowledge of his readers.

Line 623: **Hymenaeos**—Most Latin hexameters end with a correspondence of quantity and stress—see Address to the Reader. Every so often, however, a "Greek" ending is allowed. In this case, according to the Latin accent, *hymenaeos* is stressed on the first and penultimate syllables. See also Line 985: *elephanto.*

Lines 628–636: Aeneas and the Sibyl hurry to the palace of Pluto and deposit the Golden Bough.

Line 630: **Cyclopum**—The Cyclops were a race of one-eyed giants. One of their duties was to make iron for the Gods.

635   occupat Aeneas aditum corpusque recenti
spargit aqua ramumque adverso in limine figit.

his demum exactis, perfecto munere divae,
devenere locos laetos et amoena virecta
fortunatorum nemorum sedesque beatas.
640   largior hic campos aether et lumine vestit
purpureo, solemque suum, sua sidera norunt.
pars in gramineis exercent membra palaestris,
contendunt ludo et fulva luctantur harena;
pars pedibus plaudunt choreas et carmina dicunt.
645   nec non Threicius longa cum veste sacerdos
obloquitur numeris septem discrimina vocum,
iamque eadem digitis, iam pectine pulsat eburno.
hic genus antiquum Teucri, pulcherrima proles,
magnanimi heroes nati melioribus annis,
650   Ilusque Assaracusque et Troiae Dardanus auctor.
arma procul currusque virum miratur inanis;
stant terra defixae hastae passimque soluti
per campum pascuntur equi. quae gratia currum

Lines 637–678: **The enter Elysium. Aeneas asks the whereabouts of his father, Anchises. Musaeus, the Father of Poetry, offers to guide them.**

Line 638: **Devenere locos**—For Homer and the Greek poets, Elysium was not part of the Underworld, but a separate place. Vergil is original in making Heaven and Hell parts of the same Realm of the Dead.

Line 641: **Solem... norunt**—The Elysian Fields have a sun and stars of their own, distinct from those of the Upper World.

Line 645: **Threicius**—Orpheus, Ὀρφεύς , "the Thracian One," was among the mythical fathers of song, and his name was associated with revelations about the Underworld, supposed to be preserved by secret societies. He is naturally made the harper who plays while the blessed spirits dance and sing. He is called *sacerdos*.

Line 647: **Pectine**—The root meaning of *pectin* is comb, but is used here to mean a rod for striking lyre-strings.

Line 649: **Magnamini... annis**—An imitation of Catullus, 64.22-23:

      o nimis optato saeclorum tempore nati
      heroes, salvete, deum genus.

  Assaracus—Ἀσσάρακος; a son of Dardanus; the father of Ganymede.

	armorumque fuit vivis, quae cura nitentis
655	pascere equos, eadem sequitur tellure repostos.
	conspicit, ecce, alios dextra laevaque per herbam
	vescentes laetumque choro paeana canentis
	inter odoratum lauri nemus, unde superne
	plurimus Eridani per silvam voluitur amnis.
660	hic manus ob patriam pugnando vulnera passi,
	quique sacerdotes casti, dum vita manebat,
	quique pii vates et Phoebo digna locuti,
	inventas aut qui vitam excoluere per artis
	quique sui memores aliquos fecere merendo:
665	omnibus his nivea cinguntur tempora vitta.
	quos circumfusos sic est adfata Sibylla,
	Musaeum ante omnes (medium nam plurima turba
	hunc habet atque umeris exstantem suspicit altis):
	"dicite, felices animae tuque optime vates,
670	quae regio Anchisen, quis habet locus? illius ergo
	venimus et magnos Erebi tranavimus amnis."
	atque huic responsum paucis ita reddidit heros:
	"nulli certa domus; lucis habitamus opacis,
	riparumque toros et prata recentia rivis
675	incolimus. sed vos, si fert ita corde voluntas,
	hoc superate iugum, et facili iam tramite sistam."
	dixit, et ante tulit gressum camposque nitentis
	desuper ostentat; dehinc summa cacumina linquunt.

Line 656: **Per herbam**—They are feasting while sat on the grass; a simplicity of manners common in the Golden Age.

Line 659: **Eridani**—The Eridanus; the River Po.

Line 666: **Circumfusos**—Spread all about the place which Aeneas and the Sibyl are entering.

Line 667: **Musaeum**—Musaeus of Athens, Μουσαῖος, was a legendary polymath, philosopher, historian, prophet, seer, priest, poet, and musician, said to have been the Father of Poetry. He composed dedicatory and purificatory hymns and prose treatises, and oracular responses. The fragments that survive are presumed to be late forgeries.

Line 673: **Certa domus**—A fixed habitation. The possessive adjective *nostrum* is omitted.

at pater Anchises penitus convalle virenti
680   inclusas animas superumque ad lumen ituras
lustrabat studio recolens, omnemque suorum
forte recensebat numerum, carosque nepotes
fataque fortunasque virum moresque manusque.
isque ubi tendentem adversum per gramina vidit
685   Aenean, alacris palmas utrasque tetendit,
effusaeque genis lacrimae et vox excidit ore:
"venisti tandem, tuaque exspectata parenti
vicit iter durum pietas? datur ora tueri,
nate, tua et notas audire et reddere voces?
690   sic equidem ducebam animo rebarque futurum
tempora dinumerans, nec me mea cura fefellit.
quas ego te terras et quanta per aequora vectum
accipio! quantis iactatum, nate, periclis!
quam metui ne quid Libyae tibi regna nocerent!"
695   ille autem: "tua me, genitor, tua tristis imago
saepius occurrens haec limina tendere adegit;
stant sale Tyrrheno classes. da iungere dextram,
da, genitor, teque amplexu ne subtrahe nostro."
sic memorans largo fletu simul ora rigabat.
700   ter conatus ibi collo dare bracchia circum;

Lines 679–702: Anchises is in the valley beyond, surveying his future posterity, spirits that are hereafter to take flesh. He welcomes Aeneas with joy and surprise. Aeneas attempts to embrace him, but in vain.

Line 680: **Ituras**—expresses what is to happen in the course of things to come.

Line 691: **Tempora dinumerans**—Anchises has been counting the days till Aeneas was to arrive.

Line 694: **Libyae... regna**—Carthage.

Line 696: **Saepius**—Anchises appeared to Aeneas in Carthage, urging him to leave. In Book V, he orders him to go to Italy and to visit the Underworld for further directions.

Line 697: **Tyrrheno**—Tyrrhenus, Τυρρηνός was one of the founders of the Etruscan League of twelve cities. Here, the word is used to mean "the Tuscan shore."

ter frustra comprensa manus effugit imago,
par levibus ventis volucrique simillima somno.

interea videt Aeneas in valle reducta
seclusum nemus et virgulta sonantia silvae,
705   Lethaeumque domos placidas qui praenatat amnem.
hunc circum innumerae gentes populique volabant:
ac veluti in pratis ubi apes aestate serena
floribus insidunt variis et candida circum
lilia funduntur, strepit omnis murmure campus.
710   horrescit visu subito causasque requirit
inscius Aeneas, quae sint ea flumina porro,
quive viri tanto complerint agmine ripas.
tum pater Anchises: "animae, quibus altera fato
corpora debentur, Lethaei ad fluminis undam
715   securos latices et longa oblivia potant.
has equidem memorare tibi atque ostendere coram
iampridem, hanc prolem cupio enumerare meorum,
quo magis Italia mecum laetere reperta."
"o pater, anne aliquas ad caelum hinc ire putandum est
720   sublimis animas iterumque ad tarda reverti
corpora? quae lucis miseris tam dira cupido?"
"dicam equidem nec te suspensum, nate, tenebo"
suscipit Anchises atque ordine singula pandit.

Lines 700-01: **Ter... imago**—These two lines are repeated from Book II, when Aeneas tries to embrace the ghost of his wife.

Lines 703–723: **Looking at the ghost, Aeneas asks who they are. He is told they are to drink water from the River Lethe, so that they will be stripped of all memory before being sent into the world again. He wonders why they should want a new life, which leads Anchises to explain.**

Line 705: **Lethaeum... amnem**—Lethe, Λήθη, "forgetfulness," was another river of the Underworld. All who drank from it were stripped of memory and therefore of personal identity.

84

"principio caelum ac terras camposque liquentis
725 lucentemque globum lunae Titaniaque astra
spiritus intus alit, totamque infusa per artus
mens agitat molem et magno se corpore miscet.
inde hominum pecudumque genus vitaeque volantum
et quae marmoreo fert monstra sub aequore pontus.
730 igneus est ollis vigor et caelestis origo
seminibus, quantum non noxia corpora tardant
terrenique hebetant artus moribundaque membra.
hinc metuunt cupiuntque, dolent gaudentque, neque auras
dispiciunt clausae tenebris et carcere caeco.
735 quin et supremo cum lumine vita reliquit,
non tamen omne malum miseris nec funditus omnes
corporeae excedunt pestes, penitusque necesse est
multa diu concreta modis inolescere miris.
ergo exercentur poenis veterumque malorum
740 supplicia expendunt: aliae panduntur inanes
suspensae ad ventos, aliis sub gurgite vasto
infectum eluitur scelus aut exuritur igni:
quisque suos patimur manis. exinde per amplum
mittimur Elysium et pauci laeta arva tenemus,
745 donec longa dies perfecto temporis orbe
concretam exemit labem, purumque relinquit

Lines 724–751: Anchises explains that everything in nature is pervaded by one great spirit, that this in men is clogged by the body, and consequently that, after death, there has to be a longer or shorter purification, after which the souls are sent back into the world to animate other bodies.

Line 724: **Principio**—"in the first place." Probably an echo of Lucretius—*eg*, V.92:

Principio, maria ac terras caelumque tuere.

Line 725: **Titaniaque astra**—"The titanic stars," or the Sun.

Line 727: **Corpore**—The body of the universe.

Line 730: **Ollis**—An archaism for *illis*.

Line 732: **Moribunda**—A stronger word than *mortalia*, implying that the body is ready to die, and would but for the resistance of the principle of life.

aetherium sensum atque aurai simplicis ignem.
has omnis, ubi mille rotam volvere per annos,
Lethaeum ad fluvium deus evocat agmine magno,
750   scilicet inmemores supera ut convexa revisant
rursus, et incipiant in corpora velle reverti."

dixerat Anchises natumque unaque Sibyllam
conventus trahit in medios turbamque sonantem,
et tumulum capit unde omnes longo ordine posset
755   adversos legere et venientum discere vultus.

"nunc age, Dardaniam prolem quae deinde sequatur
gloria, qui maneant Itala de gente nepotes,
inlustris animas nostrumque in nomen ituras,
expediam dictis, et te tua fata docebo.
760   ille, vides, pura iuvenis qui nititur hasta,
proxima sorte tenet lucis loca, primus ad auras
aetherias Italo commixtus sanguine surget,
Silvius, Albanum nomen, tua postuma proles,
quem tibi longaevo serum Lavinia coniunx
765   educet silvis regem regumque parentem,
unde genus Longa nostrum dominabitur Alba.
proximus ille Procas, Troianae gloria gentis,
et Capys et Numitor et qui te nomine reddet

Line 747: **Aurai**—Archaic genitive of *aurum*.

Line 748: **Rotam volvere**—To spin the wheel of time.

Lines 752–755: Aeneas and Anchises and the Sibyl go up to a high place, from where they can see those who will have a future life.

Lines 756–787: Anchises shows Aeneas the long train of Alban kings, his future descendants, ending in Romulus, the founder of Rome.

Line 760: **Pura... hasta**—An ancient prize for bravery was a spear without any head.

Line 763: **Silvius**—Third king of Alba, after Aeneas and Ascanius.

Line 764: **Lavinia**—The daughter of Latinus and Amata, and the last wife of Aeneas.

Silvius Aeneas, pariter pietate vel armis
770   egregius, si umquam regnandam acceperit Albam.
qui iuvenes! quantas ostentant, aspice, viris
atque umbrata gerunt civili tempora quercu!
hi tibi Nomentum et Gabios urbemque Fidenam,
hi Collatinas imponent montibus arces,
775   Pometios Castrumque Inui Bolamque Coramque;
haec tum nomina erunt, nunc sunt sine nomine terrae.
quin et avo comitem sese Mauvortius addet
Romulus, Assaraci quem sanguinis Ilia mater
educet. viden', ut geminae stant vertice cristae
780   et pater ipse suo superum iam signat honore?
en huius, nate, auspiciis illa incluta Roma
imperium terris, animos aequabit Olympo,
septemque una sibi muro circumdabit arces,
felix prole virum: qualis Berecyntia mater
785   invehitur curru Phrygias turrita per urbes
laeta deum partu, centum complexa nepotes,
omnes caelicolas, omnes supera alta tenentis.

Lines 767-68: **Procas... Capys... Aeneas Silvius... Numitor**—The next four kings of Alba. The last of these, Numitor, was the father of Rhea Silvia, who, with Mars as their father, gave birth to Romulus and Remus.

Line 772: **Civili... quercu**—The *Corona Civica*, or wreath of oak given to any Roman who had saved another's life in battle. This was an honour given by the Senate to Augustus, who was present at the first recital of this Book.

Lines 773-75: **Gabbii... Nomentum... Fidenae... Collatia... Suesa Pometia... Castrum Inui... Cora... Bela**—Towns close to Rome; in some cases suburbs of the modern city. Bela is unknown.

Line 777: **Mauvortius**—Mars. See above.

Line 779: **Viden**—Read *videns*. The *s* is elided to produce vidĕns.

Line 784: **Berecyntia mater**—Βερεκυντία; a surname of Cybele, Κυβέλη, the Mother of the Gods, from Mount Berecyntus in Phrygia, where she was particularly worshipped. Her priests were notorious for castrating themselves in an orgiastic delirium that attended their consecration. Though Roman citizens were forbidden to join her priesthood, she was honoured as the inventress of fortifications.

huc geminas nunc flecte acies, hanc aspice gentem
Romanosque tuos. hic Caesar et omnis Iuli
790   progenies magnum caeli ventura sub axem.
hic vir, hic est, tibi quem promitti saepius audis,
Augustus Caesar, divi genus, aurea condet
saecula qui rursus Latio regnata per arva
Saturno quondam, super et Garamantas et Indos
795   proferet imperium; iacet extra sidera tellus,
extra anni solisque vias, ubi caelifer Atlas
axem umero torquet stellis ardentibus aptum.
huius in adventum iam nunc et Caspia regna
responsis horrent divom et Maeotia tellus,
800   et septemgemini turbant trepida ostia Nili.
nec vero Alcides tantum telluris obivit,
fixerit aeripedem cervam licet, aut Erymanthi

Lines 788–807: Anchises draws attention to the Julian Family, and especially Augustus, the destined conqueror of realms wider than were ever traversed by Hercules or Bacchus.

Line 789: **Iuli**—Ascanius, the son of Aeneas, was also called Iulus. Hence the "Julian Line" that ran through Julius Caesar to Augustus and his heirs.

Line 792: **Divi genus**—After his assassination, Julius Caesar was declared a god by the Senate. According to Plutarch, this was a political act, in which the Senate showed willing to an angry people that it would repeal none of his laws. It was an unintended gift to Octavian, that master of propaganda, that he could present himself to the world as the adopted son of a god.

The lines may sound hollow to us. They bring to mind the vast flattery heaped during the past century on the most worthless of men. So they might have sounded to those Romans who lived under the successors of Augustus.

Line 794: **Garamantes**—A tribe mentioned by Herodotus. They are thought to correspond to Iron Age Berber tribes in the southwest of ancient Libya. The reference is probably to the invasion of Ethiopia by Gaius Petronius in 25 BC.

Line 796: **Atlas**—Ἄτλας; the giant who was condemned to bear the world on his shoulders; eventually shown the head of Medusa by Perseus, and made into the mountain that has his name.

Line 799: **Maeotia**—The Maeotians, Μαιῶται, were an ancient people dwelling along the Sea of Azov, which was known as the "Maeotian marshes" or "Lake Maeotis."

Line 802: **Aeripedem cervam**—The deer with brazen feet pursued by Hercules.

pacarit nemora et Lernam tremefecerit arcu;
nec qui pampineis victor iuga flectit habenis
805   Liber, agens celso Nysae de vertice tigris.
et dubitamus adhuc virtutem extendere factis,
aut metus Ausonia prohibet consistere terra?

quis procul ille autem ramis insignis olivae
sacra ferens? nosco crines incanaque menta
810   regis Romani primam qui legibus urbem
fundabit, Curibus parvis et paupere terra
missus in imperium magnum. cui deinde subibit
otia qui rumpet patriae residesque movebit
Tullus in arma viros et iam desueta triumphis
815   agmina. quem iuxta sequitur iactantior Ancus
nunc quoque iam nimium gaudens popularibus auris.
vis et Tarquinios reges animamque superbam
ultoris Bruti, fascisque videre receptos?
consulis imperium hic primus saevasque securis

Line 802-03: **Erymanthi... nemora**—"The woods of Erymanthus," a mountain where Hercules hunted a giant boar.

Line 803: **Lernam**—Lerna, a place near Argos, where Hercules killed the Hydra.

Line 805: **Liber**—Another name for Bacchus, raised by the nymphs of Mount Nysa. The reference is to his travels in a chariot drawn by tigers, which were sacred to him for their common tendency to fury and enthusiastic rage. **Pampineis**—its reins were made from vine-shoots.

Line 807: **Ausonia**—Another name for Italy; taken from an ancient race who lived on the coast of Campania.

Lines 808–835: The Kings of Rome are pointed out, and the great men of the Republic, Pompey and Caesar.

Line 808: **Ille**—A reference to Numa, the second King of Rome and alleged founder of many of its institutions.

Line 814: **Tullus**—The third King of Rome.

Line 815: **Ancus**—Ancus Martius, the fourth King of Rome, after whom came the two Tarquins, with Servius between them.

Line 818: **Bruti**—Brutus, nephew of Tarquin the Proud, the last King of Rome. He roused the people to expel their King and to found the Republic. Therefore the restoration of the *fasces*, or symbol of power, to the people.

820   accipiet, natosque pater nova bella moventis
ad poenam pulchra pro libertate vocabit,
infelix, utcumque ferent ea facta minores:
vincet amor patriae laudumque immensa cupido.
quin Decios Drusosque procul saevumque securi
825   aspice Torquatum et referentem signa Camillum.
illae autem paribus quas fulgere cernis in armis,
concordes animae nunc et dum nocte prementur,
heu quantum inter se bellum, si lumina vitae
attigerint, quantas acies stragemque ciebunt,
830   aggeribus socer Alpinis atque arce Monoeci
descendens, gener adversis instructus Eois!
ne, pueri, ne tanta animis adsuescite bella
neu patriae validas in viscera vertite viris;

Lines 820-01: **Natos... ad poenam**—The story is given in Book II of Livy. Brutus was one of the first Consuls. During his time in office, his sons were charged with conspiring to restore King Tarquin. They were tried before Brutus, and he condemned them to death.

Line 824: **Decios**—A father and son who both sacrificed themselves in battle.

Druso—This may refer to Livius Drusus, who conquered Hasdrubal in the Second Punic War, or to Claudius Drusus, the son by an earlier marriage of Liva, the wife of Augustus. The Drusii are probably mentioned by way of flattering Livia, who was present at the first recital of this Book.

Line 825: **Torquatum**—Manlius Torquatus was famous for having his own son put to death for disobeying his orders on the field of battle.

Signa—Captured by the Gauls at the battle of the Allia, and recovered by Camillus when he conquered the enemy on their leaving Rome.

Camillum—Marcus Furius Camillus. According to Livy and Plutarch, he was granted four triumphs, was five times Dictator, and was honoured with the title of Second Founder of Rome.

Line 826: **Illae**—A reference to Caesar and Pompey and their civil war.

Fulgere—Normally a verb of the second declension: fulgēre. Here, it is moved, doubtless to fit the metre—to the third declension: fulgĕre.

Line 830: **Socer**—Caesar married his daughter Julia to Pompey. Her early death removed the last impediment to their civil war.

Line 830: **Monoeci**—Monaco.

Line 833: **Viscera vertite viris**—Alliteration was an occasional adornment of both prose and poetry in Latin.

tuque prior, tu parce, genus qui ducis Olympo,
835   proice tela manu, sanguis meus!—

ille triumphata Capitolia ad alta Corintho
victor aget currum caesis insignis Achivis.
eruet ille Argos Agamemnoniasque Mycenas
ipsumque Aeaciden, genus armipotentis Achilli,
840   ultus avos Troiae templa et temerata Minervae.
quis te, magne Cato, tacitum aut te, Cosse, relinquat?
quis Gracchi genus aut geminos, duo fulmina belli,
Scipiadas, cladem Libyae, parvoque potentem
Fabricium vel te sulco, Serrane, serentem?

Line 835: Another unfinished line.

Lines 836–853: Other heroes of the Republic pass in review. Anchises declares the greatness of Rome to lie not in art or science, but in war and the following peace and justice.

Line 836: **Ille… victor**—A reference to Lucius Mummius, who sacked Corinth in 146 BC. The following lines justify this act as revenge by the posterity of the Trojans against the posterity of Agamemnon and Menelaus.

Line 839: **Aeaciden**—A reference to Perseus, King of Macedon, who claimed descent from Achilles. See above.

Line 841: **Cato**—Marcus Porcius Cato, 234-149 BC; Censor in 184, and opponent of Greek cultural influence. A beast to his slaves. Famous for ending his speeches with *Ceterum censeo Carthaginem esse delendam*—despite the Roman oath to do no harm to the defeated enemy if it disarmed.

Cosse—Aulus Cornelius Cossus, who won the *Spolia Opima* in 437 BC by killing the King of Veientines in battle.

Line 842: **Gracchi genus… geminos**—The two brothers Tiberius and Gracchus who were both murdered by the Senate for trying to ensure that Roman People would share the benefits of the empire they were conquering. Though regarded as traitors to their class, they were among the ideological ancestors of Julius Caesar, and, together with Cicero, they shared in the posthumous truce that was part of the Augustan Settlement.

Line 843: **Scipiadas**—Two members of the Scipio Family, both called *Africanus*, who were prominent in the defeat and final destruction of Carthage.

Line 844: **Fabricium**—Gaius Fabricius Luscinus Monocularis; Consul in 282 BC. He directed the war against Pyrrhus. According to Plutarch, Pyrrhus was so impressed in their truce negotiations by his inability to bribe Fabricius, that he released the Roman prisoners even without a ransom.

Serrane—Atilius Regulus Serranus; Consul in 287 BC. Famed for his simplicity of life. Note the alliteration.

845   quo fessum rapitis, Fabii? tu Maximus ille es,
        unus qui nobis cunctando restituis rem.
        excudent alii spirantia mollius aera
        (credo equidem), vivos ducent de marmore vultus,
        orabunt causas melius, caelique meatus
850   describent radio et surgentia sidera dicent:
        tu regere imperio populos, Romane, memento
        (hae tibi erunt artes), pacique imponere morem,
        parcere subiectis et debellare superbos."

        sic pater Anchises, atque haec mirantibus addit:

Line 846: **Unus qui nobis...**—Quintus Fabius Maximus Cunctator; General after the disaster at Cannae in 216 BC, whose refusal to fight another battle helped save Italy from Hannibal. The line is a reworking of Ennius:

    unus homo nobis cunctando restituit rem:
    noenum rumores ponebat ante salutem:
    ergo postque magisque viri nunc gloria claret.

Line 847 *et seq.*: **Alii**—These are the Greeks. Their traditional view of the Greeks involved the Romans in some contradiction. On the one hand, the Greeks were a soft and effeminate race, conquered by Rome with barely a decent war. They were also the ancestral enemy who had burned Troy and whose conquest by Rome was just revenge. See above. On the other hand, they were the matchless Golden Race who had led the Romans from darkness into light. Every time a Roman squeezed ink from a reed pen, he was entering a world created by the Greeks. It would be indecent of Vergil to do other than confess the debt.

Line 843: **Parcere subiectis et debellare superbos**—After a three-century course of treachery and mass-murder, the Romans around the Birth of Christ found themselves masters of an empire bounded by the Rhine, the Euphrates and the Atlas Mountains. They now chose to justify this with talk of universal peace and justice. There are worse justifications.

Lines 854–887: Anchises points out the elder Marcellus, who is attended by a younger spirit. Aeneas asks who the youth is, and learns that he is destined to die young, amid the general grief of the Roman people.

855   "aspice, ut insignis spoliis Marcellus opimis
           ingreditur victorque viros supereminet omnis.
           hic rem Romanam magno turbante tumultu
           sistet eques, sternet Poenos Gallumque rebellem,
           tertiaque arma patri suspendet capta Quirino."
860   atque hic Aeneas (una namque ire videbat
           egregium forma iuvenem et fulgentibus armis,
           sed frons laeta parum et deiecto lumina vultu)
           "quis, pater, ille, virum qui sic comitatur euntem?
           filius, anne aliquis magna de stirpe nepotum?
865   qui strepitus circa comitum! quantum instar in ipso!
           sed nox atra caput tristi circumvolat umbra."
           tum pater Anchises lacrimis ingressus obortis:
           "o gnate, ingentem luctum ne quaere tuorum;
           ostendent terris hunc tantum fata nec ultra
870   esse sinent. nimium vobis Romana propago
           visa potens, superi, propria haec si dona fuissent.
           quantos ille virum magnam Mavortis ad urbem
           campus aget gemitus! vel quae, Tiberine, videbis
           funera, cum tumulum praeterlabere recentem!
875   nec puer Iliaca quisquam de gente Latinos
           in tantum spe tollet avos, nec Romula quondam
           ullo se tantum tellus iactabit alumno.
           heu pietas, heu prisca fides invictaque bello

Line 855: **Marcellus**—A double reference here. Marcus Marcellus was a general in the Second Punic War, who won the *Spolia Opima* by killing a Gaulish chieftain with his own hands. The other Marcellus was the nephew of Augustus whose early death was the first of a series of blows that left the first Emperor with no eventual choice but to leave everything to his step-son Tiberius. Octavia, the mother of Marcellus, was present at the first recital of this Book. She is said to have fainted after hearing these words. She then gave Vergil 100,000 Sesterces for each relevant line—or about £160,000 as of 2019.

Line 859: **Quirino**—Quirinus was the name given to Romulus after he was made a god. The *Spolia Opima* were won only three times in Roman history: by Romulus, by Cossus and by Marcellus.

Line 872: **Mavortis**—Mavors; another name for Mars, the God of War.

Line 873: **Campum**—The Campus Martius in Rome.

dextera! non illi se quisquam impune tulisset
880 obvius armato, seu cum pedes iret in hostem
seu spumantis equi foderet calcaribus armos.
heu, miserande puer, si qua fata aspera rumpas,
tu Marcellus eris. manibus date lilia plenis
purpureos spargam flores animamque nepotis
885 his saltem accumulem donis, et fungar inani
munere." sic tota passim regione vagantur
aeris in campis latis atque omnia lustrant.

quae postquam Anchises natum per singula duxit
incenditque animum famae venientis amore,
890 exim bella viro memorat quae deinde gerenda,
Laurentisque docet populos urbemque Latini,
et quo quemque modo fugiatque feratque laborem.
Sunt geminae Somni portae, quarum altera fertur
cornea, qua veris facilis datur exitus umbris,
895 altera candenti perfecta nitens elephanto,
sed falsa ad caelum mittunt insomnia Manes.
his ibi tum natum Anchises unaque Sibyllam

Lines 888–901: Anchises explains to Aeneas what awaits him in Italy, and then dismisses him and the Sibyl through one of the gates of sleep. Aeneas sails to Caieta.

Line 891: **Laurentis**—Laurentum was a coastal town a few miles south of Ostia. It was the seat of King Latinus, with whom Aeneas has considerable dealings in the later books of *The Aeneid.*

Line 893: **Sunt geminae Somni portae**—The Gates of Sleep are from Homer's Gates of Dreams, which are similarly described in Od. 19. 562 *et seq.* Much ingenuity has gone, during the past two thousand years, into explaining the departure of Aeneas through the Gate of False Dreams. Perhaps this is another section that Vergil would have changed had be lived. Or perhaps he is undercutting all his lush praise of Augustus by dismissing all earthly glory as a passing dream.

Line 896: **Manes**—The *Di Manes* are deities thought to represent souls of deceased loved ones. They were associated with the Lares, Lemures, Genii, and Di Penates as deities that pertained to domestic, local, and personal cults. They belonged broadly to the category of *di inferi,* "those who dwell below," the undifferentiated collective of divine dead. The Manes were honoured during the Parentalia and Feralia in February. Many Roman grave stones bear the words *Dis Manibus.*

prosequitur dictis portaque emittit eburna,
ille viam secat ad naves sociosque revisit.
900   Tum se ad Caietae recto fert litore portum.
ancora de prora iacitur; stant litore puppes.

Line 900: **Caietae**—Caieta was a coastal town in Latium.
Recto litore—Sailing straight along the shore.

TRANSLATIONS

The Argument (John Dryden, 1697)

The Sibyl foretells Aeneas the adventures he should meet with in Italy. She attends him to hell; describing to him the various scenes of that place, and conducting him to his father Anchises, who instructs him in those sublime mysteries, of the soul of the world, and the transmigration; and shows him that glorious race of heroes, which was to descend from him and his posterity.

Liber VI Interpretatio Carolus Ruaeus (1675)	Book VI Translation Joseph Davidson (1723)

Lines 1–13: Aeneas travels to Italy and lands there, and goes to the Temple of Apollo at Cumae to consult the Sibyl.

Sic loquitur plorans, et permittit navibus cursum *liberum*, et demum appellitur litori Euboico Cumarum. *Nautae* vertunt prora *ad* mare: deinde anchora sistit naves uncis tenacibus, et curvatae puppes tegunt *extremum* litus: prompta turba iuvenum exilit in terram Italicam: pars quaerit scintillas ignis latentes in venis lapidis: pars colligit ligna *arborum, quae sunt* opacae domus ferarum; et ostendit repertos fluvios.

THUS he speaks with Tears in his Eyes, and gives his Ship full Sail, and at length he makes the Eubean Coast of Cumae. They turn their Prows out to the Sea; then the Anchor with its tenacious Fluke moored the Ships and the winding Sterns line the Margin of the Shore: The youthful Crew springs forth with Ardour on the Hesperian strand: Some explore the Seeds of Fire latent in the Veins of Flint: Some plunder the copses, the close Retreat of wild Beasts, and point out Rivers newly discovered.

Sed Pius Aeneas vadit *ad* templum altum cui Apollo praeest, et ad vastam penitus cavernam et horrendum penetrale Sibyllae, cui Deus Delius inspirit magnam animam et intelligentiam, declaratque *res* futuras. Iam intrant sylvas et auratum templum Dianae.

But the pious Aeneas repairs to the Towers over which exalted Apollo presides, and to the ample dreary Cave, the Cell of the Sibyl awful at a Distance; whose great Mind and Soul the prophetic God of Delos inspires, and discloses to her Futurity. Now they enter Diana's Groves, and *Apollo's*

97

golden Roofs.

Lines 14–41: The Temple described, together with the carvings on its gates. The Sibyl calls everyone inside.

Daedalus, sicut fama perhibet, fugiens regnum Minois, ausus committere se aeri *cum* pennis velocibus, evasit ad frigidum septentrionem per viam insolitam; et volans stetit denique super arce Cumana. Appulsus primum his terris sacravit tibi remos alarum, O Apollo; et fundavit vastum templum.

Daedalus, as is famed, flying the Realms of Minos, adventuring to commit himself to the Sky on nimble Wings, failed *aloft in Air* through an untried path to the cold Regions of the North, and at length gently alighted on the Tower of Chalcis. Having landed first on those Coasts, to thee, *O Phoebus*, he consecrated his oary Wings, and reared a huge Temple.

In portis *erat sculpta* mors Androgei: deinde Athenienses iussi *in* poenam dare singulis annis septem corpora filiorum, *res* misera! Adest urna *unde* sortes eductae *erant*. Cretica insula eminens mari respondet e regione. Hic adest amor insanus Pasiphaes *erga* taurum, et Pasiphae supposita *per* fraudem et Minotaurus soboles *eius* biformis mixto genere, monimentum flagitiosae libidinis. Hic *adest* illa difficultas et error inextricabilis labyrinthi.

On the Gates was *represented* the death of Andregeos: Then the Athenians doomed, as an Attonement *for their Crime*, a piteous Case! To pay *the* yearly *Tribute of* seven of their Children; *there* stands the Urn whence the Lots were drawn: in Counterview answers the Land of Crete raised above the Sea: Here is seen Pasiphae's fierce Passion for the Bull, and she by Artifice humbled *to his Embrace*; and the Minotaur, that mingled Birth, and two formed Offsprings, *all* Monuments of execrable Lust: Here *is seen* the laboured Work of the Labyrinth, and the inextricable Mazes.

Nam Daedalus miserans magnum amorem filiae regis, ipse explicuit *Theseo* fraudes circuitus parietum, dirigens filo passus *eius* incertos.

But Daedalus, pitying the violent Love of the Princess *Ariadne*, unravels to *Theseus* the Intricacies and winding Alleys of the Structure, himself guiding his dark mazy Steps by a Thread.

Tu etiam, O Icare, haberes magnum locum in tanta sculptura, si dolor permisset. Bis conatus erat exprimere in auro calamitatem illam: bis manus paternae defecerunt.

You too, *O Icarus*, should have bore a considerable Part in that great Work, had but *the Father's Grief* permitted. Twice he essayed to figure the disastrous Story in Gold; twice the Parent's Hand misgave him.

At vero *Troiani* ulterius perlustrassent oculis omnia: nisi Achates ante praemissus *ab Aenea ad Sibyllam*, rediisset; et cum eo Deiphobe *filia* Glauci, sacerdos Apollinis ac Dianae, quae dicit haec regi:

And now *the Trojans* woujld survey the whole Work in Order, were not Achates sent before *by Aeneas* just at hand, and with him the Priestess of Phoebus and Diana, Deiphobe, Glaucus's Daughter, who thus bespeaks the King:

"Hoc tempus non petit sibi haec spectacula: nunc potius erit immolare septem iuvencos de armento *adhuc* indomito, et totidem oves electas iuxta ritum."

"This Hour admits not to be spent in these Amusements. At present it will be more suitable to sacrifice seven Bullocks from a Herd untouched *with the Yoke*, and as many chosen Ewes with usual Rites."

Lines 42–76: The Sibyl commands Aeneas to pray. He prays for a happy end to his wanderings, with a home in Italy for himself and his people.

Sacerdos allocuta Aeneam *his verbis*, invitat Troianos in altum templum: et famuli non tardant *exequi* mandata de *sacrificio*. Latus ingens rupis Cumanae excavatum *est* in *formam* antri: quo centum lati aditus et centum portae ducunt: unde erumpunt totidem voces, *quae sunt* responsa Sibyllae.

The Priestess having thus addressed Aeneas (nor are they backwards to obey her sacred Orders) summons the Trojans into the lofty Temple. The huge side of an Euboeand Rock is cut out into a Cave, whither an hundred broad Avenues lead, an hundred Doors; whence rush forth as many Voices, the Responses of the Sibyl.

Perventum erat ad os *antri*: cum Virgo dixit: "Tempus est petendi oracula: Deus, Deus adest."

They had come to the Entry *of the Cave*, when *thus* the Virgin: Now is the Time to consult your Fate: "The God, lo the God," she cries.

Cui dicenti talia ante ostia, repente non remansit facies *eadem*, non idem color, non capilli ordinate: sed pectus anhelans, et cor efferatum intumescit rabie: *coepitque* apparere maior nec loquens modo humano: ex quo correpta est spiritu Dei iam praesente.

While thus before the Gate she speaks, on a sudden her Looks change, her Colour comes and goes, her Locks are dishevelled, her Breast heaves, and her fiercely untoward Heart swells with enthusiastic Rage: she appears in a larger and more majestic Form, her Voice speaking her not a Mortal, now that she is inspired with the nearer influence of the God:

Dixit*que*: "Tardus es ad emittenda vota et preces, O Aenea Troiane!

"Do you delay, Trojan Aeneas," she says, "do you delay to pour forth Vows

Tardus es! Nam magna ostia antri terrifici non aperientur prius, *quam preces emiseris.*"

Et haec locuta siluit.

Tremor frigidus subiit in ossa dura Troianorum; et Rex *eorum* misit preces ex intimo corde:

"O Phoebe, qui *semper* misertus *es* acerborum casuum Troiae: qui direxisti sagittam Troianam et manum Paridis in corpus Achillis: te auctore ingressus sum tot maria cingentia magnas terras, et nationes Massylorum longe remotas, et litora vicina Syrtibus. Nunc denique attingimus litora Italiae recedentis. Hactenus calamitas Troianorum nos persecute fuerit. Nunc aequum est vos etiam ignoscere Troianae genti, O Dii, et Deae omnes, quibus adversabatur Troia et magna Gloria Troiadis.

"Et tu, O sanctissima Sibylla, praevidens futurum, permitte Troianos, et Deos vagos, et numina Troiae iactata, sedere in Latio: non peto regna non debita meis fatis. Tunc statuam Phoebo et Dianae templa e marmore solido, et dies festos de nomine Phoebi *dictos.* Magnum etiam sacrarium expectat te in regnis nostris. Ego enim ille recondam tua oracula, et secreta fata declarata meae genti; et dedicabo tibi viros electos, O alma: tantummodo noli inscribere carmina

and Prayers? *Instantly begin*; for not till then shall the ample Gates of this Mansion where the God thunders with his Voice, expand their Jaws."

And having thus said she ceased.

Shivering Horror ran thrilling cold through the Trojans, and penetrated even to their hard *and solid* Bones: Prince *Aeneas* pours forth these Prayers from the Bottom of his Heart:

"*Great* Apollo, always disposed to pity the grievous Calamities of Troy. Who guided the Trojan Darts and the Hand of Paris to the Body of Achilles; under thy Conduct I have entered so many Seas encompassing extensive Countries, and the Massylian Kingdoms far remote, and Regions whose Frontiers are guarded by Quicksands. Now, after all our Toils, we are in Possession of the Coast of Italy that flies from us. Let it suffice that the Fortune of Troy has persecuted us thus far. Now it is but Equity that you too spare the Trojan Race, ye Gods and Goddesses all, to whom Ilium and the high Renown of Dardania was obnoxious.

"And thou most holy Prophetess, skilled in Futurity, grant *(for I ask no Realms but what are destined to me by Fate)* that the Trojans, their wandering gods, and the persecuted deities of Troy, may settle in Latium. Then will I appoint, to Phoebus and Diana, temples of solid marble, and festival days, called by the propitious *maid*, I will deposit thy oracles, and the secret fates declared to my nation, and will consecrated chosen men *for thy service.* Only commit not thy *prophetic* verses to leaves, lest they fly about in disorder,

frondibus, ne confusa evolent *in* ludibrium rapidorum ventorum: precor *te*, loquere tu ipsa."

the sport of the rapid winds: I beg you yourself will pronounce them.

Lines 77–97: Inspired by Apollo, the Sibyl promises Aeneas every success in Italy, but only after wars as long and terrible as that of Troy.

Sic fecit finem loquendi voce.

He ended his address.

At Sibylla ingens, nondum patiens Phoebi, furit in caverna, *tentans*, an possit expellere e pectore magnum Deum: ille tanto magis exagitat os rabidum, subigens pectus efferatum, et opprimendo accommodat *ad oracula proferanda*.

But the prophetess, as yet impatient under the influence of Phoebus, raves with wild outrage in the cave, struggling if possible to disburden her soul of the mighty god: so much the more he *curbs and* harasses her wildly rebellious jaws, subduing her ferocious heart, and, by bearing down her opposition, forms *and makes her pliable*.

Et iam centum magnae portae antri apertae sunt moto proprio, et emittunt in aerem *haec* responsa Sibyllae:

And now the hundred spacious gates of the dome expanded of their own accord, and pour forth these responses into the open air:

"O qui evasisti magna pericula maris. Sed maiora expectant te *in* terra. Troiani prevenient ad regnum Lavinium, eiice hanc solicitudinem e corde: sed cupient quoque non *eo* pervenisse. Video bella, horrida bella, et Thybrim spumantem multo sanguine. Non deerunt tibi Simois, nec Xanthus, nec exercitus Graeci: alter Achilles iam paratus est *in* Latio, ipse etiam filius Deae: et Iuno infesta Troianis non aberit ullo loco. Quem tu, quas nations Italorum, et quas urbes non implorabis supplex in rebus extremis? Causa tantarum calamitatum *erit* rursus Troianis coniunx hospitio excipiens *eos*, et rursus peregrinae nuptiae.

"O thou who hast at length overpassed the vast perils of the ocean! Yet more afflictive trials by land await thee. The Trojans shall come to the realms of Lavinium (dismiss that concern from your breast); but they shall wish too they had never come *thither*. Wars, horrid wars I foresee, and Tyber foaming with a deluge of blood. Neither Simois, nor Xanthus, nor Grecian camps, shall be wanting to you there. Another Achilles is prepared *for thee* in Latium; he too the son of a goddess. Nor shall Juno, the appointed scourge of the Trojans, leave them wherever they are: while in your distress, which of the Italian states, which of its cities, shall you not humbly supplicate for aid? Once more shall a consort, a hostess, once more shall a foreign match be the cause of so great calamity to the

Trojans.

"Tu noli frangi calamitatibus: sed contra resiste audacior, quam tua fortuna te permitte *esse*. Prima salutis via aperietur *tibi* ab urbe Graeca, quod non putas."

"Sink not under the weight of your sufferings, but encounter them with the greater fortitude, the more that fortune shall oppose you. What you least expect, your first means of deliverance shall arise from a Grecian city."

Lines 98–123: Aeneas accepts the hard fate laid out for him by the Sibyl. He asks only that he should first be allowed to visit the Underworld to converse with Anchises, his late father.

Talibus verbis Cumaea Sibylla canit e recessu terrificas ambages, et reboat e caverna, obtegens vera obscuris: sic Apollo regit habenas, et agitat stimulus sub *eius* corde.

Thus from her holy cell the Cumaean Sibyl delivers her awfully mysterious oracles, and, wrapping the truth in obscurity, bellows in her cave: with such rigour Apollo shakes the reins over her as she wildly rages, and deep in her breast exerts his stimulating power.

Statim atque furor excessit, et ad os efferatum siluit; heros Aeneas coepit *loqui*:

As soon as her fury ceased, and her maddening tongue was silent, the hero Aeneas begins:

"O Virgo, nulla species laborum occurrit mihi nova et improvisa: praesensi et mecum prius mente confeci cuncta. Unum precor: quandoquidem fertur his *esse* porta regis inferni, et obscura palus Acheronte exundante: liceat *mihi* ire in conspectum et vultum dilecti patris: monstra iter, et aperi sacras portas.

"To me, O virgin, no shape of sufferings can arise new or unexpected: I have anticipated all *the ills of life*, and acted them over before-hand in my mind. My sole request is (since here at the gate of the infernal king is said to be, and the darksome lake *arising* from the overflowing of Acheron), that I may be so happy as to come into the sight and presence of my dear father, that you would show the way, and open to me the sacred avenues.

"Ego his humeris servavi illum inter flammas et mille spicula insequentia, et extraxi e mediis hostibus. Ille secutus *est* meum iter et omnia maria mecum; atque tolerabat omnes minas et coeli et maris, *quamquam* infirmus, supra

"On these shoulders I rescued him, through flames and a thousand darts pursing, and saved him from the midst of the enemy. He accompanied my path, attended me in all my voyages, and though weak and infirm, bore all the terrors both of the sea and sky,

robur et conditionum senectutis. Praeterea ipse rogans me, *simul* dabat iussa ut convenirem tuam domum.

beyond what the power and condition of old age can *usually* bear. Nay more, he it was who earnestly requested and enjoined me to come to thee a suppliant, and visit thy Temple.

"O alma precor, miserere filii et patris: nam potes cuncta: nec frustra Hecate praeposuit te sylvis infernis. Si Orpheus potuit evocare umbram uxoris, adiutus cithara Thracia et chordis sonantibus: si Pollux eripuit fratrem alterna morte, et totius it reditque per *illam eandem* viam: cur proferem Theseum; cur magnum Herculem? Mihi origo est a supremo Iove."

Propitious *Virgin*, pity, I pray, the Son and the Sire: For they Power is unlimited, nor hath Hecate in vain given thee Charge of the Athenian Groves. If Orpheus had power to recall *to Light* his Consort's ghost, assisted by his Thracian Harp and harmonious Strings: If Pollux redeemed his Brother Castor by alternate Death, and goes and comes this Way so often: What need I mention Theseus, *or* great Alcides? I too derive my Birth *as well as they* from Jove Supreme.

Lines 124–155: The Sibyl commands Aeneas to find the Golden Bough, which, like a cross against vampires, will let him pass unharmed through the Underworld. Before then, he must give proper burial to Misenus, one of his fellows who has drowned.

Talibus verbis praecabatur, et tangebat altaria. Tunc Sibylla coepit ita loqui: "O create sanguine Deorum. Troiane fili Anchisae: facilis *est* descensus *ad* inferos: porta nigri Plutonis aperta est diu noctuque: sed referre pedem, et redire ad aerem sublimem, haec est difficultas, hic labor.

In these Terms he prayed, and held the Altar, when thus the prophetess began to speak: "Offspring of the Gods, Trojan *Prince*, Son of Anchises, easy is the Path that leads down to Hell; grim Pluto's Gate stands open Night and Day: But to reascend, and escape *from thence* to the upper Regions, this is a Work, this is a Task *indeed*:

"Pauci Deorum filii, quos iustus Iupiter dilexit, vel quos generosa virtus extulit ad coelum, *id* potuerunt. Sylvae occupant omnia intervalla, et Cocytus fluens nigris flexibus circumcingit. Si tamen tantus amor et tantum desiderium inest animo, praeternavigandi bis fluvios Stygios, et videndi bis nigrum Tartarum: et *si* placet suscipere vanum laborem: audi,

"Some few, whom favouring Jove did love, or illustrious Virtue advanced to Heaven, the Sons of the Gods, effected *it*, Woods cover all the Space that lies between, and Cocytus gliding with his black winding Flood surrounds. But if your Soul be possessed with so strong a Love, so ardent a Desire, twice to sail across the Stygian Lake, twice to visit gloomy Tartarus; and you will needs fondly pursue the desperate Enterprize,

quae prius perficienda sunt.

learn what first is to be done.

"Ramus aureus et frondibus et cortice flexile, *qui* dicitur dictatus Proserpinae infernae, latet *in* umbrusa arbore: hunc omnis sylva occultat, et umbrae obscurarum vallium abscondunt. Sed non conceditur intrare *loca* secreta terrae, priusquam aliquis evulserit ex arbore aureum ramum. Iussit pulchra Proserpina ferri ad se suum illud donum. Uno decerpto alter non deest *etiam* aureus, et ramulus pullulat simili metallo. Igitur quaere *illum* erectis oculis, et inventum evelle manu *iuxta* ritum: nam ipse sponte et facile cedet *tibi evellenti*, si fata vocant te *ad inferos*; alioqui non poteris *illum* superare ullo robore, nec amputare duro ferro.

"On a Tree of deepening Shade there lies concealed a Bough, with Leaves and limber Twigs of Gold, sacred pronounced to infernal Juno: This the whole Grove covers, and Shades in dark Vallies inclose. But to none is it given to enter the hidden Recesses of the Earth till from the Tree he pluck the Bough with its golden Locks. Fair Proserpine hath ordained this to be presented to her as her peculiar Present: When the first is torn off, a second *likewise* of Gold soon succeeds, and a *new* Twig shoots forth Leaves of the same Metal. Therefore search for it with Eyes erect, and when found pluck it with the Hand as becomes: For if the Fates invite you, itself will come away spontaneous and easy: Otherwise it will not be in your Power to master it by any *natural* Strength, nor lop it off by *the artificial means of* stubborn Steel.

"Praeterea cadaver amici exanime iacet tibi, heu ignoras *id!* et funestat morte totam classem: dum requiris responsa, et suspensus *haeres* ad ianuam meam. Prius depone hunc in propria sede, et include tumulo. *Deinde* duc *ad aram* victimas nigras: hae primae sint expiationes. Ita denique videbis sylvas Stygias, regionem inaccessam viventibus."

"Besides, the Body of your Friend lies breathless (whereof you, alas, are not aware) and pollutes the whole Shore with his Corpse while you are prying into the Secrets of Heaven, and hang lingering on at my Gate. First convey him to his Place of Rest, and bury him in the Grave. *Then* bring black Cattle: Let there be the first Sacrifices of Expiation. Thus at length you shall have a View of the Stygian Groves, Realms inaccessible to the Living.

Sic locuta est, tum clauso ore tacuit.

She said, and closing her Lips was silent.

Lines 156–211: The body of Misenus is found. While preparing wood for the funeral pyre, Aeneas is led by two doves, sacred to his mother, Venus. They lead him to the Golden Bough.

Aeneas relinquens cavernam incedit

Aeneas, with Sorrow in his Looks, his

104

vultu tristi, figens oculos *in terram*; et volvit secum mente casus obscuros: cui fidelis Achates it comes, et figit pedes *agitatus* similibus curis. Iactabant inter se plurima vario colloquio: *scilicet*, quem sociorum mortuum dixisset Sibylla, quod cadaver tumulandum. At illi postquam pervenere *ad suos*, aspiciunt in litore arido Misenum occisum miseranda morte: Misenum, *filium* Aeoli, quo non *erat* alter aptior ad incitandos tuba viros, et inflammandam pugnam sonitu. Hic fuerat socius magni Hectoris, iuxta Hectora circumibat *pugnantes* conspicuus tuba et hasta. Ex quo victor Achilles privaverat vita Hectora, heros generosissimus adiunxerat se socium Aeneae Troiano, non secutus viliorem dominum. Sed modo, dum forte inconsultus sonat per mare concha excavata, et sonitu lacessit Deos ad certamen; Triton invidus, si aequum est *id* credere, submerserat spumantibus fluctibus hominem circumventum inter scopulos. Igitur omnes circum querebantur magno clamore: imprimis pius Aeneas.

Eyes fixed on the Ground, takes his Way leaving the Cave, and musing ponders the dark Event in his Mind: whom faithful Achates accompanies, and moves on with equal Concern. Many Doubts they started between them in the Variety of their Conversation; who was the lifeless Friend designed by the Prophetess, what Corpse to be interred. And as they came they see Misenus on the dry Beach, slain by a base ignoble Death; Misenus, a Son of Aeolus, than whom none more dextrous to rouze the Hero by the brazen Trumpet, and kindle the Rage of War by *martial* Sounds. He had been the Companion of great Hector, and about Hector he fought, distinguished both for *the Use of* the Clarion and Spear. After that victorious Achilles bereaved Hector of Live, the valiant Hero associated with Dardanian Aeneas, following a Chief not inferior *to the other*. But at that Time, while madly presumptuous he makes the Seas resound with his hollow Trumpet, and with *bold* Notes challenges the Gods to a Trial of Skill, Triton, jealous *of his Honour* (if the Story be worthy of Credit) having inveigled him between two Rocks, had overwhelmed him in the foaming Billows. Therefore all murmured their Lamentations around him with loud Noise, especially the pious Aeneas.

Deinde, exequuntur mandata Sibyllae plorantes, nulla mora *est*; et contendunt accumulare ex arboribus atque erigere ad coelum rogum sepulchralem. Eunt in sylvam veterem, profunda latibula ferarum; piceae cadunt, ilex resonat percussa securibus, et trunci fraxinei roburque fissile frangitur cuneis: volvunt e montibus magnas ornos.

Then forthwith they set about the Sibyl's Orders in mournful Plight, and are emulous to heap up the Altar of the Funeral pile with Trees, and raise it towards Heaven. They repair to an ancient Wood, the deep Haunts of the Savage kind: Down drop the Firs: The Holm felled by the Axes crashes, and the Ashen beams, and the yielding Oak is cleft by Wedges: Down from the

Aeneas quoque inter tales labores primus incitat socios, et instruitur similibus instrumentis.

Mountains they tumble the huge Wild ashes. Aeneas too, in chief amidst these Labours animates his Followers, and is arrayed in like Arms.

Interim ipse meditatur haec suo cum animo moesto, intuens ingentem sylvam; et ita orat voce:

Mean while he thus ruminates in his distressed Breast, surveying the spacious Wood, and thus prays aloud:

"O si iam ille ramus aureus monstret se nobis in tanta svlva: siquidem, O Misene, Sibylla nimis vere dixit cuncta de te."

"Would but that golden Bough on the Tree now present itself to our View in this ample Forest: Since, Misenus, all that the Prophetess declared of thee is true, alas, but too true."

Vix locutus erat ista: quando duae columbae forte volantes per aerem venerunt in ipsum conspectum hominis, et steterunt in viridi terra. Tunc maximus heros agnoscit volucres matris *suae*, et gaudens orat:

Scarce had he spoke these Words, when it chanced that two Pigeons in their airly Flight, came directly into the Hero's View, and lighted on the verdant Ground. Then the exalted Hero knows his Mother's Birds, and rejoicing prays:

"*O vos* estote duces, si est aliqua via: et ex aere dirigite iter *meum* in svlvam, ubi ramus pretiosus inumbrat terram foecundam: et tu, O Dea mater, ne desere *me* in rebus incertis."

"Oh *be* my Guides, wherever is my Way, and steer your Course through the Air into the Groves, where the precious Branch overshades the fertile Soil: And thou, my Goddess-mother, oh be not wanting to me in this my Perplexity."

Sic locutus continuit pedem, explorans quae dent indicia, quo pergant ire. Illae pascentes coeperunt tantum progredi subsiliendo, quantum oculi sequentium poterant observare *visu* acutissimo. Deinde postquam pervenerunt ad os foetidi Averni; attollunt se veloces, et elapsae per aerem tenuem sistunt grato loco super gemina arbore, unde splendor auri dissimilis coloris emicuit inter ramos. Quale viscum, quod propria arbor non producit, solet hyberno tempore in sylvis virescere foliis recentibus: et cingere ramusculo

Thus having said, he paused, observing what Indications they offer, *and* whither they wing their Way. They, feeding and flying *by Turns*, advanced before as far as the eyes of the Followers could trace them with their Ken. Then, having come to the Mouth of the noisome Avernus, they mount up swiftly, and gliding through the pure Air, both alight on the wished-for Place, on the Tree whence the particolourd Gleam of the Gold shone thro' the Branches. As in the Woods the Mistletoe, which springs not from the Tree whereon it grows, uses to flourish with new Leaves in the Cold of Winter,

fulvo ramos *arborum* rotundos. Talis erat forma auri pullulantis *in* densa ilice, sic lamina stridebat dulci vento.

and twine around the tapering Trunk with its yellow Offspring; such was the Appearance of the vegetable Gold on the shady Holm: In like Manner the metallic Rind tinkled with *every* gentle Breath *of* Wind.

Aeneas statim accipit *ramum*, et cupidus decerpit lentiorem, defertque in domum Sibyllae.

Forthwith Aeneas grasps, and eagerly tears off the lingering *Branch*, and bears it to the Grotto of the prophetic Sibyl.

Lines 212–235: Meanwhile, the Trojans were conducting the funeral of Misenus in all its details. Aeneas raises a tomb over his remains.

Interea Troiani non segnius plorabant in litore Misenum, et parabant ultima *officia* cadaveri moesto. Primo erexerunt magnum bustum e taedis pinguibus et quercu fissa: cuius latera ornant ramis funestis, et *in* parte anteriore collocant funebres cupressos, et desuper ornant armis splendentibus. Pars adhibent aquam calidam, et *vasa* aerea ebullientia *ex* igne: et eluunt unguuntque cadaver frigentis. Fit comploratio: deinde collocant *in* lecto membra deplorata; et superaggerunt vestes purpureas ac tegmina consueta. Pars supposuere se magno feretro, *quod est* triste officium: et retroversi porrexere suppositam facem, *ex* consuetudine maiorum: comburuntur accumulata munera thuris, et carnes, et pocula iniecti olei. Postquam cineres subsederunt, et flamma defecit; irrigaverunt vino reliquias et favillas siccas: et Chorinaeus inclusit vasculo aereo ossa collecta. Idem circumiit ter socios aqua piaculari, aspergens tenui rore *cum* ramo fertilis oleae: et expiavit viros, et protulit voces ultimas.

Mean while the Trojans were no less assiduously employed in mourning Misenus on the Shore, and in paying the last Duties to his insensible ungrateful Shade. First they rear a vast Pile unctuous with Pines and split Oak; whole Sides they interweave with black *baleful* Boughs, and place in the Front deadly Cypresses, and deck it above with glittering Arms. Some get ready warm Water and *Caldrons* bubbling from the Flames, and wash and anoint his cold Limbs. They fetch a Groan: Then lay the bewailed Body on a Couch, and throw over it the purple Robes, his wonted Apparel. Others bore up the cumbrous Bier, a mournful Office, and with their Faces turned away *from the Pile*, after the Manner of their Ancestors, underneath it is held a *lighted* Torch. Amassed together blaze Offerings of Incense, the *sacred* Viands, and whole Goblets of Oil poured *on the Pile*. After the Ashes had sunk down, and the Flames relented, they drenched the Relicks and soaking Embers in Wine: And Chorinaeus inclosed the collected Bones in a brazen Urn. Thrice too he made the Circuit of the Company with holy Water, sprinkling them with a gentle Dew, and a Branch of the lucky Olive: and thus he purified them, and pronounced the last Farewel.

Sed pius Aeneas statuit tumulum manae molis, et *in eo* propria viri *illius* arma, et remum, et tubam, sub excelso monte, qui nunc appellatur ex illo Misenus, et servat perpetuum nomen in saecula.

But the pious *humane* Aeneas erects a spacious Tomb for the Hero, with his Arms upon it, and an Oar and Trumpet, under *the Brows of* an airy Mountain; which now from him is called Misenus and retains a Name that shall be perpetuated through Ages.

Lines 236–263: Aeneas begins the preliminaries of his descent. Black cattle are sacrificed to the infernal powers at the mouth of a cave. As dawn comes, the approach of Hecate is perceived, and Aeneas and the Sibyl descend into the Underworld.

His perfectis, implet celeriter iussa Sibyllae. Fuit caverna profunda, patens lato hiatu, saxosa, defensa nigro lacu et umbris sylvarum: super quam nullae aves poterant tuto facere iter alis: talis vapor erumpens ex nigris ostiis extollebat se ad curvaturam coeli: unde Graeci appellaverunt locum nomine Avernum. Illic primo statuit *ad aras* quatuor iuvencos nigros *secundum* terga, et sacerdos effundit vinum in caput *eorum*: et secans in medio cornuum summos pilos iniicit eos in sacras flammas, *quasi* primitias sacrificii: appellans clarnorc Hecaten potentem *in* caelo et inferis. Alii suffigunt cultros, et excipiunt *in* poculis sanguinem calentem. Ipse Aeneas caedit gladio agnum nigrae pellis matri Furiarum et magnae *eius* sorori, et vaccam infoecundam tibi, O Proserpina.

This done, he speedily executes the Sibyl's Injunctions. There stood a Cave profound and hideous, with a wide yawning Mouth, stony, fenced by a black Lake and the Gloom of Woods: Over which none of the flying Kind were able to wing their Way unhurt; such *noxious* Exhalations, issuing from its grim Jaws, ascended to the vaulted Skies: Whence the Greeks called the Place by the Name of Aornus. Here first the Priestess placed four Bullocks with Backs of swarthy Hue, and poured Wine on their Foreheads, and cropping the topmost Hairs between the Horns, lays them on the sacred Flames as the first Offerings, by *mystic* Sounds invoking Hecate, whose Power extends both to Heaven and Hell. Others employ the *sacrificing* Knives, and receive the tepid Blood in Bowls. Aeneas himself smites with his Sword an Ewe-lamb of sable Fleece in Honour of the Mother of the Furies and her great Sister; and in Honour of thee, Proserpina, a barren Heifer.

Deinde facit nocturna sacrificia regi inferno, et offert *super* altaribus tota

Then he sets about the nocturnal Sacrifices to the Stygian King, and lays

108

corpora taurorum, et superfundens etiam oleum visceribus incensis. Ecce autem circa lucem et ortum primi Solis, coepit terra reboare sub pedibus, et culmina sylvarum *coeperunt* agitari: et canes visae sunt allatrare per noctem, appropinquante Hecate.

on the Flames the Carcases of Bulls solid *and unbroken*, pouring fat Oil on the broiling Entrails. Lo now, at the early Beams and Rising of the Sun, the Ground beneath their Feet began to rumble, the Mountain tops to quake, and Dogs were seen to howl thro' the Shade of the Woods, at the Approach of the Goddess.

Tunc Sibylla exclamat: "Longe, longe recedite, O profani, et exite *e* tota sylva. Et tu ingredere viam, et extrahe gladium e vagina: nunc opus est fortitudine, nunc animo constanti, Aenea."

"Hence, far hence, O ye Profane," exclaims the Prophetess, "and begone from all the Grove: And do you, Aeneas, boldly set forward, and snatch your Sword from its Sheath: Now is the Time for Fortitude, now for Firmness of Resolution."

Hoc solum locuta, infert se furens in profundum speluncae: ille *Aeneas* passibus non timidis assequitur euntem.

This said, she furiously plunged into the open Cave. He, with intrepid Steps, keeps close by his Guide, as she leads the Way.

Lines 264–267: Vergil himself prays to the Powers of Darkness for inspiration to describe what follows.

O Dii, quibus est potestas in animas, et *vos* umbrae mutae; et Chaos, et Phlegethon, loca undique tacita *per* noctem, sit mihi licitum narrare res auditas: sit *licitum per* divinitatem vestram exponere res tectas profunda terra et obscuritate.

Ye Gods, to whom the Empire of Ghosts belongs, and ye silent Shades and Chaos, and Phlegethon, Places where Silence reigns around in *the Realms of* Night; permit me to utter the Secrets I have heard: May I have your divine Permission to disclose Things buried in deep Earth and Darkness.

Lines 268—94: Description of the Entrance to the Underworld.

Incedebant soli per noctem obscuram in tenebris, et per domos vacuas et inania regna Plutonis. Quale est iter in sylvis, ad Lunam dubiam, sub luce exigua: quando aer occultat caligine coelum, et nox obscura eripuit rebus colorem.

Darkling they travelled under the solitary Night through the Shade, and through the desolate Halls, and empty Realms of Pluto. Much like Travelling in Woods by the precarious *glimmering* Moon under a *faint* malignant Light, when Jupiter hath wrapped up the Heavens in Shade, and sable Night hate stripped Objects of Colour.

Ante ipsum vestibulum et in primo aditu inferorum, Luctus et Curae vindices fixerunt cubilia: habitantque Morbi pallidi, et moesta Senectus, et Metus, et Fames suadens mala, et Paupertas infamis, spectra horrida aspectu: et Mors, et Labor: deinde Somnus frater Mortis, et Gaudia animi scelerata, et in limine opposito Bellum mortiferum, et ferrea cubicula Furiarum, et Discordia insana implicata taeniis sanguinolentis *circa* capillos anguineos.

Before the very Courts, and in the opening Jaws of Hell, Grief and vengeful *tormenting* Cares have fixed their Couches, and pale Diseases dwell, and disconsolate *sullen* Old-age and Fear, and the evil Counsellor Famine, and vile deformed Indigence, Forms ghastly to the Sight, and Death, and Toil: Then Sleep that is a-kin to Death, and criminal Joys of the Mind; and in the opposite *confronting* Threshold murderous War, and Iron Bed-chambers of the Furies, and frantic Discord, having her viperous Locks bound with bloody Fillets.

In medio *vestibulo* ulmus magna, umbrosa, explicat ramos et brachia vetera: aiunt vulgo Somnia inania occupare hunc locum, et *ipsa* sedent sub omnibus frondibus.

In the midst a gloomy Elm displays its Boughs and aged Arms: with Seat vain *fantastic* Dreams are commonly said to haunt, and under every Leaf they dwell.

Et praeterea spectra plurima aliarum ferarum manent ad portas, Centauri, Scyllae biformes, et Briareus centuplex, et Hydra Lernae sibilans horride, et Chimaera evomens ignes: Gorgones et Harpyiae, et species umbrae tricorporis.

Besides many monstrous Savages of various Forms; in the Gates Centars stable, and double-formed Scylla's, and Briareus with his hundred Hands, and the enormous Snake of Lerna hissing dreadful, and Chimaera armed with Flames; Gorgons, Harpies, and the Forms of Geryon's three-bodied Ghost.

Ille Aeneas captus repentino metu educit gladium, et intentat venientibus strictum *illius* acumen. Et nisi sapiens comes docuisset, animas *eas* leves vagari sine corpore sub inani simulacro figurae, irrumperet, et frustra feriret umbras gladio.

Here Aeneas, disconcerted with sudden Fear, grasps his Sword, and presents the naked Point to the Shades as they came up. And had not his skilful Guide put him in mind that they were airy unbodied Phantoms, fluttering about under an empty imaginary Form, he had rushed in, and with his Sword struck at the Ghosts in vain.

Lines 295–336: They approach the ferry that will carry them across the Styx. The Sibyl explains that the ghosts eager but unable to cross are of the unburied, and that they must wait a hundred years. Aeneas grieves over the fate of the unburied, seeing among them his fellow lost in the wreck between Sicily and Africa.

Inde *incipit* iter quod ducit ad aquas Acherontis inferni. Ille gurges turbidus coeno et vasta voragine, exundat, et exonerat omnem arenam in Cocytum. Charon, vector tremendus horribili squalore tenet has aquas et *hos* fluvios: huic multa est in mento canities neglecta, oculi *pleni* sunt igne, vestis sordida nodo *ligata* pendet ex humeris. Ipse impellit cymbam pertica, et adiuvat vehis, et transportat *umbras* corporum nigra cymba, iam senex: sed senectus robusta et vegeta est, *utpote* Deo.

Hence is a Path, which leads to the Floods of Tartarean Acheron: Here a Gulf turbid and impure boils up with Mire and vast Whirlpools, and disgorges all its Sand into Cocytus. A grim Ferryman guards these Floods and Rivers, Charon, of frightful Slovenliness; on whose Chin a Load of grey Hairs uncombed and neglected lies; his Eyes *all* Flame stand *glaring*: His Vestment hangs from his Shoulders by a Knot with Filth overgrown. Himself works the Barge with a Pole, and supplies it with Sails, and wafts over the Bodies in his Iron-coloured Boat, now in Years: But the God is of fresh and green Old age.

Omnis turba currebat huc effusa ad ripas: matres et viri, et corpora fortium bellatorum privata luce, pueri, et puellae innuptae, et iuvenes elati in pyras in conspectu parentum: *tam multi*, quam multae frondes excussae cadunt per sylvas primo frigore autumni: sive quam multae volucres congregantur ad terram ex alto mari, quando tempestas hiberna pellit eas ultra mare, et mittit in plagas calidas.

Hither the whole Tribe *of Ghosts* in Swarms came pouring to the Banks, Matrons and Men, the Souls of magnanimous Heroes, who had gone through *the Labours of* Life, Boys and unmarried Maids, and young Men, who had been stretched on the Funeral pile before their Parents Eyes. As numerous as withered Leaves fall in the Woods with the first *nipping* Cold of Autumn; or as numerous as Birds flock to Land from the deep Ocean, when the chilling Year drives them beyond Sea, and sends to sunny Climes.

Stabant precantes, *ut* primi traiicerent spatium, et extendebant manus desiderio ripae oppositae. Sed vector asper nunc accipit hos, nunc illos; procul autem a ripa expellit alios.

They stood praying to cross the Flood the first, and were stretching forth their Hands with fond Desire to gain the farther Bank: But the sullen Boatman admits sometimes these, sometimes those, whilst others, to a great distance removed, he debars from the Banks.

Aeneas inquit (nam obstupuit et commotus est *hoc* tumultu) "Dic, Virgo, quid significat *illa* frequentia ad fluvium? et quid poscunt animae? Vel ob quam differentiam hae recedunt *e* ripa, illae secant remis aquas pallidas?"

Aeneas (for he stood amazed, and *much* moved with the Tumult) *thus* speaks: "O Virgin, say what means that Flocking to the River? What do the Ghosts desire? Or by whgat Laws of Distinction must these recede from the Banks, *while* those sweep with Oars the livid Flood."

Sic antiqua vates breviter locuta est illi: "Fili Anchisae certissima soboles Deorum, cernis stagna profunda Cocyti, et paludem Stygiam, cuius Dii metuunt iurare et violare divinitatem. Haec omnis turba, quam vides, est egena et insepulta: vector ille, *est* Charon: hi, quos portat unda, *sunt* sepulti. Nec permittitur traiicere ripas horribiles et fluctus sonantes, antequam ossa reposita sint *in* tumulis. Vagantur per centum annos et volitant circa has ripas: tunc denique recepti transmittunt fluvios desideratos."

To him the aged Priestess thus replied: "Son of Anchises, undoubted Offspring of the Gods, you see the deep Pools of Cocytus, and the Stygian Lake, by whose Divinity the Gods dread to swear and violate *their Oath*. All that Croud, which you see, is naked and unburied; the Ferryman is Charon; these whom the Stream carries are interred. Nor is it permitted to transport them over the horrid Banks, and hoarse resounding Waves, till their Bones are quietly lodged in Urns. They wander an hundred Years, and flutter about these Shores: Then at length admitted, they visit the wished-for Lakes."

Filius Anchisae stetit, et continuit gressum, agitans plurima, et miserans animo *eorum* sortem acerbam.

The Offspring of Anchises paused and repressed his Steps, deep musing, and pitying from his Soul their unkind Lot.

Videt illic tristes, et privatos honore sepulturae, Leucaspim, et Orontem ducem Lyciae classis: quos e Troade navigantes per maria procellosa Auster demersit simul, sepeliens *in* aquis et navem et homines.

There he spies Leucaspis, and Orontes, the Commanders of the Lycian Fleet, mournful and bereaved of the Honours of the Dead: Whom, as they sailed from Troy, over the stormy Seas, the Southwind sunk together, whelming both Ship and Crew in the Waves.

Lines 337–383: Aeneas meets Palinurus, and asks how he was lost at sea, despite an apparent promise by Apollo that he would survive the voyage. Palinurus explains that he fell overboard by accident, and begs that he may either be buried or taken with Aeneas across the Styx. The Sibyl refuses him, but says he shall have a funeral, and that the place where he was killed shall bear his name.

Ecce Palinuras gubernator ferebat se *ad eum*: *is* qui nuper in navigatione, dum observat astra, ceciderat e puppe, lapsus in medias aquas. Postquam Aeneas difficile eum agnovit ob spissas tenebras, ita alloquitur prior:

Lo the Pilot Palinurus slow advanced: Who lately in his Libyan Voyage, while he was observing the Stars, had dropped from the Stern, plunged in the midst of the Waves. When with much ado, by Reason of the thick Shade, Aeneas knew him in this mournful Mood, he thus first accosts him:

"O Palinure, quis Deorum abstulit te nobis, et obruit sub medio mari? Dic, age: nam Apollo non prius inventus mihi mendax, hoc solo responso decepit mentem *meam*; quando praediccbat te futurum esse salvum *per* mare, et perventurum ad litus Italicum: an illa est fides promissorum!"

"What God, O Palinurus, snatched you from us, and overwhelmed in the middle of the Ocean? Come tell me. For Apollo, whom I never before found false, in this one Response deceived my Mind; declaring that you should be safe on the Sea, and arrive at the Ausonian Coasts? Is this the Amount of his plighted Faith?"

Ille autem *respondit*: "O dux, fili Anchisae, nec oraculum Phoebi decepit te, nec Deus mersit me mari. Nam forte cadens praeceps, abstuli mecum gubernaculum multo pondere abruptum, cui commissus custos adhaerebam, et quo moderabar cursum. Testor maria aspera, *me* nullum habuisse tantum metum pro me, ne tua navis, destituta gubernaculo, et privata gubernatore, submergeretur, *si* tanti fluctus tumescerent. Auster validus me tres noctes asperas *super* fluctibus, per vastum mare:

But he *answers*: "Neither the Oracle of Phoebus beguiled you, Prince of Anchise's Line, nor a God plunged me in the Sea: For falling headlong I drew along with me the Helm, which I chanced with great violence to tear away, as I clung to it, and steered our Course, being assigned the Guarding *of the Ship*. By the rough Seas I swear, that any Fear I had was not so much for myself, as left your Ship, spoiled of her Rudder, dispossessed of her Pilot, should sink while such high Billows were rising. The South wind drove me violently on the Water over the spacious Sea, three *rough* wintery Nights:

"vix die quarto vidi Italiam erectus

"On the fourth Day I descried Italy

ex aliis aquis. Paulatim adnatabam *ad* terram, et iam attigeram tuta *loca*: nisi natio inhumana appetiisset ferro, me gravatum ob vestem humidam, apprehendentem curvis manibus acuta cacumina rupis; et nisi malesana existimasset *me esse* praedam. Nunc fluctus tenent meum cadaver, et venti iactant ad litus.

from the high ridge of a Wave *whereon I was* raised aloft. I was swimming gradually towards Land, and now got out of Danger, had not a cruel People fallen upon me with the Sword, incumbered with my wet Garment, and grasping with crooked Hands the ragged tops of a Mountain, and ignorantly taken me for a *rich* Prey. Now the Waves possess me, and the Winds toss me on the Shore.

"Id *vero* precor te, per gratam lucem coeli et aerem, per patrem, per spem Ascanii crescentis: libera me his malis, *O dux* invicte: vel tu impone mihi terram, quandoquidem potes; et pete portum Velinum: vel tu praebe manum *mihi* misero, et trahe me tecum trans fluvium, ut saltem post mortem quiescam in tranquillis sedibus: si est aliquis modus, si Dea mater *tua* tibi monstravit aliquem; non enim, ut existimo, suscipis traiicere tantos fluvios et paludem Stygiam absqne auctoritate Deorum."

"But by the pleasant Light of Heaven, and by the *vital* Air, by him who gave you Birth, by your Hope of rising Iulus, I thee implore, invincible *Leader*, release me from these Woes: Either throw on me *some* Earth (for it is in your Power) and seek out the Velin Port; or, if there be any Means *to bring it about*, if your Goddess Mother shews you any (for it is not, I presume, without the Will of the Gods you attempt to cross such mighty Rivers and the Stygian Lake) lend your Hand to an unhappy Wretch, and bear me with you over the Waves, that in Death at least I may rest in peaceful Seas."

Talia locutus erat, Sibylla incepit talia: "O Palinure, unde *est* tibi desiderium tam impium? Tu insepultus videbis aquas Stygias, et fluvium terribilem Furiarum? Aut exibis in ripam *alteram* sine iussu Deorum? Cessa sperare fata Deorum posse mutari orando. Sed accipe memor *mea* verba, *ad* solatium acerbae calamitatis. Nam vicini *Lucaniae* populi, coacti monitis coelestibus, placabunt ossa *tua* longe et late per urbes, et erigent *tibi* sepulchrum, et ferent munera sepulchro: et locus servabit perpetuum nomen Palinuri."

Thus he spoke, when thus the Prophetess began: "Whence, O Palinurus, rises in thee this so impious a Desire? Shall you unburied see the Stygian Floods, and the grim River of the Furies, or reach the Bank against the Command of Heaven? Cease to hope that the Decrees of the Gods are to be altered by Prayers: But mindful take these Predictions as the Solace of your hard Fate. For the neighbouring People, compelled by portentous Plagues from Heaven, shall thro' their several Cities far and wide offer Attonement to thy Ashes, erect *to thee* a Tomb, and stated anniversary Offering on that Tomb present: And the Place shall retain the

Name of Palinurus for ever."

Curae *eius* sedatae *sunt* his verbis, et dolor tantisper eiectus est e moesto corde: laetatur *ob* terram sui nominis.

By these Words his Cares were removed, and Grief a while Banished from his disconsolate Heart: He joys in the Land that is to bear his Name.

Lines 384–416: As Aeneas and the Sibyl approach the Styx they are stopped by Charon, who says that living persons may not pass, and that much harm has already resulted from the breach of the rule. The Sibyl insists that Aeneas comes with good intentions, and shows the Golden Bough. Charon gives way, and carries them across the dark water.

Igitur perficiunt iter inchoatum, et accedunt ad flumen. Quos quando vector iam inde ab amne Stygio vidit per sylvam silentem, et admovere pedem *ad* litus; sic primus adoritur *eos* verbis, et ultro increpat:

They therefore accomplish their begun Journey, and approach to the River: Whom when the Boatman soon from the Stygian Wave beheld, *as they were* advancing through the silent Grove, and forward to the Bank, thus he first accost them in *these* Words, and chides them unprovoked:

"Quicunque es, qui accedis armatus ad fluvios nostros, age, dic cur venias: et iam ex isto loco siste gradum. Haec sedes est umbrarum, Somni et Noctis somniferae; non licet vehere cymba Stygia corpora viventia. Nec vero gavisus sum me transmisisse *per* hanc paludem Herculem *huc* venientem; nec Theseum, et Pirithoum: quamvis orti essent Diis, et insuperabiles robore. Ille manu deduxit in catenas infernum canem e solio ipsius Plutonis, et traxit eum trepidantem: Hi aggressi sunt extrahere reginam e lecto Plutonis."

"Whoever thou art, who advances armed to our Rivers, say quick for what End you come: and from that very Spot advance not one Step farther. This is the Region of Ghosts, of Sleep and drowsy Night: To waft of the Bodies of the Living in my Stygian Boat is not permitted. Nor indeed was it Joy to me that I received Alcides on the Lake when he came *hither*, nor *that I received* Theseus and Pirithous; though they were the Offspring of the Gods, and invincible in Might. The one with *audacious* Hand clapped in Chains the Keeper of Tartarus, and dragged him trembling from the Throne even of our King: The others attempted to carry off our Queen from Pluto's Bed-chamber."

Adversus haec ita locuta est breviter Sibylla Apollinca: "Nullae *hic* sunt insidiae tales, desine turbari, nee arma *ista* minantur vim: *per nos* licet, *ut* magnus custos in antro

In answer to which the Amphrysian Prophetess *thus* spoke: "No such Plots are here, be not disturbed, nor do these Weapons bring Violence: Fur us the huge Porter may *unmolested* bay in his

semper latrans terreat umbras incorporeas; licet, ut Proserpina pudica teneat ianuam patrui *sui*. Aeneas Troianus, illustris pietate et fortitudine, descendit ad patrem *suum* in profundas umbras. Si te nulla species tantae pietatis commovet, saltem agnosce hunc ramum."

Den for ever to the Terror of the incorporeal Shades; Proserpine inviolate in her Chastity may *for ever* remain in her Uncle's Palace. Trojan Aeneas, illustrious for Piety and Arms, descends to the deep Shades of Erebus to *visit* his Sire. If the Image of such shining Piety make no Impression on you, own a *Regard* at least *to* this Branch"

Et ostendit ramum qui tegebatur veste. Tunc corda *Charontis* quieverunt ab ira tumida. Nec plura his *dicta sunt*. Ille admirans munus venerabile fatalis rami, *quod* videbat post longum tempus, appellit nigram navem, et accedit ad ripam. Deinde eiicit alias animas, quae sedebant in scamuis longis, et evacuat tabulata: simul admittit in cymbam magnum Aeneam. Cymba compactilis gemuit sub oncre, et bibit per rimas multum aquae.

(*at the same time* she shews the Branch that was concealed under her Robe.) Then his Heart from swelling Rage is stilled: nor passed more Words than these. He with Wonder gazing on the awful Present of the fatal Branch, seen after a long Time *intervening*, turns towards them his leaden-coloured Barge, and approaches to the Bank. Thence he dislodges the other Souls that sat on the long Benches, and clears the Hatches: At the same Time receives into his Bottom the weighty Aeneas. The frail, patched Vessel groaned under the Weight, and being leaky, took in Plenty of *Water from* the Lake.

Denique transmittit ultra fluvium salvos Aeneam et Sibyllam in foedo limo et viridi herba.

At length he lands the Hero and the Prophetess safe on the other Side of the River, on the foul, slimy Strand and sea-green Weed.

Lines 417—425: They next see Cerberus, who barks furiously. The Sibyl throws him a drugged cake, which he eats, and he falls asleep.

Magnus Cerberus sonat per hanc regionem latratu e tribus gutturibus *erumpente*, decumbens vastus in spelunca opposita. Sibylla animadvertens colla *Cerberi* iam rigescere serpentibus, proiicit huic placentam conditam melle et frugibus praeparatis. Ille aperiens tria guttura, *prae* fame furiosa, devorat *hanc* proiectam, et

Huge Cerberus, with his barking from his triple Jaws howls through these Realms, stretched at his enormous Length in a Den that fronts the Gate. To whom the Prophetess, feeling his Neck now *begin to* bristle with horrid Snakes, flings a soporific Cake of Honey and medicated Grain. He in the mad Rage of Hunger opening his three mouths snatches the offered *Morsel* and spread

116

prostratus humi deficit vastis membris, et quantus *est* porrigitur *per* totam speluncam.

on the Ground relaxes his monstrous Limbs, and is extended at vast Length over all the Cave.

Custode sopito, Aeneas occupat introitum, et pervadit promptus ripam fluvii, unde non reditur.

Aeneas, now that the Keeper *of Hell* is buried *in Sleep*, seizes the Passage, and swift overpasses the Bank of that Flood, whence there is no Return.

Lines 426–439: They come to the ghosts of those who died before their time—infants, executed criminals, suicides.

Statim voces auditae *sunt*, et magnus vagitus, et animae infantum plorantes sub primis portis, quos dies funesta eripuit, privatos iucunda vita et abstractos ab ubere, et demisit morti immaturae.

Forthwith are heard Voices, loud Wailings and weeping Ghosts of Infants in the first Opening of the Gate: Whom, bereaved of sweet Life out of the Course of Nature, and snatched from the Breast, a black *unjoyous* Day cut off, and buried in an untimely Grave.

Iuxta hos *sunt, qui* addicti sunt morti *ob* iniustam calumniam. Nec vero assignantur illae sedes absque sorte, absque iudice. Minos inquisitor agitat urnam: ipse cogit coetum umbrarum, et discutit vitam ac scelera.

Next to those, are such as had been condemned to Death by false Accusations. Nor yet were those Seats assigned them, without Destination and Appointment, nor without *the Sentence of* a Judge. Minos, an Inquisitor, shakes the Urn: He summons the Council of silent *Shades*, and examines their Lives and Crimes.

Deinde tristes occupant vicina loca, qui innocentes intulerunt sibi mortem *propria* manu, et pertaesi luminis prodegerunt animas. Quam vellent nunc in superis auris tolerare et paupertatem et labores difficiles! Fata *id* prohibent, et palus odiosa implicat tristibus aquis, et Styx novies circumflua detinet.

The next Apartments in order *those* mournful *Bands* possess, who, tho' free from Crimes *that deserved Death*, procured Death to themselves with their own Hands, and sick of the Light, threw away their Lives: How gladly would they now endure Poverty and painful Toils in the upper Regions! *But* Fate opposes, and the hateful Lake *of Acheron* imprisons them with its dreary Waves, and Styx, nine Times rolling between, confines them.

Lines 440–476: They come to the Fields of Mourning, where live those who died for love. Here Aeneas sees Dido, whom he tries to soothe, telling her that he knew not what would be the consequences to her of his departure, and that he went away most unwillingly, because the gods had ordered it. She maintains sullen silence, and at last breaks away, leaving him in sorrow.

Nec longe hinc ostenduntur patentes in omnem partem campi lugentes: ita appellant illos nomine. Hic occultae semitae abscondunt *eos* quos durus amor absumpsit crudeli veneno, et sylva myrtea undique tegit *eos*, nec solicitudines deserunt post ipsam mortem. His locis videt Phaedram, et Procrin, et tristem Eriphylen ostendentem plagas *acceptas* a crudeli filio, et Evadnen, et Pasiphaen. Laodamia socia est illarum; et Caeneus olim iuvenis, modo iterum foemina et reversa in antiquam formam *per* fatum.

Not far from hence, extended on every Side, are shewn the Fields of Mourning: *For* so they call those *Fields* by Name. Here By-paths remote conceal, and Myrtle Groves cover those around, whom unrelenting Love, with his cruel envenomed Darts, consumed away. Their Cares leave them not in Death itself. In these Apartments he sees Phaedra and Procris, and disconsolate Eriphyle pointing to the Wounds she had received from her cruel Son, Evadne and Pasiphae: These Laodamia accompanies, and Caeneus, once a Man, now a Woman, and again by Fate transformed into his pristine Shape.

Inter quas Phoenicia Dido recens post vulnus *sibi inflictum* vagabatur in magno nemore. Ut Troianus heros stetit prope, et agnovit *eam* inter tenebras obscuras; qualem aliquis videt aut putat vidisse Lunam oriri inter nubes ineunte mense; effudit lachrymas, *et prae* suavi amore locutus est:

Amongst whome Phoenician Dido, fresh from her Wound, was wandering in a spacious Grove: To whom, as soon as the Trojan Hero approached nigh, and discovered faintly through the Shades, in like Manner as one sees, or thinks he sees the Moon rising through the Clouds in the Beginning of her monthly Course; he dropped Tears, and addressed her in Love's sweet Accents:

"Misera Dido! ergo verus nuntius ad me venerat, te mortuam, et gladio passam ultima *fata*. Heu! tibi auctor fui mortis. Iuro per astra, per Deos, et si aliqua est fides sub terra profunda, exivi nolens e tuo litore, O regina. Sed mandata Deorum, quae cogunt *me* nunc ire *per* has umbras, per loca horrida squalore et tenebras profundas, expulerunt me

"Hapless Dido, was it then a true Report I had of your being dead, and that you had finished your own destiny by the Sword? Was I, alas! the Cause of your Death? I swear by the Stars, by the Powers above, and if there be any Faith under the deep Earth, against my Will, O Queen, I parted from thy Coast. But the Mandates of he Gods which now compel me to travel through these

auctoritate sua. Nec potui credere me tibi allaturum *esse* tantum dolorem abitu meo. Contine gressum, et ne subducas te conspectui meo.

Shades, through noisome dreary Regions, and profound Night, drove me from you by their Authority: Nor could I believe that I should involve you in such deep Anguish by my Departure. Stay your Career, and withdraw thee not from my Sight.

"Quem fugis? hoc est ultimum *tempus*, quo tecum loquor *per* fatum."

"Whom dost thou fly? This is the last Time Fate allows me to have Intercourse with you."

Aeneas mulcebat verbis talibus animum iratae et aspere intuentis, et *conabatur ei* movere lachrymas. Illa infensa tenebat oculos defixos *in* terram. Nec magis movetur *secundum* faciem ab usque principio sermonis, quam si stet lapis durus, aut rupes Marpesia. Denique abstulit se, et fugit inimica in sylvam umbrosam: ubi prior maritus Sichaeus respondet illi solicitudine, et aequat amorem eius.

With these Words Aeneas thought to sooth her Soul inflamed, and eyeing him with stern regard, and provoked his Tears to flow. She, loathing the Sight of him, held her Eyes fixed on the Ground; nor alters her Looks one Jot more by the Conversation he had begun, than if she were fixed immoveable *like* a stubborn Flint, or Rock of Parian Marble. At length she flung away, and in Detestation fled into a shady Grove: where Sichaeus her first Lord answers her with *correspondent amorous* Cares, and returns her Love for Love.

Nihilominus Aeneas commotus acerba *eius* morte, longe sequitur euntem plorans, et miseretur *eius*.

Aeneas, nevertheless, in deep Commotion for her disastrous Fate, with weeping Eyes pursues her far, and melts with Pity toward her as she goes *from him*.

Lines 477–493: They come to the place of dead heroes. The Trojans who fell at Troy crowd about Aeneas. The Greeks are scared.

Inde persequitur iter concessum: et iam attigerant campos extremos, quos separatos incolunt *viri* insignes bello. Hic occurrit illi Tydeus, hic Parthenopaeus illustris armis, et umbra Adrasti pallidi. Hic Troiani valde deplorati inter vivos, *et* occisi in proeliis. Quos omnes ille videns longa serie suspiravit: et Glaucum, et Medonta, et Thersilochum, tres

Hence he holds on his destined Way: And now they were got to the last Fields, which by themselves apart renowned Warriors frequent. Here Tydeus appears to him, here Partheonpeus illustrious in Arms, and the Ghost of pale Adrastus. Here those Trojans, who had died in the Field of Battle, much lamented in the upper World; Whom, when he beheld

filios Antenoris, et Polyboeten sacerdotem Cereris, et Idaeum adhuc currus adhuc arma tractantem. Animae plurimae circumsistunt *ad* dextram et sinistram: Nec sufficit vidisse semel *Aeneam*: delectat *ipsas* remanere diu, et admovere pedem *propius*, et petere causas cur venerit.

altogether in a numerous Body, he inly groaned; *particularly when he saw* Glaucus, Medon, Thersilochus, the three Sons of Antenor, and Polyboetes consecrated to Ceres, and Idaeus still handling his Chariot, still his Armour. The Ghosts in Crouds around him stand on Right and Left. Nor are they satisfied with seeing him once: They are fond to detain him longer and longer, come into close Conference with him, and learn the Reasons of his Coming.

Sed duces Graecorum, et turmae Agamemnonis, quando viderunt Aeneam et arma splendentia inter tenebras; coeperunt tremere magno timore: pars obvertere dorsum, quemadmodum olim cucurrerunt *ad* naves: pars emittere parvam vocem, clamor inceptus fallit hiantes.

But so soon as the Grecian Chiefs and Agamemnon's Battalions saw the Hero, and his Arms gleaming through the Shades, they quaked with huge Dismay. Some turned their Backs, as *when* they fled once to their Ships; some raise their slender Voices; the Scream *just* begun dies in their gasping Throats.

Lines 494–547: Aeneas sees Deiphobus, cruelly mangled, and is told the story of his death. The Sibyl reminds him that they must hurry about the main business of their visit to the Underworld.

Atque hic vidit Deiphobum, filium Priami, discerptum omnibus membris, immaniter laceratum circa os: *circa* os, et utramque manum, et tempora spoliata sectis auribus et nasum truncatum indecoro vulnere. Itaque difficile agnovit trementem, et occultantem turpes plagas; et prior alloquitur *eum* voce cognita:

And here he spies Deiphobus, the Son of Priam, mangled in every Limb, his Face all cruelly torn, his Face and both his Hands, his Temples slashed, his Ears cropped, and his Nostrils slit with a hideously deformed Wound. Thus he hardly knew him quaking *for fear of being discovered*, and seeking to hide his ghastly Scars: and thus he first accosts him with well-known Accents:

"O Deiphobe bellicose, soboles e nobili sanguine Teucri: quis ausus est exigere *de te* tam dirum supplicium? cui tantum licuit contra te? Rumor pertulit mihi, te ultima nocte Troiae lassum multa strage Graecorum obiisse super cumulum confusorum cadaverum. Tunc ego ipse erexi *tibi* in litore Rhoeteo

"Deiphobus, great in Arms, sprung from Teucer's noble Blood, who could chuse to inflict *on you* such Cruelties? Or who was allowed such Power over you? To me, in that last Night, a Report was brought that you, tired with the vast Slaughter of the Greeks, had fallen at last on a Heap of mingled Carcases. Then, with my own Hands, I raised to

sepulchrum vacuum, et appellavi ter magno clamore animam tuam: locus servat nomen et arma *tua*. Non potui, O amice, te videre, et abiens tumulare *in* patria tellure."

Tum vero filius Priami *dixit:* "Nihil praetermissum est a te, O amice: omnia exhibuisti *officia* Deiphobo, et umbrae cadaveris. Sed sors mea et perniciosum crimen *Helenae* Lacedaemoniae obruerunt me his poenis: illa reliquit *mihi* haec insignia. Scis enim quomodo traduxerimus ultimam noctem in falsa laetitia; et oportet *nos* nimis recordari: quando equus fatalis venit accensu super alta Pergama, et gravidus induxit in utero milites armatos. Illa fingens choreas, ducebat circa sacra Bacchi *foeminas* Phrygias furiosas: Ipsa in medio attollebat magnam taedam, et ex alta arce invitabat Graecos.

"Tunc funestus lectus tenebat me fatigatum curis et obrutum somno: et iucunda ac profunda quies, similisque morti tranquillae, oppressit me decumbentem. Interim digna uxor aufert arma omnia domo, et subtraxerat capite *meo* gladium fidelem. Vocat Menelaum intra domum, et aperit ianuam. Nempe existimans hoc magnum fore domum amanti *marito*, et sic infamiam veteris malitiae posse deleri.

"Quid detineo *te?* Irruunt in

you an empty Tomb on the Rhoetean Shore, and thrice with loud Voice I invoked your Manes. Your Name and Arms possess the Place. Your Body, my Friend, I could not find, and, at my Departure, deposit in thy native Land.

And upon this the Son of Priam: "Nothing, my Friend, has been omitted by you: You have discharged every Duty to Deiphobus, and to the Shadow of a Corpse. But my own *unhappy* Fate, and the cursed Wickedness of Helen, plunged me in these Woes: She hath left me these Monuments *of* her Love. For how we passed that last Night amidst false *ill-grounded* Joys you know, and must needs remember but too well; when the fatal Horse came bounding over our lofty Walls, and pregnant brought armed Infantry in its Womb. She, pretending to *celebrate* a mingled Dance, led her Train of Phrygian Matrons yelling around the Orgies: Herself in the mdst *of them* held a large flaming Torch, and called to the Greeks from the lofty Tower.

"I, at that Time being oppressed with Care, and overpowered with Sleep, was lodged in my unfortunate Bedchamber, where Rest, balmy, profound, and the perfect Image of a calm peaceful Death, pressed me as I lay. Mean while my incomparable Wife removes all Arms from my Palace, and had withdrawn my trusty Sword from my Head: She calls Menelaus into the Palace, and throws open the Gates. Hoping, no doubt, that would be a mighty Favour to her amorous Husband, and that thus the Infamy of her former wicked Deeds might be extinguished.

"In short, the burst into my Chamber:

cubiculum: additur simul *iis* comes Ulysses incitator criminum. Dii reddite talia Graecis, si imprecor *iis* supplicia iusto ore.

"At age, dic vicissim, quinam casus te adduxerint *huc* viventem: an venis pulsus erroribus maris, an iussu Deorum, an aliqua *alia* sors te adigit, ut venias *in* sedes moestas absque luce, et *ad* loca tumultuosa?"

In hac vicissitudine colloquii Aurora rubieundis equis in aereo decursu iam transierat medium coelum: et forte traduceret in talibus omne tempus concessum.

Sed comes Sibylla admonuit, et breviter locuta est: "O Aenea, nox approperat, nos traducimus horas lugendo. Hic est locus, ubi via secat se in duas partes. Dextra *est*, quae extenditur usque ad palatium magni Plutonis: per hanc iter est nobis ad Elysium: at sinistra continet supplicia impiorum, et ducit ad Tartara scelerata."

Contra Deiphobus ait: "Ne irascare, O magna vates: abibo: concludam sermonem, et redibo in tenebras. I, nostra gloria, i; sequere fata feliciora."

Hoc solum locutus *est*, et in *ipso* sermone deflexit gressum.

That Traitor of Aeolus's Race, the Promoter of Villainy, is joined in Company with them. Ye Gods requite these Cruelties to the Greeks, if I supplicated Vengeance with pious Lips.

"But come now in your Turn, say what Adventure hath brought thee *hither* alive. Come you driven by the Errors of the Main, or by the Direction of the Gods? Or what Fortune stimulates thee to visit these dreary Mansions, troublous Regions, where the Sun never shines?"

In this Conversation the Sun in his rosy Chariot had now passed the Meridian in his ethereal Course; and they perhaps would in this Manner have spent the whole Time assigned them;

but the Sibyl, his Companion, put him in mind and thus briefly spoke: "Aeneas, the Night comes on apace, *while* we waste the hours in *vain* Lamentations. This is the Place where the Path divides in two; the Right is what leads to great Pluto's Walls, by this way to Elysium lies: But the Left carries on the Punishments of the Wicked, and conveys to cursed Tartarus.

On the other Hand Deiphobus: "Be not incensed, great Priestess; I shall be gone; fill up the Number *of those disconsolate Ghosts among whom I dwell*, and be rendered back to my *former* Darkness. Pass on, thou Glory of Nation; may you prove the Fates more kind."

This much he spoke, and at the Word turned his Steps.

Lines 548–627: Looking round, Aeneas sees a great and terrible fortress, groans and cries of horror coming from it. The Sibyl explains that this is the place of torment for the truly wicked. She alone of the undamned has ever gone inside. She describes the horrors within.

Aeneas respexit statim; et sub rupe sinistra cernit spatiosam urbem, cinctam tribus muris; quam Tartareus Phlegethon, rapidus fluvius, circuit ignibus torrentibus, et volvit saxa sonantia. Porta opposita magna *est*, et columna ex adamante durissimo; *ita* ut nullum robur hominum, non ipsi superi possint evertere *eam* ferro. Turris ferrea surgit in altum: et Tisiphone sedens, cincta pallio sanguinolento, custodit limen vigil et noctu et diu. Hinc coeperunt audiri gemitus, et resonare crudeles ictus: praeterea stridor ferri et tractorum vinculorum.

Aeneas stetit, et stupefactus attendit ad strepitum. "Quae *sunt illic* species criminum, dic, O Virgo, aut quibus suppliciis cruciantur? Unde tantus planctus *surgit* in auras?"

Tunc Vates sic coepit loqui: "Clarissime dux Troianorum, nulli puro fas est subire portam impium: sed quando Hecate praeposuit me sylvis infernis: ipsa mihi declaravit supplicia *constituta* a Diis, et duxit me per omnia. Rhadamanthus Cretensis obtinet hoc saevissimum imperium: et punit, et audit fraudes, et cogit fateri quaecumque facinora patrata unusquisque per vitam protulit *usque* ad tardam mortem, gaudens vana simulatione. Statim Tisiphone vindex armata flagro verberat reos illudens, et sinistra *manu* incutiens saevos serpentes,

Aeneas on a sudden looks back; and under a Rock on the Left sees spacious Prisons inclosed with a triple Wall; which Tartarean Phlegethon's rapid Flood environs with Torrents of Flame, and whirls roaring Rocks along. Fronting is a Gate of huge Dimensions, and Columns of solid Adamant, that no Strength of Men, nor the Gods themselves can with Steel demolish. And Iron Tower rises high; and *there* Tisiphone, *a* wakeful *Fury*, clad in a bloody Robe, sits to watch the Gate both Night and Day. Hence Groans are heard; the cruel Lashes resound; the Grating too of Iron, and Clank of dragging Chains.

Aeneas stopped short, and startling listened to the Din. What scenes of Guilt *are these*, O Virgin, say; with what Pains are they chastened; What hideous Yelling *ascends* to the Skies?"

Then thus the Prophetess began: Renowned Leader of the Trojans, no holy Person is allowed to tread the cursed Threshold: But Hecate, when she set me over the Groves of Avenus, taught me herself the Punishments appointed by the Gods, and led me through all. Cretan Rhadamanthus possesses these ruthless Realms, examines and punishes Frauds; and forces every one to confess what Crimes committed in the upper World he had left *unatoned* till the late Hour of Death, hugging himself in secret Crimes of no Avail. Forthwith avenging Tisiphone, armed with her

appellat crudelem turbam sororum."

Whip, scourges the Guilty with cruel Insult, and in her Left-hand shaking them over her grim Snakes, calls *to her Aid* the fierce Troops of her Sister Furies.

"Tunc denique portae aperiuntur stridentes horrisono cardine." *Pergit Sibylla*: "Vides, quale satellitium sedeat in vestibulo? Quale spectrum occupet postes? Hydra crudelior intus habet sedem, horribilis quinquaginta faucibus. Praeterea ipse Tartarus bis tantum descendit in profundum, et extenditur sub umbras, quantus *est* prospectus *inde* ad aethereum coeli Olympum. Illic iuventus Titania, antiqua soboles Terrae, prostrati fulmine versantur in imo fundo. Illic vidi quoque geminos filios Aloei, vasta corpora: qui susceperant evertere manibus magnum coelum, et expellere Iovem e regnis supernis. Vidi etiam Salmonea solventem duras poenas, quia imitatus *fuerat* ignes Iovis et tonitru coeli. Ille vectus quatuor equis et quatiens taedam, currebat exultans per gentes Graecorum, et per mediam urbem Elidis, et exigebat sibi cultum divinum: insanus! qui imitabatur *curru* aereo et impetu equorum nimbos et tonitru non imitabile. Sed pater omnipotens vibravit fulmen per opaca nubila (non ille *quidem* faces et lumina fumida taedarum, *ut Salmoneus*) et vasto turbine prostratum transfixit.

Then at length the cursed Gates, grating on their dreadful-sounding Hinge, are thrown open. See you what kind of Watch sites in the Entry? What figure guards the Gate? An overgrown Hydra, more fell *than that of Lerna*, with fifty black gaping Mouths, has her Seat within. Then Tartarus itself sinks deep down, and extends towards the Shades twice as far as is the Prospect upwards *from the Earth* to the ethereal Throne of Heaven. Here Earth's ancient Progeny, the young Titanian Brood, hurled down with Thunderbolts, welter in the profound Abyss. Here too I saw the two Sons of Aloeus, gigantic Bodies; who attempted with *impious* Hands to overturn the spacious Heavens, and thrust down Jove from his exalted Kingdom. Salmoneus likewise I beheld suffering Punishment inflexibly severe, for having imitated Jove's flaming Bolts, and the *awful* Sounds of Heaven. He, drawn in his Chariot by four Horses, and brandishing a Torch, rode triumphant through the Nations of Greece, and the midst of the City Elis, and claimed to himself the Honour of the Gods: Infatuate! Who, with brazen Wheels, and the Prancing of his Horn-hoofed Steeds, would needs counterfeit the Storms and inimitable Thunder. But the almighty Father amidst the thick Clouds threw a Bolt (not *mock Thunder* he, nor Fire brands, and smoaky Light from Torches) and hurled him down headlong in a vast *fiery* Whirlwind.

"Videre erat etiam Tityum filium terrae omniparentis: cuius corpus

"*Here* too you might have seen Tityus, the Foster-child of all-bearing Earth:

extenditur per tota novem iugera; et immanis vultur fodicans adunco rostro iecur perpetuum et viscera foecunda *ad poenas* scrutatur ea *ad cibum*, et manet intra profundum pectus: nec ulla quies permittitur fibris repullulantibus.

Whose Body is extended over nine whole Acres; and a huge Vultur with her hooky Beak pouncing on his immortal Liver and Bowels, the fruitful Source of Punishment, rummages them for her *everlasting* Meal, and dwells in the deep Recesses of his Breast; nor is any Respite given to his Fibres still springing up afresh.

"Cur commemorem Lapithas, Ixiona, et Pirithoum? super quos nigrum saxum iamiam lapsurum et simile cadenti impendet. Fulcra aurea splendent *in* laetis lectis altis, et convivia parata ante *ora cum* abundantia regali: maxima Furiarum accumbit prope, et vetat tangere mensas manibus, et surgit erigens facem, et vociferatur ore.

"Why should I mention the Lapithae, Ixion, and Pirithous, over whom hangs a black flinty Rock every Moment threatening to tumble down, and seeming to be actually falling? Golden Pillars *supporting* lofty genial Couches shine, and full in their View Banquets furnished out with regal Magnificence; *while* the Chief of the Furies sits by them, and debars them from touching the Provisions with their Hands; and *when they attempt it*, starts up, lifting her Torch on high, and thunders over them with her Voice.

"Illic, ii quibus fratres odiosi *fuerunt*, dum vita durabat, aut pater verberatus, aut dolus fabricatus clienti; aut qui soli incubuerunt opibus partis, nec dederunt partem *earum* suis, quae turba maxima est; et qui occisi *sunt* propter adulterium, et qui secuti *sunt* bella iniusta, nec timuerunt violare fidem *datam* dominis: *illi* inclusi expectant supplicium.

"Here are those who, while Life remained, had been at Enmity with their Brothers, had beaten a Parent, or wrought Deceit against a Client; or who alone brooded over their acquired Wealth, nor assigned a Portion to their own, which Class is the most numerous: Those too who were slain for Adultery, who joined in impious Wars, nor made any Scruple to violate the Faith they had plighted to their Masters; *all these*, shut up *in those doleful Prisons*, await their Punishment.

"Ne petas doceri quale supplicium *expectent*, aut quis modus et quae sors damnaverit eos. Alii versant magnum saxum, et pendent distenti radiis rotarum. Miser Theseus sedet et perpetuo sedebit; et Phlegyas

"But what kind of Punishment seek not to be informed, in what Shape *of Misery*, or *in what piteous* State they are involved. Some roll a huge unwieldy Stone, and hang fast bound to the Spokes of Wheels. There sits, and to

miserrimus admonet omnes, et testatur magno clamore inter tenebras: 'Discite *toties* admoniti aequitatem, et non spernere Deos.' Hic prodidit patriam pecunia, et *ei* imposuit tyrannum ferocem: tulit et sustulit leges pretio. Hic aggressus est pudicitiam filiae, et nuptias prohibitas.

Eternity shall sit, the unhappy Theseus: And Phlegyas most wretched is a Monitor to all, and with loud Voice proclaims through the Shades: 'Warned *by my Example* learn Righteousness, and not to contemn the Gods.' One sold his Country for Gold, and imposed *on it* a domineering Tyrant; made and unmade Laws for Money. Another invaded his Daughter's Bed, and *joined himself to her in* unlawful Wedlock:

"Omnes ausi infanda crimina et executi consilia. Si essent mihi centum linguae et centum ora, et vox ferrea, non possem complecti omnes species criminum, nec enumerare omnia nomina suppliciorum."

"All of them boldly dared some heinous Crime, and accomplished what they dared. Had I an hundred Tongues, and an hundred Mouths, and Iron Lungs, I could not comprehend all the Species of their Crimes, nor enumerate the Names of all their Punishments."

Lines 628–636: Aeneas and the Sibyl hurry to the palace of Pluto and deposit the Golden Bough.

Postquam longaeva vates Apollinis protulit haec verba, ait: "Nunc autem age, ingredere viam, et perfice inceptum officium: properemus. Video muros fabricatos *in* fornacibus Cyclopum, et portas sub opposito fornice: ubi *Dii* nos iubent deponere munera decerpta *ex arbore*."

When the aged Priestess of Phoebus had uttered these Words, she adds: "But now come set forward and finish the Task you have undertaken: Let us haste on. I see the Walls *of Pluto* wrought in the Forges of the Cyclops, and the Gates with their Arch full in our View, where our Instructions enjoin us to deposit this *our* Offering."

Sic locuta fuerat: et pariter ambulantes per tenebrosa *spatia* viarum invadunt medium iter, et appropinquant portis. Aeneas occupat aditum, et aspergit corpus recenti aqua, et affigit ramum in opposito limine.

She said, and with equal Pace advancing through the gloomy Path, they speedily traverse the intermediate Space, and approach the Gates. Aeneas springs forward to the Entry, sprinkles his Body with fresh Water, and fixes the Bough in the fronting Portal.

Lines 637–678: The enter Elysium. Aeneas asks the whereabouts of his father, Anchises. Musaeus, the Father of Poetry, offers to guide them.

Denique his absolutis, persoluto munere Proserpinae, pervenerunt *ad*

Having finished these Rites, and performed the Offering to the Goddess,

loca laeta, et prata iucunda, et sedes beatas sylvarum felicium. Hic aer agros liberior et luce purpurea: et *incolae* cognoscunt suum Solem et sua astra. Pars exercent corpora in herbosis locis, certant ludis, et luctantur *in* arena fulva. Pars agitant saltationes pedibus, et canunt cantilenas. Vates etiam Thracius cum veste longa canit numeris septem discrimina sonorum: et sonat eadem, modo digitis, modo plectro eburneo.

they came at length to the Regions of *eternal* Joy, delightful green Retreats, and blessed Abodes in Groves, where Happiness abounds. Here the Air they breathe is freer and more enlarged, and clothes the Field with radiant Light: *Here the happy Inhabitants* know their own Sun, and their own Stars. Some exercise their Limbs on the grassy Plains, in Sports contend, and wrestle on the yellow Sand: Some beat Harmony in the mingled Dances, and sing Hymns. *Orpheus* too, the Thracian Priest, in his long Robe warbles melodious Lays the seven distinguished Notes *of Music*: And now strikes the same with his Fingers, now with his Ivory Quill.

Hic *est* vetusta propago Teucri, soboles clarissima, heroes magnanimi, nati temporibus felicioribus: et Ilus, et Assaracus, et Dardanus fundator Troiae. Miratur procul arma et currus virorum vacuos. Hastae sunt fixae *in* terra, et equi liberi pascuntur passim in campis: amor curruum et armorum qui fuit viventibus, studium quod *fuit* alendi pingues equos; idem manet *iis* depositis *sub* terra.

Here is Teucer's ancient Race, a most illustrious Line, magnanimous Heroes, born in happier Times. Ilus, Assaracus, and Dardanus, the Founder of Troy. From far he views with Wonder the Arms and empty Chariots of the Chiefs. Their Spears stand fixed in the Ground, and up and down their Horses feed at large throughout the Plain. The same Fondness they had when alive for Chariots and Armes, the same Concern for training up shining Steeds, follows them deposited under the Earth.

Ecce videt alios *ad* dextram et ad sinistram epulantes super gramine, et cantantes in choro laetas cantilenas, in odorifera sylva lauri: unde magnus Eridanus decurrit per sylvam apud superos. Hic turba *est eorum*, qui certando pro patria tulerunt vulnera: et qui sacerdotes puri *fuerunt*, dum vita durabat: et qui vates pii, ac locuti *res* dignas Apolline: aut qui ornaverunt vitam *humanam* per artes repertas a se: et qui reddiderunt alios memores sui,

Lo he views others on the Right and Left feasting upon the Grass, and singing joyous Hymns to Apollo in Concert, amidst a fragrant Grove of Laurel: Whence from on high the River Eridanus rolls in copious Streams through the Wood. Here is a Band *made up of* those who sustained Wounds in fighting for their Country; Priests who preserved themselves pure and holy, while the *Temptations* of Life remained; pious Poet, who sung in Strains worthy of Apollo; those who

iis benefaciendo. Capita horum omnium coronantur taenia candida.

improved *human* life by the Invention of Arts; and who by their worthy Deeds made others remember them *with Gratitude*: All these have their Temples crowned with a Snow-white Fillet.

Quos circumstantes Sibylla sic allocuta est, prae caeteris Musaeum; nam magna turba hunc habet in medio *sui*, et admiratur superantem altis humeris:

Whom gathered around they Sibyl thus addressed, *and* Musaeus chiefly; for a numerous Croud has him in their Center, and admires him raised above them by the Heighth of the Shoulders:

"O animae fortunatae, et tu optime vates: dicite, quae regio, quis locus tenet Anchisen? illius causa venimus *huc*, et traiecimus magnos fluvios inferorum."

"Say, happy Souls, and thou, best of Poets, what Quarter, what Apartment contains Anchises? On his Account we have *hither* come, and crossed the great Rivers of Hell."

Tunc heros sic dedit ei responsum paucis *verbis*: "Nemo *nostrum* habet fixam domum: habitamus in sylvis umbrosis, et incolimus herbosas ripas, et prata *semper* nova ob rivos. Vos tamen, si cupiditas animi sic iubet, conscendite hunc collem; et *vos* deducam *ad eum* facili semita."

And thus the Hero briefly returned her an Answer: "None of us have a fixed Abode: In shady Groves we dwell, or lie upon *flowery* Couches all along the Banks, and on Meadows with Rivulets *ever* fresh *and green*: But do you, if so your Inclination leads, overpass this Eminence, and I will now set you in the easy Path."

Sic praeivit incessu, et desuper ostendit campos amoenos: deinde descendunt ex alto vertice.

He said, and advanced on before, and shews them from a rising Ground the shining Plains; then they descend from the Summit of the Mountain.

Lines 679–702: Anchises is in the valley beyond, surveying his future posterity, spirits that are hereafter to take flesh. He welcomes Aeneas with joy and surprise. Aeneas attempts to embrace him, but in vain.

Pater autem Anchises in profunda valle viridi circumspiciebat animas separatas et reversuras in lucem superiorem, considerans *eas* studiose: et forte recognoscebat omnem multitudinem suorum: et dilectos posteros, et fata, et fortunas, et mores, et facta hominum *illorum*.

But Father Anchises deep in a verdant Vale was surveying with studious Care the Souls there inclosed, who were to revisit the upper *Regions* of Light, and happened then to be reviewing the whole Number of his Race, his dear Descendants, their Fates and Fortunes, their Manners and Achievements.

Et quando ille vidit Aeneam ex adverso venientem per herbas; laetus protulit ambas manus, et lachrymae fluxerunt per genas, et vox exiit *ex* ore:

As soon as he beheld Aeneas advancing towards him across the Meads, he joyfully stretched out both his Hands, and Tears poured down his Cheeks; and these Words dropped from his Mouth:

"Venisti denique, et tua pietas certa patri superavit iter difficile! O fili, permittitur aspicere vultum tuum, et accipere ac reddere voces familiares! Certe numerans tempora, cogitabam animo et existimabam ita fore: et mea solicitudo non decepit me. O fili, *per* quales terras et per quanta maria iactatum, et quantis periculis agitatum ego te audio! Quam timui ne regna Africae tibi obstarent aliquantum!"

"Are you come at length, and has that Piety *so much* experienced by your Sire, surmounted the arduous Journey? Am I permitted, my Son, to see thy Face; to hear and return the well known Accents? So indeed I concluded in my Mind, and reckoned it would happen, computing the Time. Nor have my anxious Hopes deceived me. Over the Lands, *O* son, over what immense Seas have you, I hear, been tossed! With what Dangers harassed! how I dreaded lest you had sustained Harm from Libya's Realms;"

Aeneas vero *ait*: "Tua, O pater, tua moesta umbra saepe visa impulit me venire ad haec loca. Naves *meae* stant *in* mari Tyrrheno. Permitte *mihi*, O pater, permitte coniungere manus, et ne te subducas complexui meo."

But he: Your Ghost, your dreary Ghost, my Sire, often-times appearing, compelled me to set forward to these Mansions. My Fleet rides in the Tyrrhene Sea. Permit me, Father, to join my Right-hand *with thine*; and withdraw thee not from my Embrace."

Sic loquens, simul madefaciebat vultum copiosis lachrymis. Ter conatus erat implicare brachia collo *eius*: ter umbra frustra comprehensa elapsa est e manibus, similis ventis levibus, et simillima fugaci somno.

So saying, he at the same time watered his Cheeks with a Flood of Tears. There thrice he attempted to throw his Arms around his Neck; thrice the Phantom grasped in vain escaped his Hold, like the Air, or resembling most a fugitive Dream.

Lines 703–723: Looking at the ghost, Aeneas asks who they are. He is told they are to drink water from the River Lethe, so that they will be stripped of all memory before being sent into the world again. He wonders why they should want a new life, which leads Anchises to explain.

Interea Aeneas cernit in valle secreta sylvam separatam, et frutices sonantes per sylvam; et fluvium Lethaeum, qui praeterfluit

Mean while Aeneas sees in the retired winding Vale a Grove situate by itself, Shrubs rustling in the Woods, and the River Lethe which glides by those

129

tranquillam sedem. Gentes et populi innumeri volabant circa hunc *fluvium*. Et quemadmodum quando in pratis, suda aestate, apes adhaerent diversis floribus, et vagantur circa alba lilia: *sic* omnis campus sonat fremitu.

peaceful Dwellings. Around this *River* un-numbered Tribes and Nations of Ghosts were fluttering. And as in Meadows on a serene Summer's Day, when the Bees sit on the various Blossoms, and swarm around the Snow-white Lillies, all the Plain buzzes with their humming Noise.

Aeneas ignarus *rei* statim obstupet aspectu, et petit causas: quinam ergo sint illi fluvii, aut quinam homines occupaverint ripas tanta multitudine.

Aeneas nonplussed shudders at the unexpected Sight, and asks the Causes *of that Appearance*, what those Rivers yonder are, or what Ghosts have in such Crouds filled the Banks?

Tunc pater Anchises *ait*: "Animae quibus alia corpora destinantur *per* fatum, bibunt oblivia aeterna et liquores tutos ad aquas Lethaei fluvii. Ego certe iamdudum opto enarrare tibi, et coram monstrare illas, et enumerare sobolem illam meorum: ut magis gaudeas Italiam demum inventam *fuisse a te*."

Then father Anchises: Those Souls, for whom other Bodies are destined by Fate, at the Streams of Lethe's flood quaff Care-expelling Draughts and lasting Oblivion. Long indeed have I wished to give you a Detail of these, pointing them out before you, and enumerate this my future Race; that you may rejoice the more with me in the Possession of Italy."

"O pater," *ait Aeneas*, "an existimandum est animas aliquas illustres hinc redire in lucem, et reverti rursus in pigra corpora? quodnam est miseris tam insanum vitae desiderium?"

"O father, is it to be imagined that any Souls of an exalted Nature will go from hence to the World above, and enter again into clumsy inactive Bodies? What cursed love of Life possesses the miserable Beings?"

Respondet Anchises: "O nate, equidem dicam, nec te relinquam dubium."

"I indeed," replied Anchises, "will inform you, my Son, nor hold you longer in Suspense:"

Et *sic* explicat singula per ordinem.

And thus he unfolds each particular in Order.

Lines 724–751: Anchises explains that everything in nature is pervaded by one great spirit, that this in men is clogged by the body, and consequently that, after death, there has to be a longer or shorter purification, after which the souls are sent back into the world to animate other bodies.

"Primo spiritus fovet intus coelum,

"First *then*, the *divine* Spirit within

terram, spatia aquea, et lucidum globum Lunae, et astra Titania: et mens didita per omnia membra movet totam illam *molem*, et miscet se cum magno *illo* corpore.

sustains the Heavens, the Earth, and watery Plains, the Moon's enlightened Orb, and shining Stars; and the *eternal* Mind, diffused through all the Parts of Nature, actuates the whole stupendous Frame, and mingles with the vast Body *of the Universe.*

"Inde *oritur* genus hominum, et pecudum et vitae avium, et monstra quae mare fert sub polita planitie. Inest illis animis vis ignea, et origo coelestis; quatenus corpora noxia non gravant, et artus terreni membraque mortalia non retundunt *vim illam*. Hinc *animae* timent et desiderant, moerent et laetantur: nec suspiciunt coelum inclusae in tenebris et obscuro carcere.

"Thence *proceed* the Race of Men and Beasts, the vital Principles of the flying Kind, and the Monsters which the Ocean breeds under its smooth *crystal* Plain. These Principles have the active Force of Fire, and are of a heavenly Original, *which they exert* so far as they are not clogged by noxious Bodies, blunted by Earth-born Limbs and sickly dying Members. From this *Union and Incumbrance* they are *subjected* to various *Passions*, they fear and desire, grieve and rejoice; and shut up in Darkness, and a gloomy Prison, lose Sight of their *native* Skies.

"Praeterea quando ultima luce vita recessit: non tamen omne malum, nec omnes corporeae sordes omnino recedunt a miseris; et plane necesse est *ut* multa vitia diu conglutinata *iis adhuc* adhaerescant admirabili ratione.

"Nay, even when with the last Beams of Light their Life is gone, yet not every Ill, nor all corporeal Stains are quite removed from the unhappy Beings: And it is absolutely unavoidable that many *vicious Habits*, which have long grown up with the Soul, should be strangely confirmed and riveted therein.

"Ideo cruciantur poenis, et persolvunt supplicia preteritarum noxarum. Aliae, suspensae exponuntur levibus ventis: aliis crimen, *quo sunt* infectae, lavatur sub immenso lacu, aut absumitur flammis. *Omnes* patimur, unusquisque suos ultores.

"Therefore are they afflicted with Pains, and pay the Penalties of their former Ills. Some hung on high, are spread out to *whiten* in the empty Winds: In others the Guilt not done away with is washed out in a vast watery Abyss, or burnt away in Fire:

"Deinde inducimur in spatiosum Elysium, et pauci obtinemus laetos campos: quando longa dies confectis

"We have each of us his Demon, from whom we suffer, till Length of Time, after the fixed Period is elapsed, hath

spatiis temporum delevit congenitas sordes, ac reliquit purum sensum coelestem et simplicem fulgorem ignis. Postquam verterunt rotam per mille annos, Deus vocat eas omnes magno numero ad amnem oblivionis: nempe ut oblitae *Praeteritorum* repetant superiorem curvaturam *mundi*, et incipiant velle iterum redire in corpora."

done away the inherent Stains, and hath left celestial Reason pure *from all irregular Passions*, and the *Soul, that Spark of heavenly* Fire, in its *original* Purity and Brightness, simple and unmixed. "Then we are conveyed into Elysium, and we, *who* are the *happy* few, possess the Fields of Bliss. All these *Souls whom you see*, after they have rolled away a thousand Years, are summoned forth by the God in a great Body to the River Lethe; To the Intent, that, losing Memory *of the past*, they may revisit the upper Regions, and again become willing to return into Bodies."

Lines 752–755: Aeneas and Anchises and the Sibyl go up to a high place, from where they can see those who will have a future life.

Anchises *haec* dixerat: et ducit filium ac simul Sibyllam in medios coetus turbamque frementem: et conscendit collem, unde possit considerare longa serie omnes *sibi* obversos et intueri vultus venientium.

Anchises said: and leads his Son, together with the Sibyl, into the midst of the Assembly and noisy Throng; then chooses a rising Ground, whence he may survey them all as they stand opposite to him in a long Row, and discern their Looks as they come up.

Lines 756–787: Anchises shows Aeneas the long train of Alban kings, his future descendants, ending in Romulus, the founder of Rome.

"Age modo," *inquit Anchises*, "explicabo verbis, quis honos aliquando secuturus sit sobolem Troianam, qui posteri destinentur ex Italica familia, nobiles animas, et successuras nostro nomini: et tibi aperiam tua fata.

"Now mark, I will explain to you what Glory shall henceforth attend the Trojan Race, what Descendants await them of the Italian Nation, Souls of distinguished Worth, and who shall succeed to our Name; yourself too I will instruct in your *particular* Fate.

"Vides*ne?* Ille iuvenis qui insistit hastae nitidae, occupat sorte spatium proximum lumini, primus erumpet in aerem coelestem mixtus Italo sanguine, Sylvius, nomen Albanum, tua soboles postrema: quem uxor Lavinia in sylvis tarde pariet tibi

"See you that Youth who leans on his pointless Spear? He by Destiny holds a Station nearer to the *Regions of* Light; he shall ascend to the upper World the first *of your Race*, who shall have a Mixture of Italian Blood in his Veins, Sylvius, an Alban Name, your last

132

seniori, *futurum* regem et patrem regum: a quo familia nostra regnabit Albae Longae.

"Hic vicinus *huic*, est Procas, honor Troianae nationis: Deinde Capys, et Numitor, et Aeneas Sylvius, qui referet te nomine; aequaliter illustris armis et pietate, si tandem *aliquando* accipiat regendam Albam. Qui iuvenes vide quantum prae se ferant robur! At qui habent caput cinctum *corona* civili quercica: hi condent tibi in montibus Nomentum, et Gabios, et urbem Fidenam: hi arces Collatinas, Pometiam, et Castrum Inui, et Bolam, et Coram. Haec nomina tunc dabuntur *illis*, iam sunt terrae absque nomine.

"Quin etiam Romulus Martius, quem pariet mater Ilia ex stirpe Assaraci, adiiciet se socium avo. Videsne, ut duae cristae surgant *ex eius* capite, et *ut* pater Deorum iam insigniat *eum* suo splendore?

"Ecce, O fili, famosa illa Roma huius ductu aequabit dominationem suam terris, et animos coelo; et una cinget sibi muro septem montes. Fortunata sobole civium; qualis mater Berecynthia vehitur curru per urbes Phrygias, *coronata* turribus, gaudens proles eorum, amplexa centum nepotes, omnes incolas coeli, omnes obtinentes *spatia* alta et superiora.

Issue: late your Consort Lavinia shall in the Woods bring forth to you in your advanced Age, *himself* a King, and the Father of Kings: In whom our Line shall reign over Alba Longa.

"That next is Procas, the Glory of the Trojan Nation, and Capys, and Numitor, and Aeneas Silvius, who shall represent thee in Name, equally distinguished for Piety and Arms, if ever he receive the Crown of Alba. See what *brave* Youths *are these*, what manly Force they shew! And bear their Temples shaded with *a* Civic *Crown of* Oak; these to thy Honour shall build Nomentum, Gabii, and the City Fidena; these on the Mountains shall raise the Collatian Towers, Pometia, the Fort of Inuus, Bola, and Cora. These shall then be *famous* Names, now they are Lands nameless *and obscure.*

"Farther, martial Romulus, whom Ilia of Assaracus's Line shall bear, shall associated with his Grandsire *Numitor.* See you not how the double Plumes stand on his Head erect, and how the Father of the Gods himself already marks him out with his *distinguished* Honours?

"Lo, my Son, under his auspicious Influence Rome, that City of Renown, shall measure her Dominion by the Earth, and her Valour by the Skies, and that one City shall for herself wall around seven strong Hills, happy in a Race of Heroes. *Cloathed with* such *Majesty* as Mother Berecynthia, crowned with Turrets, rides in her Chariot through the Phrygian Towns, joyful in a Progeny of Gods, who embraces an hundred Grandchildren, all Inhabitants of Heaven, all seated in the high celestial Abodes.

Lines 788–807: Anchises draws attention to the Julian Family, and especially Augustus, the destined conqueror of realms wider than were ever traversed by Hercules or Bacchus.

"Huc, huc obverte geminos oculos: cerne hanc nationem, ei Romanos tuos. Hic *est* Caesar, et omnis proles Iulii, exitura sub magnum axem coeli. Hic est ille vir, quem saepe audis promitti tibi, Augustus Caesar, filius Deorum: qui instaurabit iterum aurea saecula per Latium, per loca olim gubernata a Saturno: et propagabit imperium ultra Garamantas atque Indos: sita est *illa* terra ultra sidera, ultra iter Solis et anni, ubi Atlas coelifer versat humeris coelum confixum stellis ardentibus.

"This way now bend both your Eyes: View this Lineage, and your own Romans. This is Caesar, and the whole Race of Iulus, who shall one Day rise to the spacious Axle of the Sky. This, this is the Man whom you have often heard promised to you, Augustus Caesar, the Offspring of a God: Who once more shall establish the golden Age in Latium, through those Lands where Saturn reigned of old, and shall extend his Empire over the Garamantes and Indians. *Their* Land lies without the Signs *of the Zodiac*, beyond the Sun's annual Course, where Atlas, supporting Heaven on his Shoulder, turns the Axle studded with flaming Stars.

"In eius expectatione iam nunc et regna Caspia, et terra Maeotica, trepidant *ob* oracula Deorum: et septem ostia Nili stupefacta commoventur. Nec certe Hercules peragravit tot terras: licet occiderit cervam aeneis pedibus, aut pacaverit sylvas Erymanthi, et arcu terruerit Lernam. Neque Bacchus, qui victor regit currum habenis pampino *vestitis*, impellens tigres ex alto cacumine Nysae.

"Against his Approach even now both the Caspian Realms and the Land about the Palus Maeotis are dreadfully dismayed at the Responses of the Gods, and quaking Mouths of seven fold Nile hurry on their troubled Waves. Nor indeed did Hercules himself run over so many Countries, though he transfixed the brazen footed Hind, quelled the Forest of Erymanthus, and made Lerna tremble with his Bow. Nor Bacchus, who in Triumph manages his Carr with Reins wrapped about with Vine-leaves, driving the *yoked* Tygers from Nysa's lofty Top.

"Et adhuc dubitamus aeternare virtutem factis? Aut timor impedit *nos* sedere in terra Italica?

"And doubt we yet to extend *the Fame of our Virtue* by *heroic* Deeds? Or is Fear a Bar to our settling in the Ausonian Land?

Lines 808–835: The Kings of Rome are pointed out, and the great men of the Republic, Pompey and Caesar.

"Quis vero procul ille spectabilis ramo olivae, portans sacras *res?* Agnosco capillos et barbam canam regis Romani: qui primus firmabit urbem legibus, missus in amplum regnum a parvis Curibus et terra paupere. Cui postea succedet Tullus, qui turbabit pacem patriae, et excitabit ad bella cives quietos et exercitum desuetum vincendi. Quem prope sequitur Ancus iactantior, et iam nunc nimis quaerens favorem populi.

"But who is he at a Distance distinguished by the Olive Boughs, bearing the sacred Utensils? I know the *venerable* Locks and hoary Beard of the Roman King; who first shall establish the City by Lwas, sent from *his* Little *City* Cures, and poor Estate, to vast Empire. Whom Tullus shall next succeed, who shall break the Peace of his Country, and rouze to Arms his inactive Subjects, and Troops now unused to Triumphs. Whom follows next vain-glorious Ancus, even now too much tickled with the Breath of popular Applause.

"Visne etiam videre reges Tarquinios, et animam gloriosam Bruti vindicis, et fasces recuperatos? Hic primus accipiet imperium Consulis et secures severas: et pro honesta libertate pater adiget ad supplicium filios parantes novum bellum, miser: quomodocumque posteri accepturi sint hoc factum, amor patriae superabit et immensum desiderium gloriae.

"Will you also see the Tarquin Kings, and the *stern* unsubmitting Soul of Brutus, the Avenger *of his Country's Wrongs*, and the Sovereignty recovered *to the People*? He first shall receive the consular Power and the Sword of Justice inflexibly severe; and the ill fated Sire shall, for the Sake of glorious Liberty, summon to Death his own Sons, raising *civil* War, *till then* new, *and unknown to Rome*: However Posterity shall interpret that Action, Love to his Country, and the unbounded Desire of Praise, shall prevail *over paternal Affection*.

"Praeterea vide longe Decios et Drusos, et Torquatum saevientem securi, et Camillum reportantem vexilla.

"See besides at some Distance the Decii, Drusi, Torquatus inflexibly severe in executing Justice, and Camillus recovering the *Roman* Standards *from the Enemy*.

"Illae autem animae, quas vides splendere in armis aequalibus, concordes nunc, et dum teguntur *his* tenebris: heu! Si pervenerint ad

"But those *two* Ghosts whom you observe to shine in equal Arms, in perfect Friendship now, and while they shall be shut up in *the Realms of* Night,

lucem vitae, quantum bellum, quantas pugnas et clades inter se excitabunt! Socer descendens e montibus Alpinis et rupe Monoeci: gener adiutus orientalibus *populis* oppositis.

ah what War, what Battles and Havock shall they between them raise, if once they have attained to the Light of Life! The Father-in-law descending from the Alpine Hills, and the Tower of Monoecus? The Son-in-law furnished with Troops of the East to oppose him.

"O pueri, ne assuefacite animum tantis bellis: neve convertite in viscera patriae firmum *eius* robur. Et tu prior, tu abstine, qui trahis originem e coelo. Proiice arma *e* manibus, *O qui* sanguis meus *es*.

"Make not, my Sons, make not such *unnatural* Wars familiar to your Minds; nor turn the powerful Supports of your Country against its own Bowels. And thou, Caesar, first forbear, thou who deriveth thy Origin from Heaven; fling those Arms out of thy Hand, O *my Offspring*, my own Blood!

Lines 836–853: Other heroes of the Republic pass in review. Anchises declares the greatness of Rome to lie not in art or science, but in war and the following peace and justice.

"Ille subacta Corintho victor impellet currum ad altum Capitolium, clarus ob interfectos Achivos. Ille destruet Argos, et Mycenas Agamemnonis, et ipsum nepotem Aeaci, sobolem bellicosi Achillis: ultus avos *suos* Troianos, et templum Minervae violatum.

"That one, having triumphed over Corinth, shall drive his Chariot victorious to the lofty Capitol, illustrious in *the Blood of* slaughtered Greeks. That other shall overthrow Argos, and Mycenae, Agamemnon's Seat, and Aeacides himself, the Descendant of valorous Achilles; avenging his Trojan Ancestors, and the vilated Temple of Minerva.

"Quis omittat te indictum, O magne Cato: aut te, O Cosse? Quis familiam Gracchorum? Aut duo fulmina belli, duos Scipiones destructores Libyae? Aut paupertate gloriosum Fabricium? Aut te seminantem *in* sulco, O Serrane? Quo *me* abripitis fatigatum, O Fabii? Tu es ille *Fabius* Maximus, qui solus nobis reparas rempublicam cunctando.

"Who can in Silence pass over thee, great Cato, or thee, Cossus? Who the Family of Gracchus, or both the Scipio's, those two Thunderbolts of War, the Bane of Afric, and Fabricius in low Fortune exalted? Or thee, Serranus, sowing in the Furrow *thy own Hands had made*? Whither, ye Fabii, do you hurry me *already* tired? Thou art that Fabius, *justly stiled* the Greatest, who sole shall repair our *sinking* State by *wise* Delay.

"Alii, opinor equidem, conflabunt

"Others, I grant indeed, shall with more

solertius aera *quasi* animata: excident e marmore vivos vultus; melius agitabunt causas, et distinguent virga circuitus coeli, et explicabunt ortum astrorum: tu, Romane, memineris gubernare gentes *cum* auctoritate: hae erunt artes tuae: et statuere conditiones pacis, et ignoscere submissis, et domare superbos."

Delicacy mould the breathing *animated* Brass; from Marble draw the Features to the Life; plead Causes better; describe with the *Astronomer's* Rod the Courses of the Heavens, and explain the rising Stars: *But* to rule the Nations with imperial Sway be thy Care, O Roman; these shall be they Arts; to impose Terms of Peace, to spare the Humbled, and crush the proud *stubborn* Foes."

Lines 854–887: Anchises points out the elder Marcellus, who is attended by a younger spirit. Aeneas asks who the youth is, and learns that he is destined to die young, amid the general grief of the Roman people.

Sic *ait* Anchises: et haec adiicit mirantibus: "Vide quomodo Marcellus incedit, notabilis ob spolia opima, et lictor assurgit super omnes viros. Hic magno tumultu furente firmabit rem Romanam equitatu: vincet Carthaginenses et Gallum rebellantem: et dicabit patri Quirino tertia spolia direpta."

Thus Father Anchises, and, as they are wondering farther, subjoins: "Behold how adorned with triumphal Spoils Marcellus stalks along, and shines above the Heroes all! He, mounted on his *fierce* Steed, shall prop the Roman state in the Rage of a formidable Insurrection; the Carthaginians he shall humble, and the rebellious Gaul, and dedicate to Father Quirinus the third *triumphal* Spoils."

Hic vero Aeneas *ait* (nam videbat simul incedere iuvenem insignem pulchritudine et armis splendentibus; sed frons parum erat *hilaris*, et oculi demissi e vultu):

"And upon this Aeneas *says*: for he beheld marching with him a Youth distinguished by his Beauty and shining Arms, but his Countenance not joyous, and his Eyes sunk and dejected;

"O pater, quis ille, qui sic comitatur virum incedentem? *An* filius *est eius?* An vero aliquis e magna serie posterorum? Quis strepitus sociorum est circa *illum!* Quanta similitudo *Marcelli* est in illo! Sed nigra nox cingit caput illius moestis tenebris."

"What *youth* is he, of Father, who thus accompanies the Hero as he walks? Is he a son, or one of the illustrious Line of his Descendants? What bustling Noise of Attendants round him! How great Resemblance in him *to the other!* But sable Night with her dreary Shade hovers around his Head."

Tunc pater Anchises erumpentibus lachrymis coepit *loqui*: "O fili, ne petas *a me* magnum dolorem tuorum. Fata monstrabunt duntaxat

Then Father Anchises, while Tears gushed *from his Eyes*, thus began: Seek not, my Son, to know the deep Disaster of thy Kindred: Him the Fates shall just

illum terris, nec permittent diutius vivere. O Dii, Romana gens visa est vobis nimis potens *futura*, si hoc munus fuisset ipsi perpetuum. Ille campus, *qui est* prope magnam urbem Martis, quantos emittet gemitus hominum! Vel, O Tyberine, quale aspicies funus, quando praeterflues sepulchrum eius novum! neque ullus puer Troiana stirpe eriget avos Latinos in tantam spem: neque terra Romulea olim adeo se efferet ullo filio.

shew on Earth, nor suffer longer to subsist: Ye Gods, Rome's Sons had seemed to powerful in your Eyes, had these your Gifts been permanent. What Groans of Heroes shall that Field by Mars's imperial City send forth! What *solemn* Funeral-pomp shall you, O Tierinus, see, when you glide by his recent Tomb! Shall any Youth of the Trojan Line in Hope exalt the Latin Fathers so high: Nor shall the Land of Romulus ever glory so much in any of her Sons.

"Heu pietas! Heu fides antiqua, et manus insuperabilis bello! Non ullus adversus impune opposuisset se illi armato: sive quando pedibus irrupisset in hostem, sive percussisset calcaribus membra spumantis equi.

"Ah *that* Piety! ah that Faith *and Integrity* of ancient Times! And that Right-hand invincible in War! none with Impunity had encountered him in Arms, whether on Foot he rushed upon the Foe, or goared with the Spur his foaming Courser's Flanks.

"Heu puer deplorande! *Si* aliquo modo evites dura fata, tu eris Marcellus. Date lilia plenis manibus: *ut* iniiciam rubicundos flores, et saltem ornem his muneribus umbram nepotis, et persolvam hoc vanum officium."

"Ah, piteous Youth! if possibly thou canst burst *the Bonds of* rigorous Fate, thou shalt be a Marcellus. Give me Lilies in Handfels; let me strow the purple *blooming* Flowers, these Offerings at least let me heap upon my Descendant's Shade, and discharge this unavailing Duty."

Lines 888–901: Anchises explains to Aeneas what awaits him in Italy, and then dismisses him and the Sibyl through one of the gates of sleep. Aeneas sails to Caieta.

Ita discurrunt ubique tota regione in vastis spatiis aeris, et circumspiciunt omnia. Postquam Anchises duxit filium per haec omnia, et inflammavit animum *eius* cupiditate gloriae futurae: deinde monstrat illi bella quae postea facienda *sunt*; et declarat illi Laurentem gentem, et urbem Latini; et qua ratione toleraturus sit aut evitaturus unumquemque laborem.

Thus up and down they roam through all the *Elysian* Regions in spacious airy Fields, and survey every Object. Through each of which when Anchises had conducted his Son, and fired his soul with the Love of future Fame; he next recounts to the Hero what Wars he must hereafter wage; informs him of the Laurentine People, and of the City of Latinus, and by what Means he may surmount or shun every Toil.

Duae sunt ianuae Somni: quarum una dicitur *esse* cornea, *per* quam permittitur liber egressus veris figuris: altera fulgens, *quia* facta e candido ebore; sed Dii inferi mittunt *per* hanc falsa somnia in mundum.

Two Gates there are of Sleep, whereof the one is said to be of Horn; by which an easy Egress is given to true Visions: The other shining, *as being* wrought of white Ivory; but *through it* the infernal Gods send up lying Dreams to the upper World.

Illic tunc Anchises alloquitur his verbis Aeneam et simul Sibyllam, et demittit per ianuam eburneam. Ille corripit viam ad naves, et repetit socios. Tunc *radens* rectum litus tendit ad portum Caietae. Anchora demittitur e prora, et puppes tegunt litus.

Here then Anchises addresses this Discourse to his Son and the Sibyl together, and dismisses them by the Ivory Gate. The Hero speeds his Way to the Ships, and revisits his Friends. Then steers directly along the Coast for the Port of Cajera: Where, *having arrived*, the Anchor is thrown out from the Forecastle, *and* the Sterns rest upon the Shore.

NAMES OF PERSONS AND PLACES

Achates   *Ἀχάτης*; a follower of Aeneas, sent ahead – *praemissus* – to give notice of the visit.

Acheron   *Ἀχέρων*; uncertain etymology. A river of the Underworld. Both Cocytus and Phlegethon flow into it.

Achilles   *Ἀχιλλεύς*; a Greek hero of the Trojan War and the central character and the greatest warrior of Homer's *Iliad*. His mother was the immortal Nereid Thetis, and his father, the mortal Peleus, was the king of the Myrmidons.

Achivi   From *Ἀχαιοί*, "the Achaeans" or "of Achaea." One of the collective names for the Greeks in *The Iliad* (used 598 times).

Adrastus   *Ἄδραστος*, "inescapable." A legendary king of Argos during the war of the Seven Against Thebes.

Aeaciden   A reference to Perseus, King of Macedon, who claimed descent from Achilles. It comes from Aeacus, a grandfather of Achilles

Aeneas   *Αἰνείας*; possibly derived from *αἰνή*, "praised." A Trojan hero; the son of the prince Anchises and the goddess Aphrodite (Venus). His father was a first cousin of King Priam of Troy (both being grandsons of Ilus, founder of Troy), making Aeneas a second cousin to Priam's children (such as Hector and Paris). He is a character in Greek mythology and is mentioned in *The Iliad*.

Aeolides   See Misenus.

Agamemnon   *Ἀγαμέμνων*; a king of Mycenae; the son of King Atreus and Queen Aerope of Mycenae; the brother of Menelaus, the husband of Clytemnestra and the father of Iphigenia, Electra or Laodike, Orestes and Chrysothemis. Legends make him the king of Mycenae or Argos, thought to be different names for the same area. When Helen, the wife of Menelaus, was taken to Troy by Paris, Agamemnon commanded the united Greek armed forces in the ensuing Trojan War.

Alba   Alba Longa an ancient Latin city in Central Italy, twelve miles south east of Rome, in the Alban Hills. Founder and head of the Latin League; it was destroyed by the Romans around the middle of the 7th century BC, and its inhabitants were forced to settle in Rome. In legend, Romulus and

Remus, founders of Rome, had come from the royal dynasty of Alba Longa, which in *The Aeneid* had been the bloodline of Aeneas, a son of Venus.

Alcides   Hercules, though a son of Jupiter, was often called Alcides on account of his mother's husband Alcaeus. The name Hercules does not fit into an hexameter, and so this alternative or some other must be used.

Aloidae   Otus and Ephialtes, supposed sons of Aloeus, but really of Neptune, who tried to overthrow the Gods by heaping the moutains Ossa on Olympus and Peion on Ossa. They were killed by Apollo.

Amphrysia   Adjective describing the Sybil, because Apollo once fed the flocks of Admetus close by the River Amphresus.

Anchises   Ἀγχίσης; a member of the royal family of Troy. He was said to have been the son of King Capys of Dardania and Themiste, daughter of Ilus, who was son of Tros. He is most famous as the father of Aeneas. His brother was Acoetes, father of the priest Laocoon. He was a mortal lover of the goddess Venus. She had pretended to be a Phrygian princess and then seduced him. She later revealed herself and informed him that they would have a son named Aeneas

Ancus Martius   The fourth King of Rome, after whom came the two Tarquins, with Servius between them.

Androgeus   Ἀνδρόγεως; a son of King Minos. He was killed by the Athenians, and the yearly tribute of Athenian youth was their punishment.

Antenor   Ἀντήνωρ; a counselor to King Priam of Troy

Aornon   See Avernus.

Apollo   Ἀπόλλων; variously recognised as a god of music, truth and prophecy, healing, the sun and light, plague, poetry, and more. The son of Zeus (Jupiter) and Leto, and has a twin sister, the chaste huntress Artemis (Diana). Known in Hellenised Etruscan mythology as Apulu. As the patron of Delphi (Pythian Apollo), Apollo was an oracular god – the prophetic deity of the Delphic Oracle.

Argos   A city in the Peloponnese. See *Agamemnon*.

Assaracus   Ἀσσάρακος; a son of Dardanus; the father of Ganymede.

Atlas   Ἄτλας; the giant who was condemned to bear the world on his shoulders; eventually shown the head of Medusa by Perseus, and made into the mountain that has his name.

Augustus	Born Gaius Octavius Thurinus; official title: *Imperator Caesar Divi Filius Augustus*; 23rd September 63 BC–19th August AD 14. Roman statesman and military leader who was the first Emperor of the Roman Empire, controlling Imperial Rome from 27 BC until his death in AD 14. He commissioned Vergil to write *The Aeneid*, and receives lavish praise throughout the work.
Aurora	Goddess of the Dawn; continuation in Latin of the Indo-European name *Housos*.
Ausonia	Another name for Italy; taken from an ancient race who lived on the coast of Campania.
Avernus	Avernus was believed to be the entrance to the Underworld. The name comes from ἄορνος; "without birds," because, according to tradition, all birds flying over the lake were destined to fall dead. This was likely due to the toxic fumes that mouths of the crater gave off into the atmosphere. In later times, the word was simply an alternate name for the underworld.
	On the shores of the lake is the grotto of the Cumaean Sibyl and the entrance to a long tunnel (*Grotta di Cocceio*, c.2,600 feet) leading toward Cumae, where her sanctuary was located. There are also the remains of temples to Apollo and Jupiter. During the civil war between Octavian and Antony, Agrippa tried to turn the lake into a military port, the Portus Julius. A waterway was dug from Lake Lucrino to Avernus to this end. The port's remains may still be seen under the lake's surface.
Berecyntia Mater	*Βερεκυντία*; a surname of Cybele, *Κυβέλη*, the Mother of the Gods, from Mount Berecyntus in Phrygia, where she was particularly worshipped. Her priests were notorious for castrating themselves in an orgiastic delirium that attended their consecration. Though Roman citizens were forbidden to join her priesthood, she was honoured as the inventress of fortifications.
Bola	A town close to Rome.
Briareus	*Βριάρεως*, "Strong," one of the three Hecatoncheires, or hundred-handed giants, who helped overthrow the Titans.
Brutus	Nephew of Tarquinius the Proud, the last King of Rome. It was Brutus who raised the people to expel their King and to found the Republic. Therefore the restoration of the *fasces*, or symbol of power, to the people.

Caeneus	Caenis was a young woman changed by Jupiter into a man. After his death as *Caeneus*, his sex was changed again.
Caesar	Gaius Julius Caesar; 13th July 100 BC–15th March 44 BC; known by his nomen and cognomen Julius Caesar. A Roman politician, military general, and historian who played a critical role in the events that led to the demise of the Roman Republic and the rise of the Roman Empire.
Caieta	A coastal town in Latium.
Camillus	Marcus Furius Camillus. According to Livy and Plutarch, he was granted four triumphs, was five times Dictator, and was honoured with the title of Second Founder of Rome.
Capitolium	The Capitoline Hill, *Mons Capitolinus*; between the Forum and the Campus Martius; one of the Seven Hills of Rome.
Capys	The fourth King of Alba.
Cato	Marcus Porcius Cato, 234-149 BC; Censor in 184, and opponent of Greek cultural influence. A beast to his slaves. Famous for ending his speeches with *Ceterum censeo Carthaginem esse delendam* – despite the Roman oath to do no harm to the defeated enemy if it disarmed.
Cecropidae	"Athenians." Derived from Cecrops, Κέρκωψ, founder of Athens.
Centauri	Κένταυροι, or occasionally hippocentauri, are mythological creatures with the upper body of a human and the lower body and legs of a horse.
Cerberus	Κέρβερος; a three-headed dog that guards the gates of the Underworld to prevent the dead from leaving. The offspring of the monsters Echidna and Typhon, and usually described as having three heads, a serpent for a tail, and snakes protruding from parts of his body. Cerberus is primarily known for his capture by Hercules in one of his Twelve Labours.
Chaos	Χάος; the empty state preceding the creation of the universe.
Charon	Χάρων; the Ferryman of the Dead; a silent and terrifying figure, who would row those souls given the right burial across the Styx.
Chimaera	Χίμαιρα, a fire-breathing hybrid monster of Lycia in Asia Minor, composed of the parts of more than one animal. It is usually depicted as a lion, with the head of a goat arising from its back, and a tail that might end with a snake's head.

Cnosia	Adjective from Cnossos, *Κνωσός*; the ancient capital of Crete, and taken as referring to the whole island. Close by the modern city of Heracleion.
Cocytus	*Κωκυτός* "lamentation," a river of the Underworld.
Corinthus	Corinth, *Κόρινθος*; a city in Greece, sacked by the Romans in 146 BC.
Corynaeus	A companion of Aeneas.
Cossus	Aulus Cornelius Cossus, who won the *Spolia Opima* in 437 BC by killing the King of Veientines in battle.
Cumae	*Κύμαι*; a town north of the Bay of Naples. It was said to be the oldest Greek settlement in Italy, and to have been founded by men from both Cyme in Asia Minor and from Chalcis in Euboea.
Cyclops	*Κύκλωψ*, plural: *Κύκλωπες*, "round-eyed." A primordial race of giants, each with a single eye in the centre of his forehead
Daedalus	*Δαίδαλος*, was a craftsman of genius. He was commisioned by King Minos to Crete, to build the Labyrinth where the Minotaur could be hidden. This was the hybrid monster— *biformis*—born of his wife's passion for a bull—*veneris monimenta nefandae*. Minos fed the Minotaur with a yearly tribute from Athens of seven youths chosen by lot.
	At last, Theseus, son of Aegeus, the King of Athens, went to Crete. There, helped by Ariadne, the daughter of Minos, he killed the Minotaur and freed the Athenians.
	Daedalus and his son, Icarus, were forbidden to leave Crete. Some say this was to keep the Royal Secret safe. Vergil takes the alternative view, that he had angered Minos by assisting Pasiphae in her unorthodox romance. He and Icarus were shut away in a tower. However, see Ovid, *Metamorphoses*, VIII.185-87:

"terras licet" inquit "et undas
obstruat: et cælum certe patet; ibimus illac:
omnia possideat, non possidet aera Minos."

	So, making wings from feathers held with wax, they flew from the island. Icarus, however, flying too close to the sun, lost his wings, and fell into the sea close by the island of Samos. Daedalus arrived safe in Italy. There he built a temple for Apollo and dedicated his wings—*remigium alarum posuit.*
Danaus	*Δαναός*; another of the collective names for the Greeks in

The Iliad (used 138 times).

Dardana	"Trojans." Adjective drawn from Dardanus, a son of Zeus who settled the area that eventually became Troy.
Deiphobe	See Sybil.
Deiphobus	Δηίφοβος, not to be confused with the Sybil. He was, with Hector and Paris, one of the sons of King Priam. After the death of Paris, he was given Helen for his wife. He was killed and mutilated during the sack of Troy.
Delius	Apollo, "the Delian One" was born on Delos.
Dido	Δῖδώ; the founder and first queen of Carthage. The temporary wife of Aenaes; committed suicide on his departure for Italy. In some sources she is also known as Elissa, Ἔλισσα.
Dis	Roman name for the Underworld.
Drusus	This may refer to Livius Drusus, who conquered Hasdrubal in the Second Punic War, or to Claudius Drusus, the son by an earlier marriage of Liva, the wife of Augustus. The Drusii are probably mentioned by way of flattering Livia, who was present at the first recital of this Book.
Elysium	The Elysian Fields, Ἡλύσιον πεδίον, a place in the Underworld reserved for mortals related to the Gods or other heroes, or those chosen by the Gods to be saved from the common fate of mortals. A place somewhat more exclusive – and more obviously enjoyable – than the Calvinist Heaven.
Eos	Ἔως; a Titaness and the Goddess of the Dawn, who rose each morning from her home at the edge of the Oceanus.
Erebus	Ἔρεβος, "deep shadow." Often conceived as a primordial deity, representing the personification of darkness. Hesiod identifies him as one of the first five beings in existence, born of Chaos.
Eridanus	The River Po.
Eriphyle	Ἐριφύλη; the wife of Amphiaraus. Bribed with a fine necklace, she persuaded him into the mission of the Seven against Thebes. When he found what she had done, he asked his sons to kill her when they grew up. One of them, Alcmaeon, did so.
Erymanthus	"The woods of Erymanthus," a mountain where Hercules hunted a giant boar.

Euboica	See Cumae.
Eumenides	*Εὐμενίδες*; three evil divinities, called "The Kindly Ones" by the Greeks out of fear and respect.
Evadne	The wife of Capaneus, another of the Seven against Thebes. She threw herself into her husband's funeral pyre.
Fabius	Quintus Fabius Maximus Cunctator; General after the disaster at Cannae in 216 BC, whose refusal to fight another battle helped wear down the first impetus of Hannibal.
Fabricius	Gaius Fabricius Luscinus Monocularis; Consul in 282 BC. He directed the war against Pyrrhus. According to Plutarch, Pyrrhus was so impressed in their truce negotiations by his inability to bribe Fabricius, that he released the Roman prisoners even without a ransom.
Gabios	A town close to Rome.
Garamantes	A tribe mentioned by Herodotus. They are thought to correspond to Iron Age Berber tribes in the southwest of ancient Libya. The reference is probably to the invasion of Ethiopia by Gaius Petronius in 25 BC.
Glaucus	See Sybil.
Gorgones	Winged she-monsters with sharp teeth and claws. Only Medusa had the power to turn men into stone.
Gracchi	The two brothers Tiberius and Gracchus who were both murdered by the Senate for trying to ensure that Roman People would share the benefits of the empire they were conquering. Though regarded as traitors to their class, they were among the ideological ancestors of Julius Caesar, and, together with Cicero, they shared in the posthumous truce that was part of the Augustan Settlement.
Harpyiae	Half-human and half-bird personification of storm winds.
Hecate	*Ἑκάτη*; a goddess most often shown holding a pair of torches or a key; in later periods depicted in triple form. She was variously associated with crossroads, entrance-ways, light, magic, witchcraft, knowledge of herbs and poisonous plants, ghosts, necromancy, and sorcery.
Hector	*Ἕκτωρ*; first-born son of King Priam and Queen Hecuba, who was a descendant of Dardanus and Tros, the founder of Troy. Married to Andromache, with whom he had an infant son, Scamandrius (whom the people of Troy called Astyanax). He acted as leader of the Trojans and their allies in the defence of Troy, and was killed by Achilles.

Hesperium	From Ἔσπερος, "the evening star," sometimes meaning "western." Also an occasional Greek name for Italy.
Hydra	A beast with nine heads that lived in Lerna, a marsh close to Argos.
Icarus	See Daedalus.
Idaeus	King Priam's charioteer.
Ilium	Troy
Iuno	The Queen of the Gods.
Iuppiter	The King of the Gods; genitive case: Iovem.
Lacaena	Λάκαινα, a Spartan woman; applied to Helen.
Laodamia	Wife of Protisilaus, the first man ashore when Troy was invaded, and killed with a spear wound in his armpit. Laodamia begged the Gods to restore him for a short while, at the end of which she died with him.
Lapithae	The Lapiths were a people who lived in the mountains of Thessaly. Their king, Ixion, was taken by Jupier on a visit to Olympus, where he tried to seduce June. His punishment was to be fixed to a wheel that revolved forever. Pirithous was his son.
Latini	The Latins were the people Aeneas encountered when he settled in Italy. The war between the Latins and the Trojans, and their eventual union, make up the last six books the *The Aeneid*.
Laurentum	Laurentum was a coastal town a few miles south of Ostia. It was the seat of King Latinus, with whom Aeneas has considerable dealings in the later books of *The Aeneid*.
Lavinia	The daughter of Latinus and Amata and the last wife of Aeneas.
Lethe	Λήθη, "forgetfulness," was s river of the Underworld. All who drank from it were stripped of memory and therefore of personal identity.
Liber	Another name for Bacchus, raised by the nymphs of Mount Nysa. The reference is to his travels in a chariot drawn by tigers.
Maeotia	The Maeotians, Μαιῶται, were an ancient people dwelling along the Sea of Azov, which was known in Antiquity as the "Maeotian marshes" or "Lake Maeotis."
Manes	The *Di Manes* are deities thought to represent souls of

deceased loved ones. They were associated with the Lares, Lemures, Genii, and Di Penates as deities that pertained to domestic, local, and personal cults. They belonged broadly to the category of *di inferi*, "those who dwell below," the undifferentiated collective of divine dead. The Manes were honoured during the Parentalia and Feralia in February. Many Roman grave stones bear the words *Dis Manibus.*

Marcellus   Marcus Marcellus was a general in the Second Punic War, who won the *Spolia Opima* by killing a Gaulish chieftain with his own hands. The other Marcellus was the nephew of Augustus whose early death was the first of a series of blows that left the first Emperor with no eventual choice but to leave everything to his step-son Tiberius. Octavia, the mother of Marcellus, was present at the first recital of this Book. She is said to have fainted after hearing these words. She then gave Vergil 100,000 Sesterces for each relevant line – or about £160,000 as of 2019.

Marpesia   Marpessa was a mountain on Paros from which a very hard marble was quarried.

Massylum   A North African race who lived to the west of Carthage.

Mauvortius   Another name for Mars, the God of War.

Mavors   Another name for Mars, the God of War.

Menelaus   Μενέλαος, "Wrath of the People." King of Sparta, was Helen's first and last husband.

Minerva   The Goddess of Wisdom. As Athena, she was the Patron Goddess of Athens.

Minos   (1) King of Crete; (2) a judge in the Underworld.

Minotaurus   The Minotaur.

Misenus   Μισηνός, was trumpeter to Aeneas. In Book IV, we learn that he had challenged the gods to a musical contest on the conch shell, and for his impudence was drowned by Triton. His being called *Aeolides* arose from the legendary connection between the Aeolian and Campanian Cumae.

Monoeci   Monaco

Musaeus   Μουσαῖος; was a legendary polymath, philosopher, historian, prophet, seer, priest, poet, and musician, said to have been the Father of Poetry. He composed dedicatory and purificatory hymns and prose treatises, and oracular responses.

Mycenae	A city in the Peloponnese. See Agamemnon
Nilus	The Nile.
Numitor	A King of Alba Longa, the father of Rhea Silvia, who, with Mars as their father, gave birth to Romulus and Remus.
Olympus	A mountain in Greece; the home of the Gods.
Orcus	A Roman god of the Underworld. The word may be cognate with "ogre."
Orpheus	Ὀρφεύς; among the mythical fathers of song, and his name was associated with revelations about the Underworld, supposed to be preserved by secret societies. He is naturally made the harper who plays while the blessed spirits dance and sing.
Palinurus	Helmsman of Aeneas. Promised by Apollo he would not drown, he instead fell overboard, and was killed by the inhabitants of the place where he swam ashore.
Paris	Πάρις, also known as Alexander, Ἀλέξανδρος; a son of King Priam and Queen Hecuba of Troy. Best known for his elopement with Helen, Queen of Sparta, which was the immediate cause of the Trojan War. Later in the war, he fatally wounds Achilles in the heel. The name Paris is probably Luwian and comparable to *Pari-zitis*, attested as a Hittite scribe's name.
Parthenopaeus	See the Seven against Thebes.
Pasiphae	Πασιφάη; wife of King Minos of Crete.
Pelasgum	The Pelasgians were said to have been the original inhabitants of Greece, conquered and displaced by the Greeks at the end of the Bronze Age. Some traces of their language – Θάλασσα, Κόρινθος, *etc.* – may survive in Greek. Here, the word is used to mean "Greeks."
Phaedram	Φαίδρα, the wife of Theseus, who, rejected by her step-son Hyppolytus, hanged herself.
Phlegethon	Φλεγέθων, "Burning," a river of the Underworld.
Phlegyas	Φλεγύας; the father of Ixion, and also of a daughter, Coronis. When Apollo seduced Coronis, Ixion was so angry, he set fire to a temple of the God, and his punishment was to be bound to a winged and fiery wheel that was always spinning.
Phoebus	From Φοῖβος, meaning "bright." One of the main epithets applied to Apollo.

150

Pirithous   *Πειρίθους*; a son of "heavenly" Dia, fathered either by Ixion or by Jupiter. He married Hippodamia, daughter of Atrax or Butes, at whose wedding the famous Battle of Lapiths and Centaurs occurred. By his wife, he became the father of Polypoetes, one of Greek leaders during the Trojan War. Peirithous was also the close friend of the hero Theseus, whom he accompanied into the Underworld to rescue Proserpina.

Pollux   Castor and Pollux were half-brothers. Pollux, being a son of Jupiter, was immortal, but Castor was mortal. When Castor was killed in a fight, the best Pollux could arrange was for each to pass half a year forever in the Underworld.

Priam   Πρίαμος; King of Troy during the Trojan War.

Procas   A King of Alba Longa

Proserpina   Prosperpina, the Queen of the Underworld. Daughter of the Goddess Ceres; stolen by Pluto and carried as his wife into the Underworld. Released by the mediation of Jupiter for only six months of the year, during which Ceres blesses the Earth with heat and plenty.

Quirinus   The name given to Romulus after he was made a god.

Rhadamanthus   *Ραδάμανθυς*; A brother of Minos and a fellow Judge of the Underworld.

Rhoeteus   The place where Deiphobus was buried.

Romulus   Son of Mars, and descendant, through his mother, of Aeneas; the founder of Rome.

Salmoneus   Salmoneus of Elis, who claimed divine honours without right.

Saturnus   God of generation, dissolution, plenty, wealth, agriculture, periodic renewal and liberation. In later developments, he also came to be a god of time. His reign was depicted as a Golden Age of plenty and peace. The Temple of Saturn in the Roman Forum housed the state treasury. In December, he was celebrated at what is perhaps the most famous of the Roman festivals, the *Saturnalia*, a time of feasting, role reversals, free speech, gift-giving and revelry. Saturn the planet and Saturday are both named after the God.

Scipiadae   Two members of the Scipio Family, both called *Africanus*, who were prominent in the defeat and final destruction of Carthage.

Scylla   *Σκύλλα*, a monster living on one side of a narrow channel, opposite her counterpart Charybdis. The two sides of the strait were within an arrow's range of each other – so close that sailors attempting to avoid Charybdis would pass dangerously close to Scylla and *vice versa*.

Seven against Thebes

When Oedipus, King of Thebes, realized he had married his own mother and had two sons and two daughters with her, he blinded himself and cursed his sons to divide their inheritance (the kingdom) by the sword. The two sons, Eteocles and Polynices, in order to avoid bloodshed, agreed to rule Thebes in alternate years. After the first year, Eteocles refused to step down, leading Polynices to raise an army of Argives to take Thebes by force. The leaders of this army were: Capaneus, Eteoclus, Hippomedon, Parthenopeus, Amphiaraus, Polynices. When they lost, King Creon ordered that their bodies should lie unburied.

Sibylla

The Sibyl of Cumae, Σίβυλλᾰ; the priestess in charge of the Oracle of Apollo. Deiphobe, daughter of Glaucus, is said to have been a most beautiful woman. She was propositioned by Apollo and promised, in return for her favours, whatever she might ask. She asked to live as many years as the grains of the sand she was holding in her hand. He granted her wish, and she still refused to sleep with him. Therefore, he construed her wish strictly, allowing her almost unending life, but not health or beauty. By the time Aeneas meets her, she has already lived seven hundred years, and has become the God's oracle.

Do not confuse Deiphobe the Sibyl with Deiphobus the third husband of Helen. Both appear in this Book.

Silvius

Third king of Alba, after Aeneas and Ascanius.

Simois

A river near Troy.

Styx

Στύξ, "hate," a river of the Underworld.

Sychaeus

First husband of Dido.

Tarquinius

Two of the final Kings of Rome.

Tartarus

The Underworld was generally a place of negative evils. Tartarus was a kind of Hell, in which the exceptionally wicked or unfortunate were positively tormented for eternity.

Teucri

– "Trojans." From Teucer, the first king of Troy and son of the river-god Scamander and the nymph Idaea. Before the arrival of Dardanus, the land eventually called Dardania (and later still the Troad) was known as Teucria and the inhabitants as Teucrians.

Theseus	*Θησεύς*; a King of Athens and slayer of the Minotaur.
Thyber	The River Tiber.
Tisiphon	*Τισιφόνη*, "Avenger of Murder," or Tilphousia, was one of the three Furies. Her sisters were Alecto and Megaera. She was the one who punished crimes of murder: parricide, fratricide and homicide.
Titania	The Titans were giants who supported Saturn against Jupiter, but were eventually consigned to the Underworld.
Tityos	*Τιτυός*; a monster who threatened Latona, the mother of Apollo and Diana.
Torquatus	Manlius Torquatus was famous for having his own son put to death for disobeying his orders on the field of battle.
Trivia	Another name for Diana.
Troia	Troy.
Tros	Trojan
Tullus	The Third King of Rome.
Tydeus	See The Seven against Thebes.
Tyrrhenus	*Τυρρηνός* was one of the founders of the Etruscan League of twelve cities. Here, the word is used to mean "the Tuscan shore."
Velia	*Ἐλέα*, a town on the west coast of Lucania.
Xanthus	*Ξάνθος*; a river near Troy.

MAIN VOCABULARY

a, ab, *prep abl* by (agent), from (departure, cause, remote origin, time); after (reference);

absisto, absistere, absistiti, – *v* (3rd) *intrans* withdraw from; desist, cease; leave off; depart, go away from; stand back;

abstruse *adv* secretly; remotely;

absum, abesse, abfui, abfuturus *v* be away, absent, distant, missing; be free, removed from; be lacking; be distinct;

ac *conj* and, and also, and besides;

accelero, accelerare, acceleravi, acceleratus *v* (1st) speed up, quicken, hurry; make haste, act quickly, hasten; accelerate;

accendo, accendere, accendi, accensus *v* (3rd) *trans* kindle, set on fire, light; illuminate; inflame, stir up, arouse; make bright;

accinctus, accincta, accinctum *adj* well girded; ready, prepared; strict (opp. negligens);

accingo, accingere, accinxi, accinctus *v* (3rd) *trans* gird on or about, surround; equip, provide (with); get ready, prepare (for);

accipio, accipere, accepi, acceptus *v* (3rd) *trans* take, grasp, receive, accept, undertake; admit, let in, hear, learn; obey;

accubo, accubare, accubui, accubitus *v* (1st) lie near or by; recline at table;

accumulo, accumulare, accumulavi, accumulatus *v* (1st) *trans* accumulate, heap, pile up, soil; add by exaggeration; add, increase, enhance;

acerbo, acerbare, acerbavi, acerbatus *v* (1st) *trans* embitter; aggravate; make disagreeable; make worse;

acervus, acervi *n* (2nd) *m* mass, heap, pile, stack; treasure, stock; large quantity; cluster; funeral pile;

acies, aciei *n* (5th) *f* sharpness, sharp edge, point; battle line, array; sight, glance; pupil of eye;

ad *prep acc* to, up to, towards; near, at; until, on, by; almost; according to;

adamantinus, adamantina, adamantinum *adj* incorruptible, impregnable; inflexible; hard as adamant, diamond, steel;

adamas, adamantis *n* *m* steel, hardest iron (early); anything hard, adamant; white sapphire; diamond;

addo, addere, addidi, additus *v* (3rd) *trans* add, insert, bring, attach to, say in addition; increase; impart; associate;

adeo *adv* to such a degree, pass, point; precisely, exactly; thus far; indeed, truly, even;

adeo, adire, adivi(ii), aditus *v* approach; attack; visit, address; undertake; take possession (inheritance);

adgredior, adgredi, adgressus sum *v* (3rd) *dep* approach, advance; attack, assail; undertake, seize (opportunity), attempt;

adhuc *adv* thus far, till now, to this point; hitherto; yet, as yet; still; besides;

adigo, adigere, adegi, adactus *v* (3rd) *trans* drive in, to (cattle), force, impel; cast, hurl; consign (curse); bind (oath);

adlabor, adlabi, adlapsus sum *v* (3rd) *dep* glide, move, flow towards (w, dat, acc); creep up; steal into; fly (missiles);

adloquor, adloqui, adlocutus sum *v* (3rd) *dep* speak to (friendly); address, harangue, make a speech (to); call on; console;

admiror, admirari, admiratus sum *v*

155

(1st) *dep* admire, respect; regard with wonder, wonder at; be surprised at, be astonished;

admitto, admittere, admisi, admissus *v* **(3rd)** *trans* urge on, put to a gallop; let in, admit, receive; grant, permit, let go;

admoneo, admonere, admonui, admonitus *v* **(2nd)** *trans* admonish, remind, prompt; suggest, advise, raise; persuade, urge; warn, caution;

adno, adnare, adnavi, adnatus *v* **(1st)** *intrans* swim to, towards, approach by swimming; sail to, towards; brought by sea (goods);

ador, adoris *n* **(3rd)** *n* coarse grain; emmer wheat; spelt;

adorior, adoriri, adortus sum *v* **(4th)** *dep* assail, assault, attack, rise against (military, political, plague); accost, address; improperly influence; undertake, try, attempt, come to grips; begin, set to work;

adsimilis, adsimilis, adsimile *adj* similar, like; close; closely resembling, very like;

adsto, adstare, adsteti, adstatus *v* **(1st)** *intrans* stand at, on, by, near; assist; stand up, upright, waiting, still, on one's feet;

adsum, adesse, adfui, adfuturus *v* be near, be present, be in attendance, arrive, appear; aid (w, dat);

adulterium, adulteri(i) *n* **(2nd)** *n* adultery; blending, mixing of different strains, ingredients; contamination;

advento, adventare, adventavi, adventatus *v* **(1st)** *intrans* approach, come to, draw near; arrive, "turn up"; come in (tide); approximate;

adverto, advertere, adverti, adversus *v* **(3rd)** turn, face to, towards; direct, draw one's attention to; steer, pilot (ship);

advolvo, advolvere, advolvi, advolutus *v* **(3rd)** *trans* roll to, towards; fall on knees (genibus advolvor), grovel, prostrate oneself;

adytum, adyti *n* **(2nd)** *n* innermost part of a temple, sanctuary, shrine; innermost recesses, chamber;

aemulus, aemula, aemulum *adj* envious, jealous, grudging, (things) comparable, equal (with, to);

aemulus, aemuli *n* **(2nd)** *m* rival, competitor, love rival; diligent imitator, follower; equal, peer;

aenus, aena, aenum *adj* copper, of copper (alloy); bronze, made of bronze, bronze-coloured; brazen;

aequo, aequare, aequavi, aequatus *v* **(1st)** *trans* level, make even, straight; equal; compare; reach as high or deep as;

aequor, aequoris *n* **(3rd)** *n* level, smooth surface, plain; surface of the sea; sea, ocean;

aequus, aequa -um, aequior -or -us, aequissimus -a -um *adj* level, even, equal, like; just, kind, impartial, fair; patient, contented;

aer, aeris *n c* air (one of 4 elements); atmosphere, sky; cloud, mist, weather; breeze; odor;

aeripes, (gen.), aeripedis *adj* brazen-footed; having, with feet of bronze;

aerius, aeria, aerium *adj* of, produced in, existing in, flying in air, airborne, aerial; towering, airy; blue;

aestas, aestatis *n* **(3rd)** *f* summer; summer heat, weather; a year;

aestuo, aestuare, aestuavi, aestuatus *v* **(1st)** *intrans* boil, seethe, foam; billow roll in waves; be agitated, hot; burn; waver;

aestus, aestus *n* **(4th)** *m* agitation, passion, seething; raging, boiling; heat, fire; sea tide, spray, swell;

aeternus, aeterna -um, aeternior -or -us, aeternissimus -a -um *adj* eternal, everlasting, imperishable;

aether, aetheris *n m* upper air; ether; heaven, sky; sky (as a god); space surrounding a deity;

aetherius, aetheria, aetherium *adj* ethereal, heavenly, divine, celestial; of the upper atmosphere; aloft; lofty;

affero, afferre, attuli, allatus *v trans* bring to (word, food), carry, convey; report, allege, announce; produce, cause;

afflo, afflare, afflavi, afflatus *v* (1st) blow, breathe (on, towards); inspire, infuse; waft; graze; breathe poison on;

affor, affari, affatus sum *v* (1st) *dep* speak to, address; be spoked to, addressed (*passive*), be decreed by fate;

agger, aggeris *n* (3rd) *m* rampart (or material for); causeway, pier; heap, pile, mound; dam, dike; mud wall;

aggredior, aggredi, aggressus sum *v* (3rd) *dep* approach, advance; attack, assail; undertake, seize (opportunity), attempt;

agito, agitare, agitavi, agitatus *v* (1st) stir, drive, shake, move about; revolve; live; control, ride; consider, pursue;

agmen, agminis *n* (3rd) *n* stream; herd, flock, troop, crowd; marching army, column, line; procession;

agna, agnae *n* (1st) *f* ewe lamb;

agnosco, agnoscere, agnovi, agnitus *v* (3rd) recognise, realise, discern; acknowledge, claim, admit to, responsibility;

ago, agere, egi, actus *v* (3rd) drive, urge, conduct, act; spend (time w, cum); thank (w, gratias); deliver (speech);

aio, -, – *v* say (defective), assert; say yes, so, affirm, assent; prescribe, lay down (law);

ala, alae *n* (1st) *f* wing; upper arm, foreleg, fin; armpit; squadron (cavalry), flank, army's wing;

alacris, alacris, alacre *adj* eager, keen, spirited; quick, brisk; active, lively; courageous, ready; cheerful;

aliquis, aliquis, aliquid *pron* anyone, anybody, anything; someone, something;

one or another;

aliter *adv* otherwise, differently; in any other way [aliter ac => otherwise than];

alius *conj* the one ... the other (alius ... alius);

alius, alia, aliud *adj* other, another; different, changed; [alii...alii => some...others]; (A+G);

alligo, alligare, alligavi, alligatus *v* (1st) *trans* bind, fetter (to); bandage; hinder, impede, detain; accuse; implicate, involve in;

alloquor, alloqui, allocutus sum *v* (3rd) *dep* speak to (friendly); address, harangue, make a speech (to); call on; console;

almus, alma, almum *adj* nourishing, kind, propitious; of a nurse, breast, providing nurture, fostering;

alter *conj* the one ... the other (alter ... alter); otherwise;

alter, altera, alterum *adj* one (of two); second, another; former, latter; either;

altum, alti *n* (2nd) *n* the deep, the sea; deep water; a height, depth; remote, obscure period, source;

alumnus, alumna, alumnum *adj* nourished, brought up; reared, fostered by; native, brought up locally;

alveus, alvei *n* (2nd) *m* cavity, hollow; tub; trough, bowl, tray; gameboard; beehive; canoe; hold (ship), ship, boat; channel, bed (river), trench;

ambages, ambagis *n* (3rd) *f* circuit; roundabout way; long story, details; riddle; ambiguity; lie; mystery;

ambio, ambire, ambivi, ambitus *v* (4th) go round, visit in rotation, inspect; solicit, canvass; circle, embrace;

amictus, amictus *n* (4th) *m* cloak, mantle; outer garment; clothing, garb; fashion; manner of dress; drapery;

amnis, amnis *n* (3rd) *m* river (real, personified), stream; current; (running) water; the river Ocean;

amo, amare, amavi, amatus *v* **(1st)** love, like; fall in love with; be fond of; have a tendency to;

amoenus, amoena -um, amoenior -or -us, amoenissimus -a -um *adj* beautiful, attractive, pleasant, agreeable, enjoyable, charming, lovely;

amor, amoris *n* **(3rd)** *m* love; affection; affair; illicit passion;

amoveo, amovere, amovi, amotus *v* **(2nd)** *trans* move, take, put away, remove, steal; banish, cause to go away; withdraw, retire;

amplexus, amplexus *n* **(4th)** *m* clasp, embrace, surrounding; sexual embrace; coil (snake); circumference;

amplus, ampla -um, amplior -or -us, amplissimus -a -um *adj* great, large, spacious, wide, ample; distinguished, important, honourable;

an *conj* can it be that (introduces question expecting negative answer, further question); whether; (utrum ... an = whether ... or); or; either;

ancora, ancorae *n* **(1st)** *f* anchor; grappling iron, hook;

anguis, anguis *n* **(3rd)** *c* snake, serpent; dragon; (constellations) Draco, Serpens, Hydra;

anhelus, anhela, anhelum *adj* panting, puffing, gasping; breath-taking; that emits hot blast, vapor, steaming;

anima, animae *n* **(1st)** *f* soul, spirit, vital principle; life; breathing; wind, breeze; air (element);

animus, animi *n* **(2nd)** *m* mind; intellect; soul; feelings; heart; spirit, courage, character, pride; air;

annosus, annosa, annosum *adj* aged, old, full of years; long-lived; immemorial;

annus, anni *n* **(2nd)** *m* year (astronomical, civil); age, time of life; year's produce; circuit, course;

ante *adv* before, previously, first, before this, earlier; in front, advance of; forwards;

antiquus, antiqua -um, antiquior -or -us, antiquissimus -a -um *adj* old, ancient, aged; time-honoured; simple, classic; venerable; archaic, outdated;

aperio, aperire, aperui, apertus *v* **(4th)** *trans* uncover, open, disclose; explain, recount; reveal; found; excavate; spread out;

apiscor, apisci, aptus sum *v* **(3rd)** *dep* reach, obtain, win (lawsuit); grasp; catch (person); attack (infection); pursue;

apricus, aprica -um, apricior -or -us, apricissimus -a -um *adj* sunny, having lots of sunshine; warmed by, exposed to, open to the sun, basking;

aptus, apta -um, aptior -or -us, aptissimus -a -um *adj* suitable, adapted; ready; apt, proper; tied, attached to; dependent on (w, ex);

apud *prep acc* at, by, near, among; at the house of; before, in the presence, writings, view of;

aqua, aquae *n* **(1st)** *f* water; sea, lake; river, stream; rain, rainfall (pl.), rainwater; spa; urine;

ara, arae *n* **(1st)** *f* altar, structure for sacrifice, pyre; sanctuary; home; refuge, shelter;

arbor, arboris *n* **(3rd)** *f* tree; tree trunk; mast; oar; ship; gallows; spearshaft; beam; squid?;

arcanum, arcani *n* **(2nd)** *n* secret, mystery; secret, hidden place;

arcesso, arcessere, arcessivi, arcessitus *v* **(3rd)** *trans* send for, summon, indict; fetch, import; invite; invoke; bring on oneself;

arcus, arcus *n* **(4th)** *m* bow, arc, coil, arch; rainbow; anything arched or curved;

ardeo, ardere, arsi, arsus *v* **(2nd)** be on fire; burn, blaze; flash; glow, sparkle;

rage; be in a turmoil, love;

arduum, ardui *n* **(2nd)** *n* steep, high place, heights, elevation; arduous, difficult, hard task; challenge;

armatus, armata -um, armatior -or -us, armatissimus -a -um *adj* armed, equipped; defensively armed, armour clad; fortified; of the use of arms;

armipotens, (gen.), armipotentis *adj* powerful, strong in arms, war, valiant, warlike;

armo, armare, armavi, armatus *v* **(1st)** *trans* equip, fit with armour; arm; strengthen; rouse, stir; incite war; rig (ship);

ars, artis *n* **(3rd)** *f* skill, craft, art; trick, wile; science, knowledge; method, way; character (pl.);

artus, artus *n* **(4th)** *m* arm, leg, limb, joint, part of the body; frame (pl.), body; sexual members, organs;

arva, arvae *n* **(1st)** *f* arable land, plowed field; soil, region; countryside; dry land; lowlands, plain;

arx, arcis *n* **(3rd)** *f* citadel, stronghold, city; height, hilltop; Capitoline hill; defense, refuge;

asper, aspera -um, asperior -or -us, asperrimus -a -um *adj* rude, unrefined; cruel, violent, savage, raging, drastic; stern, severe, bitter; hard; rough, uneven, shaggy, coarse, harsh; embossed, encrusted; (mint condition coins); sharp, pointed, jagged, irregular, rugged, severe; sour, pungent, grating, keen;

aspero, asperare, asperavi, asperatus *v* **(1st)** *trans* roughen; sharpen, point, tip; enrage, make fierce, violent; grate on; aggravate;

aspicio, aspicere, aspexi, aspectus *v* **(3rd)** *trans* look, gaze on, at, see, observe, behold, regard; face; consider, contemplate;

assisto, assistere, asstiti, asstatus *v* **(3rd)** take position, stand (near, by), attend;

appear before; set, place near; defend;

assuesco, assuescere, assuevi, assuetus *v* **(3rd)** accustom, become, grow accustomed to, used to, intimate with; make familiar;

ast *conj* but, on the other hand, contrary; but yet; at least; in that event; if further;

astrum, astri *n* **(2nd)** *n* star, heavenly body, planet, sun, moon; the stars, constellation; sky, heaven;

at *conj* but, but on the other hand; on the contrary; while, whereas; but yet; at least;

ater, atra -um, atrior -or -us, aterrimus -a -um *adj* black, dark; dark-coloured (hair, skin); gloomy, murky; unlucky; sordid, squalid; deadly, terrible, grisly (esp. connected with underworld); poisonous; spiteful;

atque *conj* and, as well, soon as; together with; and moreover, even; and too, also, now; yet;

atrium, atri(i) *n* **(2nd)** *n* atrium, reception hall in a Roman house; auction room; palace (pl.), house;

attollo, attollere, -, – *v* **(3rd)** *trans* raise, lift up, towards, to a higher position; erect, build; exalt; extol, exalt;

attonitus, attonita, attonitum *adj* astonished, fascinated; lightning, thunder-struck, stupefied, dazed; inspired;

auctor, auctoris *n* **(3rd)** *c* seller, vendor; originator; historian; authority; proposer, supporter; founder;

audeo, audere, ausus sum *v* **(2nd)** *semidep* intend, be prepared; dare, have courage (to go, do), act boldly, venture, risk;

audio, audire, audivi, auditus *v* **(4th)** hear, listen, accept, agree with; obey; harken, pay attention; be able to hear;

aura, aurae *n* **(1st)** *f* breeze, breath (of air), wind; gleam; odor, stench; vapor; air (pl.), heaven;

aureus, aurea, aureum *adj* of gold,

golden; gilded; gold bearing; gleaming like gold; beautiful, splendid;

auricomus, auricoma, auricomum *adj* golden-haired, with golden hair; flaxen-haired; with golden foliage, leaves;

auris, auris *n* **(3rd)** *f* ear; hearing; a discriminating sense of hearing, "ear" (for); pin on plow;

aurora, aurorae *n* **(1st)** *f* dawn, daybreak, sunrise; goddess of the dawn; Orient, East, peoples of the East;

aurum, auri *n* **(2nd)** *n* gold (metal, colour), gold money, riches;

auspicium, auspici(i) *n* **(2nd)** *n* divination (by birds); omen; beginning; auspices (pl.); right of doing auspices;

ausus, ausus *n* **(4th)** *m* daring, initiative; ventures (pl.);

aut *conj* or, or rather, else; either...or (aut...aut) (emphasizing one);

autem *conj* but (postpositive), on the other hand, contrary; while, however; moreover, also;

autumnus, autumna, autumnum *adj* of autumn, autumnal;

autumnus, autumni *n* **(2nd)** *m* autumn; autumn fruits, harvest;

averto, avertere, averti, aversus *v* **(3rd)** turn away from, aside, divert, rout; disturb; withdraw; steal, misappropriate;

avis, avis *n* **(3rd)** *f* bird; sign, omen, portent;

avus, avi *n* **(2nd)** *m* grandfather; forefather, ancestor;

avus, avi *n* **(2nd)** *m* grandfather; forefather, ancestor;

axis, axis *n* **(3rd)** *m* axle, axis, pole; chariot; the sky, heaven; north pole; region, clime;

bacchor, bacchari, bacchatus sum *v* **(1st)** *dep* celebrate rites of Bacchus; revel, rave, riot; run wild; be frenzied, raving

mad;

beatus, beata -um, beatior -or -us, beatissimus -a -um *adj* happy, fortunate, bringing happiness; rich, wealthy, copious, sumptuous;

bellum, belli *n* **(2nd)** *n* war, warfare; battle, combat, fight; (at, in) (the) war(s); military force, arms;

bellus, bella -um, bellior -or -us, bellissimus -a -um *adj* pretty, handsome, charming, pleasant, agreeable, polite; nice, fine, excellent;

belua, beluae *n* **(1st)** *f* beast, wild animal (incl. sea creature); monster, brute (great size, ferocity);

bibulus, bibula, bibulum *adj* fond of drinking, ever thirsty; soaking, sodden; spongy, absorbent, porous;

bidens, (gen.), bidentis *adj* two-pronged; with two teeth; two bladed; having two permanent teeth;

biduus, bidua, biduum *adj* continuing for two days, of, for two days;

biformis, biformis, biforme *adj* of double form, two formed; consisting of two parts, forms; two-faced (Janus);

bis *adv* two times; on two occasions;

bonus, bona -um, melior -or -us, optimus -a -um *adj* good, honest, brave, noble, kind, pleasant, right, useful; valid; healthy;

bracchium, bracchi(i) *n* **(2nd)** *n* arm; lower arm, forearm; claw; branch, shoot; earthwork connecting forts;

bractea, bracteae *n* **(1st)** *f* gold leaf, foil, thin sheet of metal (esp. gold), other material; veneer; show;

brattea, bratteae *n* **(1st)** *f* gold leaf, foil, thin sheet of metal (esp. gold), other material; veneer; show;

brevis, breve, brevior -or -us, brevissimus -a -um *adj* short, little, small, stunted; brief, concise, quick; narrow, shallow; humble;

breviter, brevitius, brevitissime *adv* shortly, briefly, in a nut shell; quickly; for, within a short distance, time;

brumalis, brumalis, brumale *adj* wintry; during winter; connected with winter solstice, winter;

cacumen, cacuminis *n* **(3rd)** *n* top, peak, summit; shoot, blade of grass, tip of tree, branch; zenith; limit;

cado, cadere, cecidi, casus *v* **(3rd)** *intrans* fall, sink, drop, plummet, topple; be slain, die; end, cease, abate; decay;

caducus, caduca, caducum *adj* ready to fall; tottering, unsteady; falling, fallen; doomed; perishable; futile;

cadus, cadi *n* **(2nd)** *m* jar, large jar for wine, oil, liquids; urn, funeral urn; money jar;

caecus, caeca -um, caecior -or -us, caecissimus -a -um *adj* blind; unseeing; dark, gloomy, hidden, secret; aimless, confused, random; rash;

caedo, caedere, caecidi, caesus *v* **(3rd)** *trans* chop, hew, cut out, down, to pieces; strike, smite, murder; slaughter; sodomise;

caelestis, caeleste, caelestior -or -us, caelestissimus -a -um *adj* heavenly, of heavens, sky, from heaven, sky; celestial; divine; of the Gods;

caelicola, caelicolae *n* **(1st)** *c* heaven dweller; deity, god, goddess; worshiper of heavens;

caelifer, caelifera, caeliferum *adj* supporting sky, heavens;

caelum, caeli *n* **(2nd)** *n* heaven, sky, heavens; space; air, climate, weather; universe, world;

caenum, caeni *n* **(2nd)** *n* mud, mire, filth, slime, dirt, uncleanness; (of persons) scum, filth;

caeruleus, caerulea, caeruleum *adj* blue, cerulean, dark; greenish-blue, azure; of river, sea deities; of sky, sea;

caesus, caesus *n* **(4th)** *m* cutting, cutting off;

calcar, calcaris *n* **(3rd)** *n* spur (for horse); spur, incitement, stimulus; spur of a cock;

calidus, calida -um, calidior -or -us, calidissimus -a -um *adj* warm, hot; fiery, lusty; eager, rash, on the spot; having a warm climate, place;

caligo, caliginis *n* **(3rd)** *f* mist, fog; darkness, gloom, murkiness; moral, intellectual, mental dark; dizziness;

caminus, camini *n* **(2nd)** *m* smelting, foundry furnace, forge; home stove, furnace; vent (underground fires);

campus, campi *n* **(2nd)** *m* plain; level field, surface; open space for battle, games; sea; scope; the Campus Martius in Rome;

candeo, candere, candui, – ** *v* **(2nd) be of brilliant whiteness, shine, gleam (white); become, be hot; glow, sparkle;

candidus, candida -um, candidior -or -us, candidissimus -a -um *adj* bright, clear, transparent; clean, spotless; lucid; candid; kind, innocent, pure; radiant, unclouded; (dressed in) white; of light colour; fair skinned, pale;

canis, canis *n* **(3rd)** *c* dog; hound; subordinate; "jackal"; dog-star, fish; lowest dice throw; clamp;

canities, canitiei *n* **(5th)** *f* white, gray colouring, deposit; gray, white hair, grayness of hair; old age;

cano, canere, cani, canitus *v* **(3rd)** sing, celebrate, chant; crow; recite; play (music), sound (horn); foretell;

cantus, cantus *n* **(4th)** *m* song, chant; singing; cry (bird); blast (trumpet); poem, poetry; incantation;

cantus, cantus *n* **(4th)** *m* song, chant; singing; cry (bird); blast (trumpet); poem, poetry; incantation;

capio, capere, additional, forms *v trans* take hold, seize; grasp; take bribe; arrest, capture; put on; occupy; captivate;

caput, capitis *n* **(3rd)** *n* head; person; life; leader; top; source, mouth (river); capital (punishment); heading; chapter, principal division; [~ super pedibus => head over heels];

cardo, cardinis *n* **(3rd)** *m* hinge; pole, axis; chief point, circumstance; crisis; tenon, mortise; area; limit;

carina, carinae *n* **(1st)** *f* keel, bottom of ship, hull; boat, ship, vessel; voyage; half walnut shell;

carmen, carminis *n* **(3rd)** *n* song, music; poem, play; charm; prayer, incantation, ritual, magic formula; oracle;

carpo, carpere, carpsi, carptus *v* **(3rd)** *trans* seize, pick, pluck, gather, browse, tear off; graze, crop; tease, pull out, card (wool); separate, divide, tear down; carve; despoil, fleece; pursue, harry; consume, erode;

carus, cara -um, carior -or -us, carissimus -a -um *adj* dear, beloved; costly, precious, valued; high-priced, expensive;

castigo, castigare, castigavi, castigatus *v* **(1st)** chastise, chasten, punish; correct, reprimand, dress down, castigate; neutralise;

castrum, castri *n* **(2nd)** *n* fort, fortress; camp (pl.), military camp, field; army; war service; day's march; castle, fortress; (fortified) town; [~ doloris => catafalque, coffin platform];

catena, catenae *n* **(1st)** *f* chain; series; fetter, bond, restraint; imprisonment, captivity; (chain mail);

causa, causae *n* **(1st)** *f* cause, reason, motive; origin, source, derivation; responsibility, blame; symptom; occasion, subject; plea, position; lawsuit, case, trial; proviso, stipulation; thing(s);

cautes, cautis *n* **(3rd)** *f* rough pointed, detached rock, loose stone; rocks (pl.), cliff, crag; reef;

cava, cavae *n* **(1st)** *f* hollow; cage (Ecc);

caveo, cavere, cavi, cautus *v* **(2nd)** beware, avoid, take precautions, defensive action; give, get surety; stipulate;

cedo *v* 3 1 *pres active imp* 2 S *trans* give, bring here!, hand over, come (now, here); tell, show us, out with it! behold!

celer, celeris -e, celerior -or -us, celerrimus -a -um *adj* swift, quick, agile, rapid, speedy, fast; rash, hasty, hurried; lively; early;

celero, celerare, celeravi, celeratus *v* **(1st)** quicken, accelerate; make haste, act quickly, be quick; hasten, hurry, do quickly;

celo, celare, celavi, celatus *v* **(1st)** *trans* conceal, hide, keep secret; disguise; keep in dark, in ignorance; shield;

centum, centesimus -a -um, centeni -ae -a, centie(n)s *num* one hundred;

centumgeminus, centumgemina, centumgeminum *adj* hundredfold; hundred-handed (Briareus); hundred-gated (Thebes);

cerno, cernere, crevi, cretus *v* **(3rd)** *trans* sift, separate, distinguish, discern, resolve, determine; see; examine; decide;

certamen, certaminis *n* **(3rd)** *n* contest, competition; battle, combat, struggle; rivalry; (matter in) dispute;

certo, certius, certissime *adv* certainly, definitely, really, for certain, a fact, truly; surely, firmly;

certus, certa -um, certior -or -us, certissimus -a -um *adj* fixed, settled, firm; certain; trusty, reliable; sure; resolved, determined;

cerva, cervae *n* **(1st)** *f* doe, hind; deer;

cesso, cessare, cessavi, cessatus *v* **(1st)** *intrans* be remiss, inactive; hold back, leave off, delay, cease from; rest; be free of;

ceu *adv* as, in the same way, just as; for example, like; (just) as if; as (if) it were;

chordus, chorda, chordum *adj* late-born, produced out of, late in season; second (crop of hay), aftermath;

chorea, choreae *n* (1st) *f* round, ring dance; dancers; planet movement; magistrate court; multitude; choir;

chorus, chori *n* (2nd) *m* chorus; choral passage in a play; dancing, singing performance, ers; school; round, ring dance; dancers; movement of planets; magistrate's court; multitude; choir; singing; sanctuary; those in sanctuary;

cieo, ciere, civi, citus *v* (2nd) *trans* move, set in motion; excite, rouse, stir up; urge on; summon, muster, call up; disturb, shake; provoke (war); invoke, call on by name; cite; raise, produce;

cingo, cingere, cinxi, cinctus *v* (3rd) *trans* surround, encircle, ring; enclose; beleaguer; accompany; gird, equip; ring (tree);

cinis, cineris *n* (3rd) *c* ashes; embers, spent love, hate; ruin, destruction; the grave, dead, cremation;

circa *adv* around, all around; round about; near, in vicinity, company; on either side;

circa *prep acc* around, on bounds of; about, near (space, time, numeral); concerning; with;

circum *adv* about, around; round about, near; in a circle; in attendance; on both sides;

circum *prep acc* around, about, among, near (space, time), in neighbourhood of; in circle around;

circumdo, circumdare, circumdedi, circumdatus *v* (1st) *trans* surround; envelop, post, put, place, build around; enclose; beset; pass around;

circumfero, circumferre, circumtuli, circumlatus *v* carry, hand, pass, spread, move, take, cast around (in circle); publicise; divulge;

circumfero, circumferre, circumtuli, circumlatus *v* carry, hand, pass, spread,

move, take, cast around (in circle); publicise; divulge;

circumfundo, circumfundere, circumfundi, circumfusus *v* (3rd) *trans* pour, drape, crowd around; cause (water) to go round, part; surround; distribute;

circumsto, circumstare, circumsteti, circumstatus *v* (1st) stand, gather, crowd around, surround, beset; be on either side;

circumvenio, circumvenire, circumveni, circumventus *v* (4th) *trans* encircle, surround; assail, beset; enclose; circumvent; defraud, trick; surpass;

circumvolo, circumvolare, circumvolavi, circumvolatus *v* (1st) fly, hover, flutter around; run, hasten, rush around;

circus, circi *n* (2nd) *m* race course; circus in Rome, celebration of games; circle; orbit;

cithara, citharae *n* (1st) *f* cithara, lyre; lute, guitar;

civilis, civilis, civile *adj* of, affecting fellow citizens; civil; legal; public; political; unassuming;

clades, cladis *n* (3rd) *f* defeat, reverse; casualties, slaughter, carnage, devastation; ruins; dissolution; disaster, ruin, calamity; plague; pest, bane, scourge (cause of disaster);

clamo, clamare, clamavi, clamatus *v* (1st) proclaim, declare; cry, shout out; shout, call name of; accompany with shouts;

clamor, clamoris *n* (3rd) *m* shout, outcry, protest; loud shouting (approval, joy), applause; clamour, noise, din; war-cry, battle-cry; roar (thunder, surf); cry of fear, pain, mourning; wailing;

clamor, clamoris *n* (3rd) *m* shout, outcry, protest; loud shouting (approval, joy), applause; clamor, noise, din; war-cry, battle-cry; roar (thunder, surf); cry of fear, pain, mourning; wailing;

clarus, clara -um, clarior -or -us,

clarissimus -a -um *adj* clear, bright, gleaming; loud, distinct; evident, plain; illustrious, famous;

classis, classis *n* **(3rd)** *f* class, division of Romans; grade (pupils); levy, draft; fleet, navy; group, band;

claudo, claudere, clausi, clausus *v* **(3rd)** *trans* close, shut, block up; conclude, finish; blockade, besiege; enclose; confine;

cliens, clientis *n* **(3rd)** *c* client, dependent (of a patron), vassal; client state, its citizens, allies;

coepio, coepere, -, – *v* **(3rd)** begin, commence, initiate;

coerceo, coercere, coercui, coercitus *v* **(2nd)** *trans* enclose, confine; restrain, check, curb, repress; limit; preserve; punish;

cognomen, cognominis *n* **(3rd)** *n* surname, family, 3rd name; name (additional, derived from a characteristic);

collabor, collabi, collabsus sum *v* **(3rd)** *dep* collapse, fall down, in ruin; fall in swoon, exhaustion, death; slip, slink (meet);

collus, colli *n* **(2nd)** *m* neck; throat; head and neck; severed head; upper stem (flower); mountain ridge;

color, coloris *n* **(3rd)** *m* colour; pigment; shade, tinge; complexion; outward appearance, show; excuse, pretext

coluber, colubri *n* **(2nd)** *m* snake; serpent; (forming hair of mythical monsters);

columba, columbae *n* **(1st)** *f* pigeon; dove; (term of endearment); (bird of Venus, symbol of love, gentleness);

columna, columnae *n* **(1st)** *f* column, pillar (building, monument, pedestal, waterclock), post, prop; portico (pl.); stanchion (press, ballista); water-spout; pillar of fire; penis (rude);

coma, comae *n* **(1st)** *f* hair, hair of head,

mane of animal; wool, fleece; foliage, leaves; rays;

comes, comitis *n* **(3rd)** *c* comrade, companion, associate, partner; soldier, devotee, follower of another;

comitatus, comitatus *n* **(4th)** *m* company of soldiers, mercenaries; war band; company, throng, crowd; rank and file; escort, retinue (of slaves, clients); court of a king; combination, association; county;

comitor, comitari, comitatus sum *v* **(1st)** *dep* join as an attendant, guard, escort; accompany, follow; attend (funeral); go, be carried with; be retained, stay, grow, join with; be connected with; occur;

commissum, commissi *n* **(2nd)** *n* undertaking, enterprise; trust, secret; thing entrusted, confiscated; crime;

compello, compellere, compuli, compulsus *v* **(3rd)** *trans* drive together (cattle), round up; force, compel, impel, drive; squeeze; gnash;

complaceo, complacere, complacui, complacitus *v* **(2nd)** *intrans* please, take fancy of, capture affections of, be acceptable, agreed to;

complector, complecti, complexus sum *v* **(3rd)** *dep* embrace, hug; welcome; encircle, encompass; attain; include, bring in, involve; lay hold of, grip; seize; grasp, take in, up; sum up; include in scope, cover;

compleo, complere, complevi, completus *v* **(2nd)** *trans* fill (up, in); be big enough to fill; occupy space, crowd; furnish, supply, man; finish, complete, perfect; make pregnant; fulfill, make up, complete, satisfy;

complexus, complexus *n* **(4th)** *m* surrounding, encompassing, encircling; clasp, grasp, hold, embrace; inclusion; sexual intercourse (w, Venerius, femineus); hand-to-hand fighting; stranglehold;

comprehendo, comprehendere, comprehendi, comprehensus *v* **(3rd)**

trans catch, seize, grasp firmly; arrest; take hold, root, fire, ignite; conceive (baby); embrace; include, cover, deal with (in speech, law); express (by term, symbol);

comprimo, comprimere, compressi, compressus *v* **(3rd)** *trans* press, squeeze together, fold, crush; hem, shut, keep, hold in; copulate (male); suppress, control, stifle, frustrate, subdue, cow, put down; hold breath; silence;

comptus, compta -um, comptior -or -us, comptissimus -a -um *adj* adorned, decorated, dressed, arranged, brushed (hair), smart; ornate, embellished; elegant (writing, writers), neat, in order, polished, smoothed;

concha, conchae *n* **(1st)** *f* mollusk, murex, oyster, scallop; pearl, mollusk-shell; Triton horn;

concilium, concili(i) *n* **(2nd)** *n* public gathering, meeting; popular assembly, council; hearing; debate, discussion; association, society, company; union, connection (of objects); league of states; sexual union, coition; close conjunction; bond of union; plant iasione blossom;

conclamo, conclamare, conclamavi, conclamatus *v* **(1st)** cry, shout aloud, out; make resound w, shouts; give a signal; summon; bewail, mourn;

concordia, concordiae *n* **(1st)** *f* concurrence, mutual agreement, harmony, peace; rapport, amity, concord, union; friend;

concordo, concordare, concordavi, concordatus *v* **(1st)** harmonise; be in harmony, agreement, on good terms, friendly; agree; go by pattern;

concretus, concreta -um, concretior -or -us, concretissimus -a -um *adj* composed, formed; composite; concrete; solid, hard, stiff, frozen; matted; dense; condensed; curdled, clotted; cohering, closed up; constipated; ingrained (sin);

concursus, concursus *n* **(4th)** *m* running

to and fro, together, collision, charge, attack; assembly, crowd; tumult; encounter; combination, coincidence; conjunction, juxtaposition; joint right;

concutio, concutere, concussi, concussus *v* **(3rd)** *trans* shake, vibrate, agitate violently; wave, brandish; (sound) strike (the ear); strike together, to damage; weaken, shake, shatter; harass, intimidate; rouse;

condo, condere, condidi, conditus *v* **(3rd)** *trans* put, insert (into); store up, put away, preserve, bottle (wine); bury, inter; sink; build, found, make; shut (eyes); conceal, hide, keep safe; put together, compose; restore; sheathe (sword); plunge, bury (weapon in enemy); put out of sight;

confero, conferre, contuli, collatus *v trans* bring together, carry, convey; collect, gather, compare; unite, add; direct, aim; discuss, debate, confer; oppose; pit, match against another; blame; bestow, assign;

conficio, conficere, additional, forms *v trans* make, construct; prepare, complete, accomplish; cause; perform; do thoroughly; compose; amass, collect; raise (troops); traverse; eat up, consume; expend; finish off; kill, dispatch; defeat finally, subdue, reduce, pacify; chop, cut up;

congero, congerere, congessi, congestus *v* **(3rd)** *trans* collect, bring, get together, amass; heap, pile up, on; build, construct; compile; consign (to one's stomach); assemble, crowd together; give repeatedly, shower;

congesto, congestare, congestavi, congestatus *v* **(1st)** *trans* bring, carry together;

conicio, conicere, conieci, coniectus *v* **(3rd)** *trans* throw, put, pile together; conclude, infer, guess; assign, make go; classify, put; throw, cast, fling (into area); devote, pour (money); thrust, involve; insert;

coniugium, coniugi(i) *n* **(2nd)** *n* marriage, wedlock; husband, wife; couple; mating (animal), pair; close connection;

coniunx, coniugis *n* **(3rd)** *c* spouse, mate, consort; husband, wife, bride, fiancee, intended; concubine; yokemate;

conlabor, conlabi, conlabsus sum *v* **(3rd)** *dep* collapse, fall down, in ruin; fall in swoon, exhaustion, death; slip, slink (meet);

conor, conari, conatus sum *v* **(1st)** *dep* attempt, try, endeavour, make an effort; exert oneself; try to go, rise, speak;

consanguineus, consanguinea, consanguineum *adj* of the same blood; related by blood; kindred; fraternal; brotherly, sisterly;

consido, considere, consedi, consessus *v* **(3rd)** *intrans* sit down, be seated; hold sessions, sit (judge), try; alight; subside, sink (in); encamp, bivouac; take up a position; stop, stay, make one's home, settle; lodge;

consilium, consili(i) *n* **(2nd)** *n* debate, discussion, deliberation, consultation; advice, counsel, suggestion; adviser; decision, resolution; intention, purpose, policy, plan, action; diplomacy, strategy; deliberative, advisory body; state council, senate; jury; board of assessors; intelligence, sense, capacity for judgment, invention; mental ability; choice;

consisto, consistere, constiti, constitus *v* **(3rd)** stop, stand, halt, cease; pause, linger; stop spreading, flowing; take a position; stand together, fast; consist of, be reckoned in; rest, depend upon; be unaltered; make a stand; stay, remain (fixed), stand still, erect, upright; correspond to; come about, exist; fall due (tax); be established; remain valid, applicable;

conspicio, conspicere, conspexi, conspectus *v* **(3rd)** *trans* observe, see, witness; notice; watch; gaze, stare on; catch, be in sight of; face; have appearance; attract attention; discern;

(*passive*) be conspicuous, visible;

constituo, constituere, constitui, constitutus *v* **(3rd)** set up, in position, erect; place, dispose, locate; (call a) halt; plant (trees); decide, resolve; decree, ordain; appoint, post, station (troops); settle (colony); establish, create, institute; draw up, arrange, set in order; make up, form; fix;

consto, constare, constiti, constatus *v* **(1st)** *intrans* agree, correspond, fit, be correct; be dependent, based upon; exist, continue, last; be certain, decided, consistent, sure, fixed, established, well-known, apparent, plain; stand firm, still, erect, together; remain motionless, constant; consist of, in;

consul, consulis *n* **(3rd)** *m* consul (highest elected Roman official - 2, year); supreme magistrate elsewhere;

consultus, consultus *n* **(4th)** *m* decision, resolution, plan; decree (of senate, other authority); oracular response;

contendo, contendere, contendi, contentus *v* **(3rd)** stretch, draw tight, make taut; draw, bend (bow, catapult); tune; stretch out; compete, contend (fight, law), dispute; compare, match, contrast; demand, press for; strain, tense; make effort, strive for; speak seriously, passionately; assert; hurl, shoot; direct; travel; extend; rush to, be in a hurry, hasten;

conticesco, conticescere, conticui, – *v* **(3rd)** *intrans* cease to talk, fall silent, lapse into silence; cease to function, become idle;

contra *prep acc* against, facing, opposite; weighed against; as against; in resistance, reply to; contrary to, not in conformance with; the reverse of; otherwise than; towards, up to, in direction of; directly over, level with; to detriment of;

convallis, convallis *n* **(3rd)** *f* valley (much shut in), ravine, deep, narrow, enclosed valley, glen; (also pl.);

conveho, convehere, convexi, convectus *v* **(3rd)** *trans* bring, carry, bear together, to one place; collect, gather; get in (harvest);

conventus, conventus *n* **(4th)** *m* agreement, covenant; coming together; conjunction (astrology); Roman district; gathering, meeting; assembly, people in assembly; provincial court, "assize"; convent, monastery; religious community; convention (Ecc);

cor, cordis *n* **(3rd)** *n* heart; mind, soul, spirit; intellect, judgment; sweetheart; souls, persons (pl.);

coram *adv* in person, face-to-face; in one's presence, before one's eyes; publicly, openly;

coram *prep abl* in the presence of, before; (may precede or follow object); personally;

corneus, cornea, corneum *adj* of horn, made of horn, horn-; resembling horn (hardness, appearance); horny;

cornipes, cornipedis *n* **(3rd)** *m* hoofed animal; (horse); (centaur);

cornu, cornus *n* **(4th)** *n* horn; hoof; beak, tusk, claw; bow; horn, trumpet; end, wing of army; mountain top;

corporeus, corporea, corporeum *adj* corporeal, material, physical, endowed w, body; fleshy, composed of animal tissue;

corporo, corporare, corporavi, corporatus *v* **(1st)** *trans* kill, strike dead; form into a body, furnish w, a body; form (corporate society);

corpus, corporis *n* **(3rd)** *n* body; person, self; virility; flesh; corpse; trunk; frame(work); collection, sum; substantial, material, concrete object, body; particle, atom; corporation, guild;

corripio, corripere, corripui, correptus *v* **(3rd)** *trans* seize, grasp, snatch up, lay hold of; sweep off; carry away; appropriate, arrogate; censure, reproach, rebuke, chastise; shorten, abridge; hasten (upon); catch (fire);

cortina, cortinae *n* **(1st)** *f* cauldron, (of Delphi oracle), kettle; water-organ; vault, arch; curtain;

crater, crateris *n* **(3rd)** *m* mixing bowl; depression, volcano crater, basin of fountain; Cup (constellation);

creatrix, creatricis *n* **(3rd)** *f* mother, she who brings forth; creator (of the world); authoress, creatress;

credo, credere, credidi, creditus *v* **(3rd)** trust, entrust; commit, consign; believe, trust in, rely on, confide; suppose; lend (money) to, make loans, give credit; believe, think, accept as true, be sure;

cremo, cremare, cremavi, crematus *v* **(1st)** *trans* burn (to ash), cremate; consume, destroy (fire); burn alive; make burnt offering;

crepito, crepitare, crepitavi, crepitatus *v* **(1st)** *intrans* rattle, clatter; rustle, crackle; produce rapid succession of sharp, shrill noises;

crimen, criminis *n* **(3rd)** *n* indictment, charge, accusation; blame, reproach, slander; verdict, judgment; sin, guilt; crime, offense, fault; cause of a crime, criminal; adultery;

crinis, crinis *n* **(3rd)** *m* hair; lock of hair, tress, plait; plume (helmet); tail of a comet;

crista, cristae *n* **(1st)** *f* crest, comb (bird, beast); plume (helmet); plant yellow-rattle; clitoris;

croceus, crocea, croceum *adj* yellow, golden; saffron-coloured; of saffron, its oil, saffron-; scarlet (Ecc);

crudelis, crudele, crudelior -or -us, crudelissimus -a -um *adj* cruel, hardhearted, unmerciful, severe, bloodthirsty, savage, inhuman; harsh, bitter;

crudeliter, crudelius, crudelissime *adv* cruelly, savagely, relentlessly; with cruel effect;

crudus, cruda -um, crudior -or -us,

crudissimus -a -um *adj* raw; bloody, bleeding; crude, cruel, rough, merciless; fierce, savage; grievous; youthful, hardy, vigourous; fresh, green, immature; undigested; w, undigested food;

cruentus, cruenta -um, cruentior -or - us, cruentissimus -a -um *adj* bloody, bleeding, discharging blood; gory; blood red; polluted w, blood-guilt; bloodthirsty, insatiably cruel, savage; accompanied by, involving bloodshed;

cruor, cruoris *n* **(3rd)** *m* blood; (fresh, clotted from wound); (spilt in battle); vegetable, other juice; gore; murder, bloodshed, slaughter; blood (general); stream, flow of blood;

cubile, cubilis *n* **(3rd)** *n* bed, couch, seat; marriage bed; lair, den, nest, pen, hive of bees; base, bed;

culter, cultri *n* **(2nd)** *m* knife; (weapon, sacrificial, hunt); pruner edge; spear point; plowshare;

cum *adv* when, at the time, on each occasion, in the situation that; after; since, although; as soon; while, as (well as); whereas, in that, seeing that; on, during which;

cum *prep abl* with, together, jointly, along, simultaneous with, amid; supporting; attached; under command, at the head of; having, containing, including; using, by means of;

cumba, cumbae *n* **(1st)** *f* skiff, small boat; (esp. that in which Charon ferried the dead across the Styx);

cumulo, cumulare, cumulavi, cumulatus *v* **(1st)** *trans* heap, pile up, high, gather into a pile, heap; accumulate, amass; load, fill full; increase, augment, enhance; perfect, finish up; (*passive*) be made, composed of;

cuncto, cunctare, cunctavi, cunctatus *v* **(1st)** delay, impede, hold up; hesitate, tarry, linger; be slow to act; dawdle; doubt;

cuneus, cunei *n* **(2nd)** *m* wedge; wedge-shaped stone, area, rack, block of seats; battalion, etc in a wedge;

cupido, cupidinis *n* **(3rd)** *c* desire, love, wish, longing (passionate); lust; greed, appetite; desire for gain;

cupio, cupere, cupivi, cupitus *v* **(3rd)** *trans* wish, long, be eager for; desire, want, covet; desire as a lover; favour, wish well;

cupressus, cupressi *n* **(2nd)** *f* cypress-tree; cypress oil, wood, cypress-wood casket, spear of cypress-wood;

cura, curae *n* **(1st)** *f* concern, worry, anxiety, trouble; attention, care, pains, zeal; cure, treatment; office, task, responsibility, post; administration, supervision; command (army);

curro, currere, cucurri, cursus *v* **(3rd)** *intrans* run, trot, gallop, hurry, hasten, speed, move, travel, proceed, flow swiftly, quickly;

currus, currus *n* **(4th)** *m* chariot, light horse vehicle; triumphal chariot; triumph; wheels on plough; cart;

cursus, cursus *n* **(4th)** *m* running; speed, zeal; charge, onrush; forward movement, march; revolution (wheel); course, direction, line of advance, orbit; voyage, passage; race; career; series; lesson;

curvus, curva, curvum *adj* curved, bent, arched; crooked; morally wrong; stooped, bowed; winding; w, many bends

custodia, custodiae *n* **(1st)** *f* protection, safe-keeping, defense, preservation; custody, charge; prisoner; watch, guard, picket; guard post, house; prison; confinement; protective space;

custos, custodis *n* **(3rd)** *c* guard; sentry, watch; guardian, protector, keeper; doorkeeper, watchman, janitor; jailer, warden; poll watcher; spy; garrison; container; replacement vine shoot;

cymba, cymbae *n* **(1st)** *f* skiff, small boat; (esp. that in which Charon ferried the dead across the Styx);

damno, damnare, damnavi, damnatus *v* (1st) *trans* pass, pronounce judgment, find guilty; deliver, condemn, sentence; harm, damn, doom; discredit; seek, secure condemnation of; find fault; bind, oblige under a will;

daps, dapis *n* (3rd) *f* sacrificial feast, meal; feast, banquet; food composing it; food, meal of animals;

de *prep abl* down, away from, from, off; about, of, concerning; according to; with regard to;

dea, deae *n* (1st) *f* goddess;

debello, debellare, debellavi, debellatus *v* (1st) fight out, to a finish; bring a battle, war to an end; vanquish, subdue;

debeo, debere, debui, debitus *v* (2nd) owe; be indebted, responsible for, obliged, bound, destined; ought, must, should;

decedo, decedere, decessi, decessus *v* (3rd) *intrans* withdraw, retire, go off, away, depart, leave; relinquish, cease; desert, abandon; quit office and return home; make, get out of the way; yield; wane; fall short; stray, digress; pass away, depart life, die; subside, cease (feelings); disappear;

decerpo, decerpere, decerpsi, decerptus *v* (3rd) *trans* pluck, pull, tear, snip off, pick; cull; reap, procure, gather; catch, snatch; remove

decoro, decorare, decoravi, decoratus *v* (1st) adorn, grace, embellish, add beauty to; glorify, honour, add honour to; do credit to;

decus, decoris *n* (3rd) *n* glory, splendor; honour, distinction; deeds; dignity, virtue; decorum; grace, beauty;

deduco, deducere, deduxi, deductus *v* (3rd) *trans* lead, draw, , pull, bring, stretch down, away, out, off; escort; eject, evict (claimant); divert, draw (water); draw (sword); spin; deduct, reduce, lessen; describe; deduce launch, bring downstream (ship); remove (force); entice; found, settle (colony);

deficio, deficere, defeci, defectus *v* (3rd) *intrans* fail, falter; run short, out; grow weak, faint; come to end; revolt, rebel, defect; ass away; become extinct, die, fade out; subside, sink; suffer eclipse, wane;

defungor, defungi, defunctus sum *v* (3rd) *dep* have done with (*abl*), finish, bring, come to end, be quit, done, rid of; discharge; settle a case (for so much); make do; discharge; die; (*perf*) to have died;

dehinc *adv* hereafter, henceforth, from here, now on; afterwards; for, in the future, next; then, after that, thereupon; at a later stage; for the rest; next (in order);

dehisco, dehiscere, dehivi, – *v* (3rd) *intrans* gape, yawn, split open; part, divide, develop, leave a gap, leak; be, become apart;

deicio, deicere, deieci, deiectus *v* (3rd) *trans* throw, pour, jump, send, put, push, force, knock, bring down; cause to fall, drop; hang; overthrow, bring down, depose; kill, destroy; shoot, strike down; fell (victim); unhorse; let fall; shed; purge, evacuate bowel; dislodge, rout; drive, throw out;

deinde *adv* then, next, afterward; thereon, henceforth, from there, then; in next position, place;

deludo, deludere, delusi, delusus *v* (3rd) deceive, dupe; play false, mock, make sport; play through, complete a performance;

demens, dementis (gen.), **dementior -or -us, dementissimus -a -um** *adj* out of one's mind, senses; demented, mad, wild, raving; reckless, foolish;

demitto, demittere, demisi, demissus *v* (3rd) *trans* drop, let fall; sink; send, cast, go, flow, float, slope down; flow, shed, let (blood); bend, stoop, bow, sag; lower (eyes); let (clothes, hair, beard) hang down; bring, strike down; plunge, insert, thrust, plant; dismiss, demote; depose; absorb; descend by race, birth; leave (will); let issue rest (on evidence); fell (tree);

demum *adv* finally, at last; at length, in the end, eventually; [tum demum => only then]; other possibilities being dismissed; only, alone, and no other, nowhere else;

dens, dentis *n* **(3rd)** *m* tooth; tusk; ivory; tooth-like thing, spike; destructive power, envy, ill will;

dependo, dependere, dependi, depensus *v* **(3rd)** *trans* pay over, down; pay (penalty); expend (time, labour); spend, lay out; bestow;

depono, deponere, deposui, depostus *v* **(3rd)** *trans* put, lay down, aside, away; let drop, fall; give up; resign; deposit, entrust, commit; lift off; take off (clothes); have (hair, beard, nails) cut; shed (tusks); ull down, demolish; plant (seedlings); set up, place; lay to rest; fire;

descendo, descendere, descendi, descensus *v* **(3rd)** *intrans* descend, climb, march, come, go, flow, run, hang down; dismount; penetrate, sink; stoop; demean; drop, become lower (pitch); be reduced; trace descent, come down;

descensus, descensus *n* **(4th)** *m* decent, climbing, getting down; action, means, way of descent; lying down (rude);

describo, describere, descripsi, descriptus *v* **(3rd)** *trans* describe, draw, mark, trace out; copy, transcribe, write; establish (law, right)

desino, desinare, desavi, desatus *v* **(1st)** stop, end, finish, abandon, leave, break off, desist, cease; come to, at end, close;

desum, deesse, defui, defuturus *v* be wanting, lacking; fail, miss; abandon, desert, neglect; be away, absent, missing;

detrudo, detrudere, detrusi, detrusus *v* **(3rd)** *trans* push, thrust, drive, force off, away, aside, from, down; expel; dispossess; postpone;

deturbo, deturbare, deturbavi, deturbatus *v* **(1st)** *trans* upset, topple, bring tumbling down; dislodge; strike, beat to ground; drive, pull, knock, cast, thrust, strike down, off; deprive of;

deus, dei *n* **(2nd)** *m* god; divine essence, being, supreme being; statue of god;

devenio, devenire, deveni, deventus *v* **(4th)** *intrans* come to, arrive, turn up (at); go (to see, stay); reach; land; turn to; extend to;

dexter, dextra -um, dexterior -or -us, dextimus -a -um *adj* right, on, to the right hand, side; skillful, dexterous, handy; favourable, fortunate, pretentious; opportune; proper, fitting, suitable;

dextera, dexterae *n* **(1st)** *f* right hand; weapon, greeting, shaking hand; right side; soldier; ledge, contract; metal model of hand as token of agreement;

dico, dicere, dixi, dictus *v* **(3rd)** say, declare, state; allege, declare positively; assert; plead (case); talk, speak; make speech; play (instrument); pronounce, articulate; utter; mean; name, call; appoint, fix, set (date); designate, declare intention of giving;

dies, diei *n* **(5th)** *c* day; daylight; (sunlit hours); (24 hours from midnight); open sky; weather; specific day; day in question; date of letter; festival; lifetime, age; time;

differo, differre, distuli, dilatus *v* postpone, delay, differ; put off, keep waiting; give respite to; differ, disagree; spread abroad; scatter, disperse; separate; defame; confound, bewilder, distract;

digitus, digiti *n* **(2nd)** *m* finger; toe; finger's breadth, inch; (1, 16 of a pes); twig;

dignus, digna -um, dignior -or -us, dignissimus -a -um *adj* appropriate, suitable; worthy, deserving, meriting; worth (w, *abl*, *gen*);

dinumero, dinumerare, dinumeravi, dinumeratus *v* **(1st)** *trans* count, calculate (number of); enumerate; reckon; count, pay out (money);

dirigo, dirigere, direxi, directus *v* **(3rd)** *trans* arrange, set in line, direction; align; set in order; form up, fall in (army); mark, fix (boundary); demarcate; straighten (out); level; square (up); oint; direct (word, attention); bring proceedings; end word w, inflection; direct (course, steps), turn, steer, guide; propel, direct (missiles, blows);

dirus, dira -um, dirior -or -us, dirissimus -a -um *adj* awful, dire, dreadful (omen); ominous, frightful, terrible, horrible; skillful;

discedo, discedere, discessi, discessus *v* **(3rd)** go, march off, depart, withdraw; scatter, dissipate; abandon; lay down (arms);

disco, discere, didici, discitus *v* **(3rd)** *trans* learn; hear, get to know, become acquainted with; acquire knowledge, skill of, in;

discolor, (gen.), discoloris *adj* another colour, not of the same colour; of different, party colours; variegated;

discordia, discordiae *n* **(1st)** *f* disagreement, discord;

discrimen, discriminis *n* **(3rd)** *n* crisis, separating line, division; distinction, difference;

dispicio, dispicere, dispexi, dispectus *v* **(3rd)** look about (for), discover espy, consider;

distringo, distringere, distrinxi, districtus *v* **(3rd)** *trans* stretch out, apart; detain; distract; pull in different directions;

diu, diutius, diutissime *adv* (for) a long, considerable time, while; long since;

diva, divae *n* **(1st)** *f* goddess;

diverbero, diverberare, diverberavi, diverberatus *v* **(1st)** split; strike violently;

dives, divitis (gen.), divitior -or -us, divitissimus -a -um *adj* rich, wealthy; costly; fertile, productive (land); talented, well endowed;

divus, diva -um, -, divissimus -a -um *adj* divine; blessed, saint;

do, dare, dedi, datus *v* **(1st)** *trans* give; dedicate; sell; pay; grant, bestow, impart, offer, lend; devote; allow; make; surrender, give over; send to die; ascribe, attribute; give birth, produce; utter;

doceo, docere, docui, doctus *v* **(2nd)** teach, show, point out;

doctus, docta -um, doctior -or -us, doctissimus -a -um *adj* learned, wise; skilled, experienced, expert; trained; clever, cunning, shrewd;

doleo, dolere, dolui, dolitus *v* **(2nd)** hurt; feel, suffer pain; grieve; be afflicted, pained, sorry; cause pain, grief;

dolor, doloris *n* **(3rd)** *m* pain, anguish, grief, sorrow, suffering; resentment, indignation;

dolus, doli *n* **(2nd)** *m* trick, device, deceit, treachery, trickery, cunning, fraud;

dominus, domini *n* **(2nd)** *m* owner, lord, master; the Lord; title for ecclesiastics, gentlemen;

domo, domare, domui, domitus *v* **(1st)** subdue, master, tame; conquer;

domus, domus *n* **(4th)** *f* house, building; home, household;

donec *conj* while, as long as, until;

donum, doni *n* **(2nd)** *n* gift, present; offering;

dubito, dubitare, dubitavi, dubitatus *v* **(1st)** doubt; deliberate; hesitate (over); be uncertain, irresolute;

dubius, dubia, dubium *adj* doubtful, dubious, uncertain; variable, dangerous; critical;

duco, ducere, duxi, ductus *v* **(3rd)** lead, command; think, consider, regard; prolong;

ductor, ductoris *n* **(3rd)** *m* leader, commander;

dulcis, dulce, dulcior -or -us, dulcissimus -a -um *adj* pleasant, charming; sweet; kind, dear; soft, flattering, delightful;

dum *conj* while, as long as, until; provided that;

duo -ae o, secundus -a -um, bini -ae -a, bis *num* two (pl.);

durus, dura -um, durior -or -us, durissimus -a -um *adj* hard, stern; harsh, rough, vigourous; cruel, unfeeling, inflexible; durable;

dux, ducis *n* (3rd) *m* leader, guide; commander, general;

eburneus, eburnea, eburneum *adj* ivory, of ivory; white as ivory, ivory-coloured;

ecce *interj* behold! see! look! there! here!

edo, edare, edidi, editus *v* (1st) *trans* eject, emit; put, give forth (buds); beget; bear (fruit); display, evince, exhibit; utter solemnly; pronounce, decree (oracle); deliver (message); issue (command); publish; disclose, tell, relate, make known; declare, make formal statement; cause; see birth of;;

edo, edere, edi, essus *v* (3rd) *trans* eat, consume, devour; eat away (fire, water, disease); destroy; spend money on food;

educo, educere, eduxi, eductus *v* (3rd) lead out; draw up; bring up; rear;

effero, efferre, extuli, elatus *v* carry out; bring out; carry out for burial; raise;

effingo, effingere, effinxi, effictus *v* (3rd) fashion, form, mold; represent, portray, depict; copy; wipe away;

effor, effari, effatus sum *v* (1st) *dep* utter, say (solemn words); declare, announce, make known; speak, express;

effugio, effugere, effugi, effugitus *v* (3rd) flee, escape; run, slip, keep away (from), eschew, avoid; baffle, escape notice;

effundo, effundere, effudi, effusus *v* (3rd) *trans* pour out, away, off; allow to drain; shower; volley (missiles); send, stream forth; shed (blood, tears); discharge (vomit, urine), debouch, emit; flow out, overflow; break out; bear, yield, bring forth; expend, use up; unseat, eject, drop, discard; stretch, spread out, extend; spread (sail); loosen, slacken, fling, give rein;

egenus, egena, egenum *adj* in want of, destitute of;

egeo, egere, egui, - *v* (2nd) need (w, gen, *abl*), lack, want; require, be without;

ego, mei *pron pers* I, me;

egregius, egregia, egregium *adj* singular; distinguished; exceptional; extraordinary; eminent; excellent;

elephas, elephantis *n m* elephant; ivory; large variety of lobster, large sea creature;

elido, elidere, elisi, elisus *v* (3rd) strike or dash out; expel; shatter; crush out; strangle; destroy;

eluo, eluere, elui, elutus *v* (3rd) wash clean; wash away, clear oneself (of);

emico, emicare, emicui, emicatus *v* (1st) leap, dash, bolt, jump, spurt, burst, break, shine out; spring, dart, shoot forth, up; appear suddenly, quickly; make sudden movement up, out; give a jump; stand out;

emitto, emittere, emisi, emissus *v* (3rd) hurl; let go; utter; send out; drive; force; cast; discharge; expel; publish;

emo, emere, emi, emptus *v* (3rd) buy; gain, acquire, obtain;

emoveo, emovere, emovi, emotus *v* (2nd) move away, remove, dislodge;

en *interj* behold! see! lo! here! hey! look at this!;

enim *conj* namely (postpos.); indeed; in fact; for; I mean, for instance, that is to say;

eno, enare, enavi, enatus *v* (1st) swim out;

ensis, ensis *n* (3rd) *m* sword;

enumero, enumerare, enumeravi, enumeratus *v* **(1st)** count up, pay out; specify, enumerate;

eo, ire, ivi(ii), itus *v* go, walk; march, advance; pass; flow; pass (time); ride; sail;

epula, epulae *n* **(1st)** *f* courses (pl.), food, dishes of food; dinner; banquet; feast for the eyes;

epulum, epuli *n* **(2nd)** *n* feast; solemn or public banquet; entertainment;

eques, equitis *n* **(3rd)** *m* horseman, cavalryman, rider; horsemen (pl.), cavalry; equestrian order; knight (*abb* eq.); (wealthy enough to own his own horse); horse;

equidem *adv* truly, indeed; for my part;

equus, equi *n* **(2nd)** *m* horse; steed;

ergo *adv* therefore; well, then, now;

eripio, eripere, eripui, ereptus *v* **(3rd)** snatch away, take by force; rescue;

erro, errare, erravi, erratus *v* **(1st)** wander, go astray; make a mistake, err; vacillate;

error, erroris *n* **(3rd)** *m* wandering; error; winding, maze; uncertainty; deception;

eruo, eruere, erui, erutus *v* **(3rd)** pluck, dig, root up, overthrow, destroy; elicit;

et *conj* and, and even; also, even; (et ... et = both ... and);

etiam *conj* and also, besides, furthermore, in addition, as well; even, actually; yes, indeed; now too, as yet, still, even now; yet again; likewise; (particle); (et-iam);

evado, evadere, evasi, evasus *v* **(3rd)** evade, escape; avoid;

eveho, evehere, evexi, evectus *v* **(3rd)** carry away, convey out; carry up; exalt; jut out, project;

evoco, evocare, evocavi, evocatus *v* **(1st)** call forth; lure, entice out; summon, evoke;

ex *prep abl* out of, from; by reason of; according to; because of, as a result of;

exanimus, exanima, exanimum *adj* dead; lifeless;

exaudio, exaudire, exaudivi, exauditus *v* **(4th)** hear clearly; comply with, heed; hear from afar; understand;

excido, excidere, excidi, excisus *v* **(3rd)** cut out, off, down; raze, destroy;

excipio, excipere, excepi, exceptus *v* **(3rd)** take out; remove; follow; receive; ward off, relieve;

excolo, excolere, excolui, excultus *v* **(3rd)** improve; develop, honour;

exerceo, exercere, exercui, exercitus *v* **(2nd)** exercise, train, drill, practice; enforce, administer; cultivate;

exigo, exigere, exegi, exactus *v* **(3rd)** drive out, expel; finish; examine, weigh;

exiguus, exigua, exiguum *adj* small; meager; dreary; a little, a bit of; scanty, petty, short, poor;

eximo, eximere, exemi, exemptus *v* **(3rd)** *trans* remove, extract, take, lift out, off, away; banish, get rid of; free, save, release;

exinde *adv* thence; after that, next in order, thereafter, then; furthermore; by that cause;

exitialis, exitialis, exitiale *adj* destructive, deadly;

exitus, exitus *n* **(4th)** *m* exit, departure; end, solution; death; outlet, mouth (of river);

exopto, exoptare, exoptavi, exoptatus *v* **(1st)** long for;

expedio, expedire, expedivi, expeditus *v* **(4th)** disengage, loose, set free; be expedient; procure, obtain, make ready;

expendo, expendere, expendi, expensus *v* **(3rd)** pay; pay out; weigh, judge; pay a penalty;

expleo, explere, explevi, expletus *v* **(2nd)** fill out; fill, fill up, complete, finish; satisfy, satiate;

expono, exponere, exposui, expositus *v* **(3rd)** set, put forth, out; abandon, expose; publish; explain, relate; disembark;

exsanguis, exsanguis, exsangue *adj* bloodless, pale, wan, feeble; frightened;

exscindo, exscindere, exscidi, exscissus *v* **(3rd)** *trans* demolish, destroy, raze to ground (town, building); exterminate, destroy (people);

exsequor, exsequi, exsecutus sum *v* **(3rd)** *dep* follow, go along, on with; pursue for vengeance, punishment; strive, search after; ersist in; execute, carry out; rehearse; attain, arrive at, accomplish;

exsomnis, exsomnis, exsomne *adj* sleepless, wakeful;

exspecto, exspectare, exspectavi, exspectatus *v* **(1st)** lookout for, await; expect, anticipate, hope for;

exstinguo, exstinguere, exstinxi, exstinctus *v* **(3rd)** put out, extinguish, quench; kill, destroy;

exsto, exstare, -, - *v* **(1st)** stand forth, out; exist; be extant, visible; be on record;

exsurgo, exsurgere, exsurrexi, exsurrectus *v* **(3rd)** *intrans* bestir oneself, take action; swell, rise, move, extend up, out, to higher moral level; rise (to one's feet, from bed, moon, in revolt); stand, rear, get up; come to being;

extemplo *adv* immediately, forthwith;

extendo, extendere, extendi, extentus *v* **(3rd)** *trans* stretch, thrust out; make taut; extend, prolong, continue; enlarge, increase; make even, straight, smooth; stretch out in death, (*passive*) lie full length;

externus, externa, externum *adj* outward, external; foreign, strange;

exterreo, exterrere, exterrui, exterritus *v* **(2nd)** strike with terror, scare;

exto, extare, extiti, - *v* **(1st)** stand out or forth, project be visible, exist, be on record;

extra *adv* outside;

extra *prep* *acc* outside of, beyond, without, beside; except;

extremum, extremi *n* **(2nd)** *n* limit, outside; end;

exuro, exurere, exussi, exustus *v* **(3rd)** *trans* burn (up, out, completely); destroy, devastate by fire; dry up, parch; scald;

facies, faciei *n* **(5th)** *f* shape, face, look; presence, appearance; beauty; achievement;

facilis, facile, facilior -or -us, facillimus -a -um *adj* easy, easy to do, without difficulty, ready, quick, good natured, courteous;

facio, facere, feci, factus *v* **(3rd)** *trans* make, build, construct, create, cause, do; have built, made; fashion; work (metal); act, take action, be active; (bowels); act, work (things), function, be effective; roduce; produce by growth; bring forth (young); create, bring into existence; compose, write; classify; provide; do, perform; commit crime; suppose, imagine;

fallax, fallacis (gen.), fallacior -or -us, fallacissimus -a -um *adj* deceitful, treacherous; misleading, deceptive; false, fallacious; spurious;

fallo, fallere, fefelli, falsus *v* **(3rd)** deceive; slip by; disappoint; be mistaken, beguile, drive away; fail; cheat;

falsus, falsa, falsum *adj* wrong, lying, fictitious, spurious, false, deceiving, feigned, deceptive;

fama, famae *n* **(1st)** *f* rumour; reputation; tradition; fame, public opinion, ill repute; report, news;

fames, famis *n* **(3rd)** *f* hunger; famine; want; craving;

fas, undeclined *n* **N** divine, heaven's law,

will, command; that which is right, lawful, moral, allowed;

fascis, fascis *n* **(3rd)** *m* bundles of rods (w, ax) (pl.); (carried by lictors before high Roman magistrate);

fatalis, fatalis, fatale *adj* fated, destined; fatal, deadly;

fateor, fateri, fassus sum *v* **(2nd)** *dep* admit, confess (w, acc); disclose; acknowledge; praise (w, dat);

fatigo, fatigare, fatigavi, fatigatus *v* **(1st)** weary, tire, fatigue; harass; importune; overcome;

fatisco, fatiscere, -, - *v* **(3rd)** gape, crack; crack open, part asunder; grow weak or exhausted, droop;

fatum, fati *n* **(2nd)** *n* utterance, oracle; fate, destiny; natural term of life; doom, death, calamity;

faux, faucis *n* **(3rd)** *f* pharynx (usu pl.), gullet, throat, neck, jaws, maw; narrow pass, shaft, strait; chasm;

favilla, favillae *n* **(1st)** *f* glowing ashes, embers; spark; ashes;

fax, facis *n* **(3rd)** *f* torch, firebrand, fire; flame of love; torment;

fecundus, fecunda -um, fecundior -or - us, fecundissimus -a -um *adj* fertile, fruitful; productive (of offspring), prolific; abundant; imaginative;

felix, felicis (gen.), felicior -or -us, felicissimus -a -um *adj* happy; blessed; fertile; favourable; lucky; successful, fruitful;

femina, feminae *n* **(1st)** *f* woman; female;

feralis, feralis, ferale *adj* funereal; deadly, fatal;

feretrum, feretri *n* **(2nd)** *n* bier;

ferio, feriare, feriavi, feriatus *v* **(1st)** rest from work, labour; keep, celebrate holiday; be idle; abstain from;

fero, ferre, tuli, latus *v* bring, bear; tell,

speak of; consider; carry off, win, receive, produce; get;

ferreus, ferrea, ferreum *adj* iron, made of iron; cruel, unyielding; (blue);

ferrugineus, ferruginea, ferrugineum *adj* of the colour of iron-rust, somber;

ferrum, ferri *n* **(2nd)** *n* iron; any tool of iron; weapon, sword;

ferus, feri *n* **(2nd)** *c* wild beast, animal; wild, untamed horse, boar;

fessus, fessa, fessum *adj* tired, wearied, fatigued, exhausted; worn out, weak, feeble, infirm, sick;

festino, festinare, festinavi, festinatus *v* **(1st)** hasten, hurry;

festus, festa, festum *adj* festive, joyous; holiday; feast day; merry; solemn;

fetus, fetus *n* **(4th)** *m* offspring, young (animals); children (of a parent); brood, litter; fetus, fetus, young while still in the womb; embryo; birth, bringing forth young; laying (egg); bearing young, breeding; conception; fruit of plant; produce, crop; offshoot, branch, sucker, sapling; bearing fruit;

fides, fidei *n* **(5th)** *f* faith, loyalty; honesty; credit; confidence, trust, belief; good faith;

fido, fidere, fisus sum *v* **(3rd)** *semidep* trust (in), have confidence (in) (w, dat or *abl*);

fidus, fida, fidum *adj* faithful, loyal; trusting, confident;

figo, figere, fixi, fixus *v* **(3rd)** fasten, fix; pierce, transfix; establish;

figura, figurae *n* **(1st)** *f* shape, form, figure, image; beauty; style; figure of speech;

filius, fili *n* **(2nd)** *m* son;

filum, fili *n* **(2nd)** *n* thread, string, filament, fiber; texture, style, nature;

findo, findere, fidi, fissus *v* **(3rd)** split,

cleave, divide;

fingo, fingere, finxi, fictus *v* **(3rd)** *trans* mold, form, shape; create, invent; produce; imagine; compose; devise, contrive; adapt, transform into; modify (appearance, character, behaviour); groom; make up (story, excuse); pretend, pose; forge, counterfeit; act insincerely;

finis, finis *n* **(3rd)** *c* boundary, end, limit, goal; (pl.) country, territory, land;

finitimus, finitima, finitimum *adj* neighbouring, bordering, adjoining;

fio, feri, factus sum *v* *semidep* happen, come about; result (from); take place, be held, occur, arise (event); be made, created, instituted, elected, appointed, given; be prepared, done; develop; be made, become; (facio *passive*); [fiat => so be it, very well; it is being done];

firmo, firmare, firmavi, firmatus *v* **(1st)** strengthen, harden; support; declare; prove, confirm, establish;

firmus, firma -um, firmior -or -us, firmissimus -a -um *adj* firm, steady; substantial, solid, secure, safe; strong, robust, sturdy, stout, durable; loyal, staunch, true, constant; stable, mature; valid, convincing, well founded;

fissilis, fissilis, fissile *adj* easily split; split;

flagellum, flagelli *n* **(2nd)** *n* whip, lash, scourge; thong (javelin); vine shoot; arm, tentacle (of polyp);

flamma, flammae *n* **(1st)** *f* flame, blaze; ardor, fire of love; object of love;

flecto, flectere, flexi, flexus *v* **(3rd)** bend, curve, bow; turn, curl; persuade, prevail on, soften;

fleo, flere, flevi, fletus *v* **(2nd)** cry for; cry, weep;

flos, floris *n* **(3rd)** *m* flower, blossom; youthful prime;

fluctus, fluctus *n* **(4th)** *m* wave; disorder; flood, flow, tide, billow, surge;

turbulence, commotion;

fluentum, fluenti *n* **(2nd)** *n* stream, river; flood; (waters of) lake; flow; current, draft, draught of air;

flumen, fluminis *n* **(3rd)** *n* river, stream; any flowing fluid; flood;

fluo, fluere, fluxi, fluxus *v* **(3rd)** flow, stream; emanate, proceed from; fall gradually;

fluvius, fluvi(i) *n* **(2nd)** *m* river, stream; running water;

folium, foli(i) *n* **(2nd)** *n* leaf;

for, fari, fatus sum *v* **(1st)** *dep* speak, talk; say;

foris, foris *n* **(3rd)** *f* door, gate; (the two leaves of) a folding door (pl.); double door; entrance;

forma, formae *n* **(1st)** *f* form, figure, appearance; beauty; mold, pattern;

formido, formidare, formidavi, formidatus *v* **(1st)** dread, fear, be afraid of; be afraid for (the safety of) (w, dat);

formido, formidinis *n* **(3rd)** *f* fear, terror, alarm; religious dread, awe; thing, reason which scares, bogy, horror; rope strung with feathers used by hunters to scare game;

formo, formare, formavi, formatus *v* **(1st)** form, shape, fashion, model;

fornix, fornicis *n* **(3rd)** *m* arch, vault, vaulted opening; monument arch; brothel, cellar for prostitution;

fors, fortis *n* **(3rd)** *f* chance; luck, fortune; accident;

fortis, forte, fortior -or -us, fortissimus -a -um *adj* strong, powerful, mighty, vigourous, firm, steadfast, courageous, brave, bold;

fortuna, fortunae *n* **(1st)** *f* chance, luck, fate; prosperity; condition, wealth, property;

fortuno, fortunare, fortunavi,

fortunatus *v* (1st) *trans* make happy, bless, prosper;

forum, fori *n* (2nd) *n* market; forum (in Rome); court of justice;

frater, fratris *n* (3rd) *m* brother; cousin;

fraus, fraudis *n* (3rd) *f* fraud; trickery, deceit; imposition, offense, crime; delusion;

fraxineus, fraxinea, fraxineum *adj* of ash; ashen;

fremo, fremere, fremui, fremitus *v* (3rd) roar; growl; rage; murmur, clamor for;

frenum, freni *n* (2nd) *n* bridle, harness, rein, bit; harnessed horses, team; check, restraint, brake; mastery;

frequento, frequentare, frequentavi, frequentatus *v* (1st) frequent; repeat often; haunt; throng; crowd; celebrate;

fretus, freta, fretum *adj* relying on, trusting to, supported by (w, *abl*);

frigeo, frigere, -, - *v* (2nd) be cold; lack vigour; get cold reception; fail to win favour; fall flat (words);

frigidus, frigida -um, frigidior -or -us, frigidissimus -a -um *adj* cold, cool, chilly, frigid; lifeless, indifferent, dull;

frigor, frigoris *n* (3rd) *m* cold; chill;

frondeo, frondere, frondui, fronditus *v* (2nd) *intrans* have, put forth leaves, be in leaf; be leafy, full of trees (place); (in spirit);

frondesco, frondescere, -, - *v* (3rd) become leafy, shoot; put forth leaves;

frons, frondis *n* (3rd) *f* foliage, leaves, leafy branch, green bough, frond;

frons, frontis *n* (3rd) *c* forehead, brow; face; look; front; fore part of anything;

frustra *adv* in vain; for nothing, to no purpose;

frux, frugis *n* (3rd) *f* crops (pl.), fruits, produce, legumes; honest men;

fugio, fugere, fugi, fugitus *v* (3rd) flee, fly, run away; avoid, shun; go into exile;

fugo, fugare, fugavi, fugatus *v* (1st) put to flight, rout; chase away; drive into exile;

fulcrum, fulcri *n* (2nd) *n* fulcrum; point of support for lever;

fulgeo, fulgere, fulsi, - *v* (2nd) flash, shine; glow, gleam, glitter, shine forth, be bright;

fulmen, fulminis *n* (3rd) *n* lightning, flash; thunderbolt; crushing blow;

fulvus, fulva, fulvum *adj* tawny, reddish yellow; yellow;

fumeus, fumea, fumeum *adj* smoky;

funditus *adv* utterly, completely, without exception; from the bottom, to the ground, by the root;

fundo, fundare, fundavi, fundatus *v* (1st) establish, found, begin; lay the bottom, lay a foundation; confirm;

fungor, fungi, functus sum *v* (3rd) *dep* perform, execute, discharge (duty); be engaged in (w, *abl* of function);

funus, funeris *n* (3rd) *n* burial, funeral; funeral rites; ruin; corpse; death;

furo, furere, -, - *v* (3rd) rave, rage; be mad, furious; be wild;

furor, furoris *n* (3rd) *m* madness, rage, fury, frenzy; passionate love;

furtum, furti *n* (2nd) *n* theft; trick; deception; stolen article;

fusus, fusa, fusum *adj* spread out, broad, flowing;

futurus, futura, futurum *adj* about to be; future;

gaudeo, gaudere, gavisus sum *v* (2nd) *semidep* be glad, rejoice;

gaudium, gaudi(i) *n* (2nd) *n* joy, delight, gladness; source, cause of joy; physical, sensual delight; everlasting blessedness; gaud, gaudy, bead of rosary;

gelidus, gelida, gelidum *adj* ice cold, icy;

geminus, gemina, geminum *adj* twin, double; twin-born; both;

gemitus, gemitus *n* (4th) *m* groan, sigh; roaring;

gemo, gemere, gemui, gemitus *v* (3rd) moan, groan; lament (over); grieve that; give out a hollow sound (music, hit);

gener, generi *n* (2nd) *m* son-in-law;

genero, generare, generavi, generatus *v* (1st) beget, father, produce, procreate; spring, descend from *passive*;

genitor, genitoris *n* (3rd) *m* father; creator; originator;

gens, gentis *n* (3rd) *f* tribe, clan; nation, people; Gentiles;

genus, generis *n* (3rd) *n* birth, descent, origin; race, family, house, stock, ancestry; offspring, descent; noble birth; kind, sort, variety; class, rank; mode, method, style, fashion, way;

gero, gerere, gessi, gestus *v* (3rd) bear, carry, wear; carry on; manage, govern; (se gerere = to conduct oneself);

globus, globi *n* (2nd) *m* ball, sphere; dense mass, close packed throng, crowd; clique, band; globe;

glomero, glomerare, glomeravi, glomeratus *v* (1st) collect, amass, assemble; form into a ball;

gloria, gloriae *n* (1st) *f* glory, fame; ambition; renown; vainglory, boasting;

glorior, gloriari, gloriatus sum *v* (1st) *dep* boast, brag; glory, pride oneself;

gnatus, gnati *n* (2nd) *m* son; child; children (pl.);

gradior, gradi, gressus sum *v* (3rd) *dep* walk, step, take steps, go, advance;

gradus, gradus *n* (4th) *m* step; position;

gramen, graminis *n* (3rd) *n* grass, turf; herb; plant;

gramineus, graminea, gramineum *adj* of grass, grassy; made of grass or turf;

gratia, gratiae *n* (1st) *f* popularity, esteem, credit (w, bona); partiality, favouritism; unpopularity (w, mala); favour, goodwill, kindness, friendship; influence; gratitude; thanks (pl.); Graces; agreeableness, charm; grace;

gravatus, gravata -um, gravatior -or - us, gravatissimus -a -um *adj* heavy; loaded down;

gravis, grave, gravior -or -us, gravissimus -a -um *adj* heavy; painful; important; serious; pregnant; grave, oppressive, burdensome;

gravo, gravare, gravavi, gravatus *v* (1st) *trans* load, weigh down; burden, oppress; pollute (air); accuse, incriminate; aggravate;

grex, gregis *n* (3rd) *c* flock, herd; crowd; company; crew; people, animals assembled; set, faction, class;

gubernaculum, gubernaculi *n* (2nd) *n* helm, rudder, steering oar of ship;

gubernator, gubernatoris *n* (3rd) *m* helmsman, pilot; one who directs, controls;

gurges, gurgitis *n* (3rd) *m* whirlpool; raging abyss; gulf, the sea; "flood", "stream";

guttur, gutturis *n* (3rd) *m* throat, neck; gullet; (reference to gluttony, appetite); swollen throat, goiter;

habena, habenae *n* (1st) *f* thong, strap; whip; halter; reins (pl.); direction, management, government;

habeo, habere, habui, habitus *v* (2nd) have, hold, consider, think, reason; manage, keep; spend, pass (time);

habito, habitare, habitavi, habitatus *v* (1st) inhabit, dwell; live, stay;

hactenus *adv* as far as this, to this place, point, time, extent, thus far, til now, hitherto;

haereo, haerere, haesi, haesus *v* **(2nd)** stick, adhere, cling to; hesitate; be in difficulties (sticky situation?);

halitus, halitus *n* **(4th)** *m* breath, steam, vapor;

harena, harenae *n* **(1st)** *f* sand, grains of sand; sandy land or desert; seashore; arena, place of contest;

hasta, hastae *n* **(1st)** *f* spear, lance, javelin; spear stuck in ground for public auction, centumviral court;

haud *adv* not, not at all, by no means; not (as a particle);

haurio, haurire, hausi, haustus *v* **(4th)** draw up, out; drink, swallow, drain, exhaust;

hebeto, hebetare, hebetavi, hebetatus *v* **(1st)** *trans* blunt, deaden, make dull, faint, dim, torpid, inactive (light, plant, senses), weaken;

herba, herbae *n* **(1st)** *f* herb, grass;

heros, herois *n* **(3rd)** *m* hero; demigod;

heu *interj* oh! ah! alas! (an expression of dismay or pain);

hiatus, hiatus *n* **(4th)** *m* opening, cleft, fissure, split, crevice; (maybe rude); chasm; wideopen jaw, expanse; hiatus; action of gaping, yawning, splitting open; greedy desire (for w, gen);

hibernus, hiberna, hibernum *adj* wintry; stormy, of, for winter time, rainy season; [hiberno => in winter];

hic *adv* here, in this place; in the present circumstances;

hinc *adv* from here, from this source, cause; hence, henceforth;

hio, hiare, hiavi, hiatus *v* **(1st)** be wide open, gape; be greedy for; be open-mouthed (with astonishment, etc);

homo, hominis *n* **(3rd)** *m* man, human being, person, fellow;

honor, honoris *n* **(3rd)** *m* honour; respect, regard; mark of esteem, reward; dignity, grace; public office;

hora, horae *n* **(1st)** *f* hour; time; season; [Horae => Seasons];

horrendus, horrenda, horrendum *adj* horrible, dreadful, terrible;

horreo, horrere, horrui, – *v* **(2nd)** dread, shrink from, shudder at; stand on end, bristle; have rough appearance;

horresco, horrescere, horrui, – *v* **(3rd)** dread, become terrified; bristle up; begin to shake, tremble, shudder, shiver;

horridus, horrida, horridum *adj* wild, frightful, rough, bristly, standing on end, unkempt; grim; horrible;

horrisonus, horrisona, horrisonum *adj* sounding dreadfully;

hortator, hortatoris *n* **(3rd)** *m* inciter; encourager, exhorter; urger (sight, sound) of horses in chariot races;

hortor, hortari, hortatus sum *v* **(1st)** *dep* encourage; cheer; incite; urge; exhort;

hospes, hospitis *n* **(3rd)** *m* host; guest; visitor, stranger; soldier in billets; one who billets soldiers;

hospitus, hospita, hospitum *adj* hospitable, harbouring, affording hospitality; received as guest; foreign, alien;

hostis, hostis *n* **(3rd)** *c* enemy (of the state); stranger, foreigner; the enemy (pl.);

huc *adv* here, to this place; to this point;

humus, humi *n* **(2nd)** *f* ground, soil, earth, land, country;

iaceo, iacere, iacui, iacitus *v* **(2nd)** *intrans* lie; lie down; lie ill, in ruins, prostrate, dead; sleep; be situated;

iacio, iacere, ieci, iactus *v* **(3rd)** throw, hurl, cast; throw away; utter;

iacto, iactare, iactavi, iactatus *v* **(1st)** throw away, throw out, throw, jerk about; disturb; boast, discuss;

179

iam *adv* now, already, by, even now; besides;

iampridem *adv* long ago, since; well before now, then; for a long time now, past;

ianua, ianuae *n* (1st) *f* door, entrance;

ibi *adv* there, in that place; thereupon;

ictus, ictus *n* (4th) *m* blow, stroke; musical, metrical beat; measure (music);

idem, eadem, idem *pron* (w, -dem ONLY, idem, eadem, idem) same, the same, the very same, also;

ignarus, ignara, ignarum *adj* ignorant; unaware, having no experience of; senseless; strange;

igneus, ignea, igneum *adj* fiery, hot; ardent;

ignis, ignis *n* (3rd) *m* fire, brightness; passion, glow of passion;

ilex, ilicis *n* (3rd) *f* holm-oak, great scarlet oak, tree or wood; its acorn;

ille, illa, illud *pron* that; those (pl.); also *demonstrative*; that person, thing; the well known; the former;

illic *adv* in that place, there, over there;

illustris, illustre, illustrior -or -us, illustrissimus -a -um *adj* bright, shining, brilliant; clear, lucid; illustrious, distinguished, famous;

imago, imaginis *n* (3rd) *f* likeness, image, appearance; statue; idea; echo; ghost, phantom;

imitabilis, imitabilis, imitabile *adj* that may be imitated;

immensus, immensa, immensum *adj* immeasurable, immense, vast, boundless, unending; infinitely great; innumerable;

immortalis, immortalis *n* (3rd) *m* immortal, god;

immortalis, immortalis, immortale *adj* immortal, not subject to death; eternal, everlasting, perpetual; imperishable;

imperium, imperi(i) *n* (2nd) *n* command; authority; rule, supreme power; the state, the empire;

impius, impia, impium *adj* wicked, impious, irreverent; showing no regard for divinely imposed moral duty;

impono, imponere, imposui, impositus *v* (3rd) impose, put upon; establish; inflict; assign, place in command; set;

impune, impunius, impunissime *adv* with impunity; without punishment, retribution, restraint, consequences, harm;

imus, ima, imum *adj* inmost, deepest, bottommost, last; (inferus);

in *prep abl* in, on, at (space); in accordance with, regard to, the case of; within (time);

in *prep acc* into; about, in the mist of; according to, after (manner); for; to, among;

inamabilis, inamabilis, inamabile *adj* disagreeable, unattractive;

inanis, inanis, inane *adj* void, empty, hollow; vain; inane, foolish;

incanus, incana, incanum *adj* quite gray, hoary;

incendo, incendere, incendi, incensus *v* (3rd) *trans* set on fire; set fire to, kindle, burn; cause to flame, burn; keep fire burning; scorch; make fiery hot (fever, thirst); light up; cause to glow; intensify; inspire, fire, rouse, excite, inflame; provoke, incense, aggravate;

incesto, incestare, incestavi, incestatus *v* (1st) pollute, defile;

incipio, incipere, incepi, inceptus *v* (3rd) begin; start, undertake;

includo, includere, inclusi, inclusus *v* (3rd) shut up, in, imprison, enclose; include;

inclutus, incluta -um, inclutior -or -us, inclutissimus -a -um *adj* celebrated, renowned, famous, illustrious, glorious;

inclytus, inclyta -um, inclytior -or -us, inclytissimus -a -um *adj* celebrated, renowned, famous, illustrious, glorious;

incoho, incohare, incohavi, incohatus *v* (1st) begin, start (work); set going, establish; draft, sketch, outline; enter upon;

incola, incolae *n* (1st) *c* inhabitant; resident, dweller; resident alien; foreigner;

incolo, incolare, incolavi, incolatus *v* (1st) live, dwell, reside (in); inhabit; sojourn;

incolo, incolere, incolui, – *v* (3rd) live, dwell, reside (in); inhabit; sojourn;

incolumis, incolumis, incolume *adj* unharmed, uninjured; alive, safe; unimpaired;

increpo, increpare, increpavi, increpatus *v* (1st) *trans* rebuke, chide, reprove; protest at, indignantly, complain loudly, scornfully;

incultus, inculta -um, incultior -or -us, incultissimus -a -um *adj* uncultivated (land), overgrown; unkempt; rough, uncouth; uncourted;

incultus, incultus *n* (4th) *m* want of cultivation or refinement, uncouthness, disregard;

incumbo, incumbere, incumbui, incumbitus *v* (3rd) lean forward, over, on, press on; attack, apply force; fall on (one's sword);

inde *adv* thence, thenceforth; from that place, time, cause; thereupon;

indebitus, indebita, indebitum *adj* that is not owed, not due;

indignus, indigna -um, indignior -or - us, indignissimus -a -um *adj* unworthy, undeserving, undeserved; unbecoming; shameful; intolerable; cruel;

indulgeo, indulgere, indulsi, indultus *v* (2nd) *dat* indulge; be indulgent, lenient, kind; grant, bestow; gratify oneself; give in to;

inextricabilis, inextricabilis, inextricabile *adj* impossible to disentangle or sort out;

infans, infantis *n* (3rd) *c* infant; child;

infectus, infecta, infectum *adj* unfinished, undone, incomplete; infecta re = without having accomplished it;

infelix, infelicis (gen.), infelicior -or -us, infelicissimus -a -um *adj* unfortunate, unhappy, wretched; unlucky, inauspicious; unproductive (plant);

infernus, inferna, infernum *adj* lower, under; underground, of the lower regions, infernal; of hell;

inferus, infera -um, inferior -or -us, infimus -a -um *adj* below, beneath, underneath; of hell; vile; lower, further down; lowest, last;

inferus, inferi *n* (2nd) *m* those below (pl.), the dead;

inficio, inficere, infeci, infectus *v* (3rd) corrupt, infect, imbue; poison; dye, stain, colour, spoil;

ingemo, ingemere, ingemui, ingemitus *v* (3rd) groan, moan, sigh (at, over); utter cry of pain, anguish; creak, groan (objects);

ingens, ingentis (gen.), ingentior -or -us, ingentissimus -a -um *adj* not natural, immoderate; huge, vast, enormous; mighty; remarkable, momentous;

ingratus, ingrata, ingratum *adj* unpleasant; ungrateful; thankless;

ingredior, ingredi, ingressus sum *v* (3rd) *dep* advance, walk; enter, step, go into; undertake, begin;

ingressus, ingressus *n* (4th) *m* entry; going in, embarking on (topic, speech); point of entry, approach; steps;

inhonestus, inhonesta -um, inhonestior -or -us, inhonestissimus -a -um *adj* shameful, not regarded with honour, respect; degrading (appearance);

inhumatus, inhumata, inhumatum *adj*

unburied;

inicio, inicere, inieci, iniectus *v* **(3rd)** *trans* hurl, throw, strike in, into; inject; put on; inspire, instill (feeling, etc);

inimicus, inimica -um, inimicior -or -us, inimicissimus -a -um *adj* unfriendly, hostile, harmful;

iniquus, iniqua -um, iniquior -or -us, iniquissimus -a -um *adj* unjust, unfair; disadvantageous, uneven; unkind, hostile;

iniussus, iniussa, iniussum *adj* unbidden, voluntary, of one's own accord; without orders, command; forbidden;

inlustris, inlustre, inlustrior -or -us, inlustrissimus -a -um *adj* bright, shining, brilliant; clear, lucid; illustrious, distinguished, famous;

inmanis, inmane, inmanior -or -us, inmanissimus -a -um *adj* huge, vast, immense, tremendous, extreme, monstrous; inhuman, savage, brutal, frightful;

inmanis, inmane, inmanior -or -us, inmanissimus -a -um *adj* huge, vast, immense, tremendous, extreme, monstrous; inhuman, savage, brutal, frightful;

inmemor, (gen.), inmemoris *adj* forgetful (by nature); lacking memory; heedless (of obligations, consequences);

inmissio, inmissionis *n* **(3rd)** *f* insertion, engrafting, action of putting, sending in, of allowing to enter;

inmitto, inmittere, inmisi, inmissus *v* **(3rd)** send in, to, into, against; cause to go; insert; hurl, throw in; let go, in; allow;

innubo, innubere, innupsi, innuptus *v* **(3rd)** *dat* marry (into a family);

innumerus, innumera, innumerum *adj* innumerable, countless, numberless; without number; immense;

innuptus, innupta, innuptum *adj* unmarried;

inolesco, inolescere, inolevi, inolitus *v*

(3rd) grow in or on;

inopinus, inopina, inopinum *adj* unexpected;

inops, (gen.), inopis *adj* weak, poor, needy, helpless; lacking, destitute (of), meager;

inops, (gen.), inopis *adj* weak, poor, needy, helpless; lacking, destitute (of), meager;

inremediabilis, inremediabilis, inremediabile *adj* fatal; irredeemable; beyond cure; for which there is no remedy;

inrumpo, inrumpere, inrupi, inruptus *v* **(3rd)** invade; break, burst, force, rush in, upon, into, penetrate; intrude on; interrupt;

inruo, inruere, inrui, inrutus *v* **(3rd)** rush, dash, run in, upon, headlong, attack, charge; throw self on; enter eagerly in;

insanus, insana -um, insanior -or -us, insanissimus -a -um *adj* mad, raging, insane, demented; frenzied; wild; possessed, inspired; maddening;

inscius, inscia, inscium *adj* not knowing, ignorant; unskilled;

insidia, insidiae *n* **(1st)** *f* ambush, ambuscade (pl.); plot; treachery, treacherous attack, device; trap, snare;

insidiator, insidiatoris *n* **(3rd)** *m* one lying in ambush, wait (attack, rob); lurker; who plots, sets traps; deceiver;

insignis, insignis, insigne *adj* conspicuous, manifest, eminent, notable, famous, distinguished, outstanding;

insisto, insistere, institi, - *v* **(3rd)** stand, tread upon, stand, stop; press on, persevere (with); pursue, set about;

insomnis, insomnis, insomne *adj* sleepless;

insomnium, insomni(i) *n* **(2nd)** *n* wakefulness; vision, dream;

inspiro, inspirare, inspiravi, inspiratus *v* **(1st)** inspire; excite, inflame; instill, implant; breathe into; blow upon, into;

instar, undeclined *n* N image, likeness, resemblance; counterpart; the equal, form of (w, gen);

instauro, instaurare, instauravi, instauratus *v* (1st) renew, repeat, restore;

instituo, instituere, institui, institutus *v* (3rd) set up, establish, found, make, institute; build; prepare; decide;

instructus, instructa -um, instructior -or -us, instructissimus -a -um *adj* equipped, fitted out, prepared; learned, trained, skilled; drawn up, arranged;

instruo, instruere, instruxi, instructus *v* (3rd) construct, build; prepare, draw up; fit out; instruct, teach;

insuetus, insueta, insuetum *adj* unused, unaccustomed to (w, gen, dat), unusual;

insum, inesse, infui, infuturus *v* be in, on, there; belong to; be involved in;

intactus, intacta, intactum *adj* untouched, intact; untried; virgin;

intento, intentare, intentavi, intentatus *v* (1st) point (at); point (weapons, etc) in a threatening manner, threaten;

intentus, intenta -um, intentior -or -us, intentissimus -a -um *adj* eager, intent, closely attentive; strict; intense, strenuous; serious, earnest;

inter *prep acc* between, among; during;

interea *adv* meanwhile;

interfusus, interfusa, interfusum *adj* poured, flowing, spread out between, suffused here and there;

intexo, intexere, intexui, intextus *v* (3rd) weave (into), embroider (on); cover by twining; insert (into a book, etc);

intono, intonare, intonavi, intonatus *v* (1st) thunder;

intono, intonare, intonui, intonitus *v* (1st) thunder;

intra *prep acc* within, inside; during;

under;

intus *adv* within, on the inside, inside; at home;

invado, invadere, invasi, invasus *v* (3rd) enter, attempt; invade; take possession of; attack (with in +acc.);

invalidus, invalida, invalidum *adj* infirm, weak feeble ineffectual;

inveho, invehere, invexi, invectus *v* (3rd) carry, bring in, import; ride (*passive*), drive, sail, attack;

invenio, invenire, inveni, inventus *v* (4th) come upon; discover, find; invent; contrive; reach, manage to get;

inventor, inventoris *n* (3rd) *m* inventor; author; discoverer;

invergo, invergere, -, – *v* (3rd) tip, pour (liquids) upon; incline;

invictus, invicta, invictum *adj* unconquered; unconquerable, invincible;

invideo, invidere, invidi, invisus *v* (2nd) envy, regard with envy, ill will; be jealous of; begrudge, refuse;

invius, invia, invium *adj* impassable; inaccessible;

involvo, involvere, involvi, involutus *v* (3rd) wrap (in), cover, envelop; roll along;

ipse, ipsa, ipsum *pron* himself, herself, itself; the very, real, actual one; in person; themselves (pl.);

ira, irae *n* (1st) *f* anger; ire, wrath; resentment; indignation; rage, fury, violence; bad blood;

irremeabilis, irremeabilis, irremeabile *adj* along or across which one cannot return;

irremediabilis, irremediabilis, irremediabile *adj* fatal; irredeemable; beyond cure; for which there is no remedy;

irrumpo, irrumpere, irrupi, irruptus *v* (3rd) invade; break, burst, force, rush in, upon, into, penetrate; intrude on; interrupt;

is, ea, id *pron* he, she, it, they (by gender number); *demonstrative*: that, he, she, it, they, them;

iste, ista, istud *pron* that, that of yours, that which you refer to; such;

istinc *adv* from (over) there, thence; from where you are; on the other side; from here;

itaque *conj* and so, therefore;

iter, itineris *n* **(3rd)** *n* journey; road; passage, path; march;

iterum *adv* again; a second time; for the second time;

itus, itus *n* **(4th)** *m* going, gait; departure;

iubar, iubaris *n* **(3rd)** *n* radiance of the heavenly bodies, brightness; first light of day; light source;

iubeo, iubere, iussi, iussus *v* **(2nd)** *trans* order, tell, command, direct; enjoin, command; decree, enact; request, ask, bid; pray;

iucundus, iucunda -um, iucundior -or -us, iucundissimus -a -um *adj* pleasant, agreeable, delightful, pleasing (experience, person, senses); congenial;

iudex, iudicis *n* **(3rd)** *m* judge; juror;

iugum, iugi *n* **(2nd)** *n* yoke; team, pair (of horses); ridge (mountain), summit, chain;

iungo, iungere, iunxi, iunctus *v* **(3rd)** join, unite; bring together, clasp (hands); connect, yoke, harness;

iuramentum, iuramenti *n* **(2nd)** *n* oath;

iure *adv* by right, rightly, with justice; justly, deservedly;

iuro, iurare, iuravi, iuratus *v* **(1st)** swear; call to witness; vow obedience to; [jus jurandum => oath]; conspire;

iussum, iussi *n* **(2nd)** *n* order, command, decree, ordinance, law; physician's prescription;

iustitia, iustitiae *n* **(1st)** *f* justice; equality; righteousness;

iuvencus, iuvenci *n* **(2nd)** *m* young bull; young man;

iuvenis, iuvenis *n* **(3rd)** *c* youth, young man, woman;

iuvo, iuvare, iuvi, iutus *v* **(1st)** help, assist, aid, support, serve, further; please, delight, gratify;

iuxta *adv* nearly; near, close to, near by, hard by, by the side of; just as, equally;

iuxta *prep acc* near, (very) close to, next to; hard by, adjoining; on a par with; like;

labor, labi, lapsus sum *v* **(3rd)** *dep* slip, slip and fall; slide, glide, drop; perish, go wrong;

labor, laboris *n* **(3rd)** *m* labour, toil, exertion, effort, work; task, undertaking; production; childbirth; preoccupation, concern; struggle, suffering, distress, hardship, stress; wear+tear;

lacer, lacera, lacerum *adj* mangled, torn, rent, mutilated; maimed, dismembered;

lacrima, lacrimae *n* **(1st)** *f* tear; exuded gum, sap; bit of lead; quicksilver from ore; weeping (pl.); dirge;

lacrimo, lacrimare, lacrimavi, lacrimatus *v* **(1st)** shed tears, weep;

lacus, lacus *n* **(4th)** *m* basin, tank, tub; lake, pond; reservoir, cistern, basin, trough; lime-hole; bin; pit;

laetor, laetari, laetatus sum *v* **(1st)** *dep* be glad, joyful, delighted; rejoice; be fond (of), delight in; flourish (on, in);

laetus, laeta -um, laetior -or -us, laetissimus -a -um *adj* happy, cheerful, joyful, glad; favourable, propitious; prosperous, successful; luxuriant, lush, rich, sleek; fertile (land); teeming, abounding; pleasing, welcome;

laeva, laevae *n* **(1st)** *f* left hand;

lampas, lampados/is *n f* lamp, lantern; light, torch, flame, flambeau; link;

firebrand; meteor (like torch);

lanio, laniare, laniavi, laniatus *v* **(1st)** tear, mangle, mutilate, pull to pieces;

largior, largiri, largitus sum *v* **(4th)** *dep* grant; give bribes, presents corruptly; give generously, bountifully;

lateo, latere, latui, – *v* **(2nd)** lie hidden, lurk; live a retired life, escape notice;

later, lateris *n* **(3rd)** *m* brick; brickwork, bricks; block; bar, ingot; tile;

latex, laticis *n* **(3rd)** *m* water; (any) liquid, fluid; running, stream, spring water; juice;

latro, latrare, latravi, latratus *v* **(1st)** bark, bark at;

laudo, laudare, laudavi, laudatus *v* **(1st)** recommend; praise, approve, extol; call upon, name; deliver eulogy on;

laurus, lauri *n* **(2nd)** *f* laurel, bay tree, foliage, sprig, branch (medicine, magic); triumph, victory; honour;

laus, laudis *n* **(3rd)** *f* praise, approval, merit; glory; renown;

lavo, lavare, lavi, lautus *v* **(1st)** wash, bathe; soak;

laxo, laxare, laxavi, laxatus *v* **(1st)** loosen, slaken, relax, weaken; expand, open up, extend;

laxus, laxa -um, laxior -or -us, laxissimus -a -um *adj* wide, spacious, ample, roomy; loose, not close packed; slack, not tight; lax; unstrung; relaxed, at ease; unrestricted; breached, wide open; distant (time);

lectus, lecta -um, lectior -or -us, lectissimus -a -um *adj* chosen, picked, selected; choice, excellent; (pl. as subst = picked men);

lego, legere, legi, lectus *v* **(3rd)** read; gather, collect (cremated bones); furl (sail), weigh (anchor); pick out;

lenis, lene, lenior -or -us, lenissimus -a -um *adj* gentle, kind, light; smooth, mild,

easy, calm;

levis, leve, levior -or -us, levissimus -a -um *adj* light, thin, trivial, trifling, slight; gentle; fickle, capricious; nimble; smooth; slippery, polished, plain; free from coarse hair, harsh sounds;

lex, legis *n* **(3rd)** *f* law; motion, bill, statute; principle; condition;

libamen, libaminis *n* **(3rd)** *n* drink-offering; first fruits;

libertas, libertatis *n* **(3rd)** *f* freedom, liberty; frankness of speech, outspokenness;

licet *conj* although, granted that; (with subjunctive);

licet, licere, licuit, licitus est *v* **(2nd)** *impers* it is permitted, one may; it is all right, lawful, allowed, permitted;

lilium, lili(i) *n* **(2nd)** *n* lily;

limen, liminis *n* **(3rd)** *n* threshold, entrance; lintel; house;

lingua, linguae *n* **(1st)** *f* tongue; speech, language; dialect;

linquo, linquere, liqui, lictus *v* **(3rd)** leave, quit, forsake; abandon, desist from; allow to remain in place; bequeath;

litus, litoris *n* **(3rd)** *n* shore, seashore, coast, strand; river bank; beach, landing place;

lituus, litui *n* **(2nd)** *m* curved staff carried by augurs; a kind of war-trumpet curved at one end;

lividus, livida, lividum *adj* livid, slate-coloured; discoloured by bruises; envious, spiteful;

loco *adv* for, in the place of, instead of;

locus, loci *n* **(2nd)** *m* place, territory, locality, neighbourhood, region; position, point; aim point; site;

longaevus, longaeva, longaevum *adj* aged; of great age, ancient;

longe, longius, longissime *adv* far (off),

distant, a long way; by far; for a long while, far (in future, past);

longus, longa -um, longior -or -us, longissimus -a -um *adj* long; tall; tedious, taking long time; boundless; far; of specific length, time;

loquor, loqui, locutus sum *v* **(3rd)** *dep* speak, tell; talk; mention; say, utter; phrase;

luceo, lucere, luxi, – *v* **(2nd)** shine, emit light (heavenly body); dawn; cause to shine; be clear, evident; sparkle, glitter, shine w, reflected light; be conspicuous in merit, excel; be bright, resplendent; be visible, show up; [lucet => it is (becoming) light];

ludibrium, ludibri(i) *n* **(2nd)** *n* mockery; laughingstock;

ludus, ludi *n* **(2nd)** *m* game, play, sport, pastime, entertainment, fun; school, elementary school;

lumen, luminis *n* **(3rd)** *n* light; lamp, torch; eye (of a person); life; day, daylight;

luna, lunae *n* **(1st)** *f* moon; month;

lustro, lustrare, lustravi, lustratus *v* **(1st)** purify cermonially (w, procession), cleanse by sacrifice, expiate;

lux, lucis *n* **(3rd)** *f* light, daylight, light of day; life; world; day; [prima luce => at daybreak];

luxus, luxus *n* **(4th)** *m* luxury, soft living; sumptuousness;

macto, mactare, mactavi, mactatus *v* **(1st)** magnify, honour; sacrifice; slaughter, destroy;

madidus, madida, madidum *adj* wet, moist; dripping, juicy; sodden, drenched; drunk, tipsy; steeped in;

maestus, maesta -um, maestior -or -us, maestissimus -a -um *adj* sad, unhappy; mournful, gloomy; mourning; stern, grim; ill-omened, inauspicious;

magis *adv* to greater extent, more nearly; rather, instead; more; (forms COMP w, DJ);

magister, magistri *n* **(2nd)** *m* teacher, tutor, master, expert, chief; pilot of a ship; rabbi;

magnanimus, magnanima, magnanimum *adj* brave, bold, noble in spirit (esp. kings, heroes); generous;

magnus, magna -um, maior -or -us, maximus -a -um *adj* large, great, big, vast, huge; much; powerful; tall, long, broad; extensive, spacious; great (achievement); mighty; distinguished; skilled; bold, confident; proud; full, complete, utter, pure; intense; loud; at high price; notable, famous; old;

maior, maioris *n* **(3rd)** *m* ancestors (pl.);

malesuadus, malesuada, malesuadum *adj* ill-advising;

malignus, maligna, malignum *adj* spiteful; niggardly; narrow;

malum, mali *n* **(2nd)** *n* evil, mischief; disaster, misfortune, calamity, plague; punishment; harm, hurt;

mandatum, mandati *n* **(2nd)** *n* order, command, commission; mandate; commandment;

mando, mandare, mandavi, mandatus *v* **(1st)** entrust, commit to one's charge, deliver over; commission; order, command;

mando, mandare, mandavi, mandatus *v* **(1st)** entrust, commit to one's charge, deliver over; commission; order, command;

maneo, manere, mansi, mansus *v* **(2nd)** remain, stay, abide; wait for; continue, endure, last; spend the night (sexual);

manus, manus *n* **(4th)** *f* hand, fist; team; gang, band of soldiers; handwriting; (elephant's) trunk;

mare, maris *n* **(3rd)** *n* sea; sea water;

marmor, marmoris *n* **(3rd)** *n* marble, block of marble, marble monument, statue; surface of the sea;

marmoreus, marmorea, marmoreum *adj* marble; of marble; marble-like;

mater, matris *n* (3rd) *f* mother, foster mother; lady, matron; origin, source, motherland, mother city;

maternus, materna, maternum *adj* maternal, motherly, of a mother;

maximus, maxima, maximum *adj* greatest, biggest, largest; longest; oldest; highest, utmost; leading, chief;

meatus, meatus *n* (4th) *m* movement along line, course, path; progress; line followed; channel; passage-way;

medium, medi(i) *n* (2nd) *n* middle, center; medium, mean; midst, community, public; publicity;

membrum, membri *n* (2nd) *n* member, limb, organ; (esp.) male genital member; apartment, room; section;

memor, (gen.), memoris *adj* remembering; mindful (of w, gen), grateful; unforgetting, commemorative;

memoro, memorare, memoravi, memoratus *v* (1st) remember; be mindful of (w, gen, acc); mention, recount, relate, remind, speak of;

mens, mentis *n* (3rd) *f* mind; reason, intellect, judgment; plan, intention, frame of mind; courage;

mensa, mensae *n* (1st) *f* table; course, meal; banker's counter;

mereor, mereri, meritus sum *v* (2nd) *dep* earn; deserve, merit, have right; win, gain, incur; earn soldier, whore pay, serve;

mergo, mergere, mersi, mersus *v* (3rd) dip, plunge, immerse; sink, drown, bury; overwhelm;

metallum, metalli *n* (2nd) *n* metal; mine; quarry;

metuo, metuere, metui, – *v* (3rd) fear; be afraid; stand in fear of; be apprehensive, dread;

metus, metus *n* (4th) *m* fear, anxiety; dread, awe; object of awe, dread;

meus, mea, meum *adj* my (personal possession); mine, of me, belonging to me; my own; to me;

mille, milis *n* (3rd) *n* thousand; thousands (men, things); miles;

ministerium, ministeri(i) *n* (2nd) *n* office, attendance, service, employment, body of helpers; occupation, work;

ministro, ministrare, ministravi, ministratus *v* (1st) *dat* attend (to), serve, furnish; supply;

minor, minoris *n* (3rd) *m* those inferior in rank, grade, age, subordinate; descendants (pl.);

minus *adv* less; not so well; not quite;

miror, mirari, miratus sum *v* (1st) *dep* be amazed, surprised, bewildered (at); look in wonder, awe, admiration at; admire, revere; wonder; marvel at;

mirus, mira, mirum *adj* wonderful, strange, remarkable, amazing, surprising, extraordinary;

misceo, miscere, miscui, mixtus *v* (2nd) mix, mingle; embroil; confound; stir up;

miser, misera -um, miserior -or -us, miserrimus -a -um *adj* poor, miserable, wretched, unfortunate, unhappy, distressing;

miserandus, miseranda, miserandum *adj* pitiable, unfortunate;

misereor, misereri, miseritus sum *v* (2nd) *dep* pity, feel pity; show, have mercy, compassion, pity for (w, gen);

misero, miserare, miseravi, miseratus *v* (1st) (with genitive) pity, feel sorry for; view with compassion; (vocal sorrow, compassion);

mitto, mittere, misi, missus *v* (3rd) send, throw, hurl, cast; let out, release, dismiss; disregard;

modo *adv* only, merely; just now; recently, lately; presently;

modo *conj* but, if only; but only;

moene, moenis *n* **(3rd)** *n* defensive, town walls (pl.), bulwarks; fortifications; fortified town; castle;

moles, molis *n* **(3rd)** *f* large mass; rock, boulder; heap, lump, pile, bulk; monster; mole, jetty, dam, dike; large structure, building; military structure, wall, ramp; causeway, embankment; crowd, throng; heavy responsibility, burden; difficulty, danger; might, force;

monimentum, monimenti *n* **(2nd)** *n* monument;

mons, montis *n* **(3rd)** *m* mountain; huge rock; towering heap;

monstro, monstrare, monstravi, monstratus *v* **(1st)** show; point out, reveal; advise, teach;

monstrum, monstri *n* **(2nd)** *n* monster; portent, unnatural thing, event regarded as omen, sign, portent;

monumentum, monumenti *n* **(2nd)** *n* reminder; memorial, monument, tomb; record, literary work, history, book;

mora, morae *n* **(1st)** *f* delay, hindrance, obstacle; pause;

morbus, morbi *n* **(2nd)** *m* sickness, illness, weakness; disease; distemper; distress; vice;

moribundus, moribunda, moribundum *adj* dying;

morior, mori, mortuus sum *v* **(3rd)** *dep* die, expire, pass, die, wither away, out; fail, come to an end; decay; erish; become obsolete (word), fall into disuse; be forgotten; become obsolete (word), fall into disuse; be forgotten; faint, languish; become void, moot (lawsuit); be extinguished (fire, light), go out;

moror, morari, moratus sum *v* **(1st)** *dep* delay; stay, stay behind; devote attention to;

mors, mortis *n* **(3rd)** *f* death; corpse; annihilation;

mortalis, mortalis, mortale *adj* mortal, transient; human, of human origin;

mortifer, mortifera, mortiferum *adj* deadly, fatal, death bringing; destructive;

motus, motus *n* **(4th)** *m* movement, motion; riot, commotion, disturbance; gesture; emotion;

moveo, movere, movi, motus *v* **(2nd)** move, stir, agitate, affect, provoke, disturb;

mugio, mugire, mugivi, mugitus *v* **(4th)** low, bellow; make a loud deep noise;

multus, multa -um, -, plurimus -a -um *adj* much, many, great, many a; large, intense, assiduous; tedious;

munus, muneris *n* **(3rd)** *n* service; duty, office, function; gift; tribute, offering; bribes (pl.);

murmur, murmuris *n* **(3rd)** *m* murmur, mutter; whisper, rustle, hum, buzz; low noise; roar, growl, grunt, rumble;

myrteus, myrtea, myrteum *adj* of myrtle;

nam *conj* for, on the other hand; for instance;

nascor, nasci, natus sum *v* **(3rd)** *dep* be produced spontaneously, come into existence, being; spring forth, grow; live; be born, begotten, formed, destined; rise (stars), dawn; start, originate; arise;

natus, nati *n* **(2nd)** *m* son; child; children (pl.);

nauta, nautae *n* **(1st)** *m* sailor, seaman, mariner;

navis, navis *n* **(3rd)** *f* ship; [navis longa => galley, battleship; ~ oneraria => transport, cargo ship];

navita, navitae *n* **(1st)** *m* sailor, seaman, mariner; (early, late, and poetic);

ne *adv* not; (intro clause of purpose with subj verb); [ne....quidem => not even]; truly, indeed, verily, assuredly; (particle of assurance); (w, personal pron);

nec *adv* nor; and not, not, neither, not even;

nec *conj* nor, and..not; not..either, not even;

necesse, undeclined *adj* necessary, essential; unavoidable, compulsory, inevitable; a natural law; true;

nefandus, nefanda, nefandum *adj* impious, wicked; abominable;

nefas, undeclined *n* N sin, violation of divine law, impious act; [fas et nefas => right and wrong];

nemus, nemoris *n* (3rd) *n* wood, forest;

nepos, nepotis *n* (3rd) *c* grandson, daughter; descendant; spendthrift, prodigal, playboy; secondary shoot;

neque *adv* nor; and not, not, neither;

nequiquam *adv* in vain;

nescio, nescire, nescivi, nescitus *v* (4th) not know (how); be ignorant, unfamiliar, unaware, unacquainted, unable, unwilling;

neu *conj* or not, and not; (for negative of IMP); [neve ... neve => neither ... nor];

ni *conj* if ... not; unless;

nigro, nigrare, nigravi, nigratus *v* (1st) be black; make black;

nihil, undeclined *n* N nothing; no; trifle, thing not worth mentioning; nonentity; nonsense; no concern;

nimbus, nimbi *n* (2nd) *m* rainstorm, cloud;

nimium *adv* too, too much; very, very much, beyond measure, excessive, too great;

nimius, nimia, nimium *adj* excessive, too great;

niteo, nitere, nitui, - *v* (2nd) shine, glitter, look bright; be sleek, in good condition; bloom, thrive;

nitor, niti, nixus sum *v* (3rd) *dep* press,

lean upon; struggle; advance; depend on (with abl.); strive, labour;

niveus, nivea, niveum *adj* snowy, covered with snow; white;

no, nare, navi, – *v* (1st) swim, float;

noceo, nocere, nocui, nocitus *v* (2nd) harm, hurt; injure (with dat);

nocturnus, nocturna, nocturnum *adj* nocturnal, of night, at night, by night;

nodus, nodi *n* (2nd) *m* knot; node;

nomen, nominis *n* (3rd) *n* name, family name; noun; account, entry in debt ledger; sake; title, heading;

nondum *adv* not yet;

nos, nostrum/nostri *pron pers* we (pl.), us;

nosco, noscere, nosse novi, notus *v* (3rd) *trans* get to know; learn, find out; become cognisant of, acquainted, familiar with; examine, study, inspect; try (case); recognise, accept as valid, true; recall;

noster, nostra, nostrum *adj* our;

notus, noti *n* (2nd) *m* friends (pl.), acquaintances;

novem, nonus -a -um, noveni -ae -a, novie(n)s *num* nine;

novissimus, novissima, novissimum *adj* last, rear; most recent; utmost;

novus, nova -um, novior -or -us, novissimus -a -um *adj* new, fresh, young; unusual, extraordinary; (novae res, f. pl. = revolution);

nox, noctis *n* (3rd) *f* night [prima nocte => early in the night; multa nocte => late at night];

noxia, noxiae *n* (1st) *f* crime, fault;

nubilus, nubila, nubilum *adj* cloudy; lowering;

nullus, nulla, nullum (gen -ius) *adj* no; none, not any; (pronominal adj)

numen, numinis *n* (3rd) *n* divine will,

divinity; god;

numerus, numeri *n* **(2nd)** *m* number, sum, total, rank; (superior) numerical strength, plurality; category; tally; rhythm, cadence, frequency; meter, metrical foot, line; melody; exercise movements;

nunc *adv* now, today, at present;

nuntius, nunti(i) *n* **(2nd)** *m* messenger, herald, envoy; message (oral), warning; report; messenger's speech;

nuper, -, nuperrime *adv* recently, not long ago; in recent years, our own time; (superlative) latest in series;

o *interi* Oh!;

ob *prep acc* on account of, for the sake of, for; instead of; right before;

obeo, obire, obivi(ii), obitus *v* go to meet; attend to; fall; die;

obicio, obicere, obieci, obiectus *v* **(3rd)** *trans* throw before, to, cast; object, oppose; upbraid; throw in one's teeth; present;

oblivium, oblivi(i) *n* **(2nd)** *n* forgetfulness, oblivion;

obloquor, obloqui, oblocutus sum *v* **(3rd)** *dep* interpose remarks, interrupt;

obmutesco, obmutescere, obmutui, - *v* **(3rd)** lose one's speech, become silent;

obruo, obruere, obrui, obrutus *v* **(3rd)** cover up, hide, bury; overwhelm, ruin; crush;

obscurus, obscura -um, obscurior -or - us, obscurissimus -a -um *adj* dim, dark, obscure; dusky, shadowy, only faintly, dimly seen; dingy; gloomy; not, barely visible, hidden from sight; imperceptible; muted, muffled, inaudible; little known, undistinguished, insignificant, humble, obscure (person); secret; not open; vague, uncertain, dim, faint, poorly known; unclear; incomprehensible;

observo, observare, observavi, observatus *v* **(1st)** watch, observe; heed;

obsto, obstare, obstiti, - *v* **(1st)** oppose, hinder; (w, dat);

obverto, obvertere, obverti, obversus *v* **(3rd)** turn or direct towards; direct against;

obvius, obvia, obvium *adj* in the way, easy; hostile; exposed (to);

occupo, occupare, occupavi, occupatus *v* **(1st)** seize; gain; overtake; capture, occupy; attack;

occurro, occurrere, occucurri, occursus *v* **(3rd)** run to meet; oppose, resist; come to mind, occur (with dat);

oculus, oculi *n* **(2nd)** *m* eye;

odoratus, odorata, odoratum *adj* smelling, having smell, odor, scent; fragrant, perfumed, sweet smelling;

offa, offae *n* **(1st)** *f* lump of food, cake;

offero, offerre, obtuli, oblatus *v* offer; present; cause; bestow;

oleo, olere, olui, – *v* **(2nd)** smell of, smell like;

oleum, olei *n* **(2nd)** *n* oil;

oliva, olivae *n* **(1st)** *f* olive; olive tree;

olivum, olivi *n* **(2nd)** *n* olive-oil; wrestling;

olla

omnipotens, (gen.), omnipotentis *adj* all-powerful, omnipotent;

omnis, omnis *n* **(3rd)** *c* all men (pl.), all persons;

opaco, opacare, opacavi, opacatus *v* **(1st)** shade, overshadow;

opimus, opima, opimum *adj* rich, fertile; abundant; fat, plump; [opima spolia => spoils from a general];

opto, optare, optavi, optatus *v* **(1st)** choose, select; wish, wish for, desire;

opus, operis *n* **(3rd)** *n* need; work; fortifications (pl.), works;

orbis, orbis *n* **(3rd)** *m* circle; territory, region; sphere; [orbis terrarum => world, (circle of lands)];

ordo, ordinis *n* **(3rd)** *m* row, order, rank; succession; series; class; bank (oars);

origo, originis *n* **(3rd)** *f* origin, source; birth, family; race; ancestry;

orior, oriri, ortus sum *v* **(4th)** *dep* rise (sun, river); arise, emerge, crop up; get up (wake); begin; originate from; be born, created; be born of, descend, spring from; proceed, be derived (from);

oro, orare, oravi, oratus *v* **(1st)** beg, ask for, pray; beseech, plead, entreat; worship, adore;

ortus, ortus *n* **(4th)** *m* rising (sun, star); sunrise, daybreak, dawn, east; the East; beginning, dawning; birth; ancestry; coming into being; source; springing up (wind);

os, oris *n* **(3rd)** *n* mouth, speech, expression; face; pronunciation;

os, ossis *n* **(3rd)** *n* bone; (implement, gnawed, dead); kernel (nut); heartwood (tree); stone (fruit);

ostendo, ostendere, ostendi, ostensus *v* **(3rd)** show; reveal; make clear, point out, display, exhibit;

ostento, ostentare, ostentavi, ostentatus *v* **(1st)** show, display; point out, declare; disclose, hold out (prospect);

ostium, osti(i) *n* **(2nd)** *n* doorway; front door; starting gate; entrance (underworld); (river) mouth;

otium, oti(i) *n* **(2nd)** *n* leisure; spare time; holiday; ease, rest, peace, quiet; tranquility, calm; lull;

ovo, ovare, ovavi, ovatus *v* **(1st)** rejoice;

paco, pacare, pacavi, pacatus *v* **(1st)** pacify, subdue;

palaestra, palaestrae *n* **(1st)** *f* palaestra, wrestling school; gymnasium;

palla, pallae *n* **(1st)** *f* palla, a lady's outer garment;

palleo, pallere, pallui, – *v* **(2nd)** be, look pale; fade; become pale at;

palma, palmae *n* **(1st)** *f* palm, width of the hand; hand; palm tree, branch; date; palm award, first place;

palus, pali *n* **(2nd)** *m* stake, pile, pole, unsplit wood; peg, pin; execution stake; wood sword; fence (pl.);

pampineus, pampinea, pampineum *adj* of, covered with vine shoots, foliage, tendrils;

pando, pandere, pandi, passus *v* **(3rd)** spread out [passis manibus => with hands outstretched];

par, paris (gen.), -, parissimus -a -um *adj* equal (to); a match for; of equal size, rank, age; fit, suitable, right, proper; equal in power, prestige, importance, rank, status, office, authority; comparable; corresponding in degree, proportionate, commensurate (unlike qualities); measuring up, adequate, matching; well-matched; fair, equitable, reasonable; balanced, level;

parco, parcere, parcui, parsus *v* **(3rd)** forbear, refrain from; spare; show consideration; be economical, thrifty with;

parens, parentis *n* **(3rd)** *c* parent, father, mother;

pariter *adv* equally; together;

pars, partis *n* **(3rd)** *f* part, region; share; direction; portion; piece; party, faction, side; role (of actor); office, function, duty (usu. pl.);

partus, partus *n* **(4th)** *m* birth; offspring;

parum, minus, minime *adv* too, very little, not enough, so good, insufficient; less; (superlative) not at all;

parumper *adv* for a short, little while; for a moment; in a short time; quickly, hurriedly;

parvus, parva -um, minor -or -us, minimus -a -um *adj* small, little, cheap;

unimportant; (superlative) smallest, least;

pasco, pascere, pavi, pastus *v* **(3rd)** feed, feed on; graze;

passim *adv* here and there; everywhere;

pateo, patere, patui, – *v* **(2nd)** stand open, be open; extend; be well known; lie open, be accessible;

pater, patris *n* **(3rd)** *m* father; [pater familias, patris familias => head of family, household];

patior, pati, passus sum *v* **(3rd)** *dep* suffer; allow; undergo, endure; permit;

patria, patriae *n* **(1st)** *f* native land; home, native city; one's country;

patrius, patria, patrium *adj* father's, paternal; ancestral;

paucus, pauca -um, paucior -or -us, paucissimus -a -um *adj* little, small in quantity, extent; few (usu. pl.); just a few; small number of;

paulatim *adv* little by little, by degrees, gradually; a small amount at a time, bit by bit;

pauper, pauperis (gen.), pauperior -or - us, pauperrimus -a -um *adj* poor, meager, unproductive; scantily endowed; cheap, of little worth; of poor man;

pavor, pavoris *n* **(3rd)** *m* fear, panic;

pecten, pectinis *n* **(3rd)** *m* comb; rake; quill (playing lyre); comb-like thing, pubic bone, region; scallop;

pecto, pectere, pexi, pectitus *v* **(3rd)** comb; card (wool, etc);

pectus, pectoris *n* **(3rd)** *n* breast, heart; feeling, soul, mind;

pecus, pecudis *n* **(3rd)** *f* sheep; animal;

pedes, peditis *n* **(3rd)** *m* foot soldier, infantryman; pedestrian, who goes on foot; infantry (pl.);

pelagus, pelagi *n* **(2nd)** *n* **(Greek word)** sea; the open sea, the main; (-us neuter, only sing.);

pello, pellere, pepuli, pulsus *v* **(3rd)** beat; drive out; push; banish, strike, defeat, drive away, rout;

pendeo, pendere, pependi, – *v* **(2nd)** hang, hang down; depend; [~ ab ore => hang upon the lips, listen attentively];

pendo, pendere, pependi, pensus *v* **(3rd)** weigh out; pay, pay out;

penetrale, penetralis *n* **(3rd)** *n* inner part of a place; inner shrine; sanctuary of the household gods; innermost parts, chambers, self (pl.); spirit, life of soul; gimlet;

penitus *adv* inside; deep within; thoroughly;

penna, pennae *n* **(1st)** *f* feather, wing;

per *prep* *acc* through (space); during (time); by, by means of;

per *prep* *acc* through (space); during (time); by, by means of;

perago, peragere, peregi, peractus *v* **(3rd)** disturb; finish; kill; carry through to the end, complete;

percurro, percurrere, percucurri, percursus *v* **(3rd)** quickly move, run, travel, hasten, pass through, over; form continuous line; stroke; review, run over (in thought, words), run through in sequence; skim over; touch upon different points in quick succession; fill offices in succession; travel quickly from end to end; make rapid tour, visit in quick succession;

percutio, percutere, percussi, percussus *v* **(3rd)** beat, strike; pierce;

peredo, peredere, peredi, peresus *v* **(3rd)** eat up, consume, waste;

perfectus, perfecta, perfectum *adj* perfect, complete; excellent;

perfero, perferre, pertuli, perlatus *v* carry through; bear, endure to the end, suffer; announce;

perficio, perficere, perfeci, perfectus *v* **(3rd)** complete, finish; execute; bring about, accomplish; do thoroughly;

pergo, pergere, perrexi, perrectus *v* (3rd) go on, proceed;

periculum, periculi *n* (2nd) *n* danger, peril; trial, attempt; risk; responsibility for damage, liability; *periclum* – shortened for metre;

perlego, perlegere, perlegi, perlectus *v* (3rd) *trans* read over, through (silent, aloud); scan, survey, run one's eyes over; recount;

persono, personare, personavi, personatus *v* (1st) *trans* make loud, continuous, pervasive noise, loud music; ring, resound; chant, shout out;

pes, pedis *n* (3rd) *m* foot;

pestis, pestis *n* (3rd) *f* plague, pestilence, curse, destruction;

peto, petere, petivi, petitus *v* (3rd) attack; aim at; desire; beg, entreat, ask (for); reach towards, make for;

piaculum, piaculi *n* (2nd) *n* expiatory offering or rite; sin; crime;

piceus, picea, piceum *adj* pitch black;

pietas, pietatis *n* (3rd) *f* responsibility, sense of duty; loyalty; tenderness, goodness; pity; piety;

pinguis, pingue, pinguior -or -us, pinguissimus -a -um *adj* fat; rich, fertile; thick; dull, stupid;

pius, pia -um, -, piissimus -a -um *adj* conscientious; upright; faithful; patriotic, dutiful, respectful; righteous, good; affectionate, tender, devoted, loyal (to family); pious, devout; holy, godly;

placidus, placida, placidum *adj* gentle, calm, mild, peaceful, placid;

plangor, plangoris *n* (3rd) *m* outcry, shriek;

plaudo, plaudere, plausi, plausus *v* (3rd) clap, strike (w, flat hand), pat; beat (wings); applaud; express (dis)approval;

plenus, plena -um, plenior -or -us, plenissimus -a -um *adj* full, plump; satisfied;

plurimus, plurima, plurimum *adj* most, greatest number, amount; very many; most frequent; highest price, value;

poena, poenae *n* (1st) *f* penalty, punishment; revenge, retribution; [poena dare => to pay the penalty];

Poenus, Poena, Poenum *adj* Carthaginian, Punic; of, associated w, Carthage; Phoenician; scarlet, bright red;

pondus, ponderis *n* (3rd) *n* weight, burden, impediment;

pono, ponere, posui, positus *v* (3rd) *trans* put, place, set; station, post (troops); pitch (camp); situate; set up; erect; specify, put down; cite, quote; locate; depict; classify; assume, suppose; bury; lay (foundation, keel); found (town), build; plant (trees); provide, serve; ut, lay down (load, arms), take off (clothes); shed (leaves); cut (nails); esteem, value, count; impose; ordain; lend, put out, offer, wager; rid, drop;

pontus, ponti *n* (2nd) *m* sea;

populus, populi *n* (2nd) *m* people, nation, State; public, populace, multitude, crowd; a following; members of a society, sex; region, district; army;

porrigo, porrigere, porrexi, porrectus *v* (3rd) stretch out, extend;

porro *adv* at distance, further on, far off, onward; of old, formerly, hereafter; again;

portitor, portitoris *n* (3rd) *m* ferry man;

porto, portare, portavi, portatus *v* (1st) carry, bring;

portus, portus *n* (4th) *m* port, harbour; refuge, haven, place of refuge;

posco, poscere, poposci, – *v* (3rd) ask, demand;

possum, posse, potui, – *v* be able, can;

post *adv* behind, afterwards, after;

post *prep acc* behind (space), after (time); subordinate to (rank);

postquam *conj* after;

postumus, postuma, postumum *adj* late, last born (child), born late in life, after will; posthumous; last, final;

potior, potiri, potitus sum *v* **(4th)** *dep* obtain, acquire; grasp; attain, reach (goal); come by (experiences); seize, capture; control; have, possess; reign over; win sexually; be, become master of (w, gen, *abl*), get possession, submission, hold of;

poto, potare, potavi, potatus *v* **(1st)** drink; drink heavily, convivially, tipple; swallow; absorb, soak up;

praeceps, praecipitis *n* **(3rd)** *n* edge of abyss; great danger;

praeceptum, praecepti *n* **(2nd)** *n* teaching, lesson, precept; order, command;

praecipio, praecipere, praecepi, praeceptus *v* **(3rd)** take or receive in advance; anticipate; warn; order; teach, instruct;

praecipito, praecipitare, praecipitavi, praecipitatus *v* **(1st)** throw headlong, cast down;

praecipuus, praecipua, praecipuum *adj* particular, especial;

praeda, praedae *n* **(1st)** *f* booty, loot, spoils, plunder, prey;

praeficio, praeficere, praefeci, praefectus *v* **(3rd)** put in charge, place in command (with *acc* and dat);

praemitto, praemittere, praemisi, praemissus *v* **(3rd)** send ahead or forward;

praenato, praenatare, praenatavi, praenatatus *v* **(1st)** swim by; flow by;

praescius, praescia, praescium *adj* having foreknowledge, prescient;

praesideo, praesidere, praesedi, - *v* **(2nd)** *dat* keep, watch, stand, , guard

(over); preside (over); supervise, govern, control;

praestans, praestantis (gen.), praestantior -or -us, praestantissimus -a -um *adj* excellent, outstanding (in quality, worth, degree, importance), surpassing all;

praesto *adv* ready, available, at hand, waiting, on the spot, at one's service;

praesto, praestare, praestavi, praestatus *v* **(1st)** excel, surpass, be outstanding, superior, best, greater, preferable (to); prevail; furnish, supply, make available, hand over; tender, offer, present; play part; apply, bring to bear; fulfill, make good; keep word; be responsible for;

praetendo, praetendere, praetendi, praetentus *v* **(3rd)** stretch out; spread before; extend in front; allege in excuse;

praeterea *adv* besides, thereafter; in addition;

praeterlabor, praeterlabi, praeterlapsus sum *v* **(3rd)** *dep* glide or slip past;

praetexo, praetexere, praetexui, praetextus *v* **(3rd)** *trans* border; adorn; D:tragedy;

pratum, prati *n* **(2nd)** *n* meadow, meadowland; meadow grass, crop; broad expanse, field, plain (land, sea);

precor, precari, precatus sum *v* **(1st)** *dep* beg, implore, entreat; wish, pray for, to; pray, supplicate, beseech;

prehendo, prehendere, prehendi, prehensus *v* **(3rd)** *trans* catch, capture; take hold of, possession of, in hand, arrest; occupy; seize, grasp; catch up with; reach shore, harbour; understand, comprehend; get a grip on;

prehenso, prehensare, prehensavi, prehensatus *v* **(1st)** *trans* grasp, clutch at, constantly; lay hold of; accost, buttonhole; canvass, solicit;

premo, premere, pressi, pressus *v* **(3rd)**

press, press hard, pursue; oppress; overwhelm;

prendo, prendere, prendi, prensus *v* **(3rd)** *trans* catch, capture; take hold of, possession of, in hand, arrest; occupy; seize, grasp; catch up with; reach shore, harbour; understand, comprehend; get a grip on;

pretium, preti(i) *n* **(2nd)** *n* price, value, worth; reward, pay; money; prayer;

prex, precis *n* **(3rd)** *f* prayer, request;

primo *adv* at first; in the first place; at the beginning;

primus, prima, primum *adj* first, foremost, best, chief, principal; nearest, next; [in primis => especially];

principio, principiare, principiavi, principiatus *v* **(1st)** begin to speak;

principium, principi(i) *n* **(2nd)** *n* beginning;

prior, prior, prius *adj* ahead, in front, leading; previous, earlier, preceding, prior; former; basic;

priscus, prisca, priscum *adj* ancient, early, former;

pristinus, pristina, pristinum *adj* former, oldtime, original; pristine;

prius *adv* earlier, before, previously, first;

prius, prioris *n* **(3rd)** *n* earlier times, events, actions; a logically prior proposition

pro *prep abl* on behalf of; before; in front, instead of; for; about; according to; as, like;

procerus, procera -um, procerior -or - us, procerissimus -a -um *adj* tall; long; high, lofty, upraised; grown, extended to great height, length;

procul *adv* away; at distance, far off;

procumbo, procumbere, procubui, procubitus *v* **(3rd)** sink down, lie down, lean forward;

prodigium, prodigi(i) *n* **(2nd)** *n* portent; prodigy, wonder;

profanus, profana, profanum *adj* secular, profane; not initiated; impious;

profundus, profunda, profundum *adj* deep, profound; boundless; insatiable;

progenies, progeniei *n* **(5th)** *f* race, family, progeny;

prohibeo, prohibere, prohibui, prohibitus *v* **(2nd)** hinder, restrain; forbid, prevent;

proicio, proicere, proieci, proiectus *v* **(3rd)** *trans* throw down, throw out; abandon; throw away;

proles, prolis *n* **(3rd)** *f* offspring, descendant; that springs by birth, descent; generation; race, breed;

promitto, promittere, promisi, promissus *v* **(3rd)** promise;

propago, propagare, propagavi, propagatus *v* **(1st)** propagate; extend, enlarge, increase;

properus, propera, properum *adj* quick, speedy;

propinquus, propinqua, propinquum *adj* near, neighbouring;

propior, propior, propius *adj* nearer, closer; more recent;

proprius, propria, proprium *adj* own, very own; individual; special, particular, characteristic;

prora, prorae *n* **(1st)** *f* prow;

prosequor, prosequi, prosecutus sum *v* **(3rd)** *dep* pursue; escort; describe in detail;

prospicio, prospicere, prospexi, prospectus *v* **(3rd)** foresee; see far off; watch for, provide for, look out for;

protinus *adv* straight on, forward; immediately; without pause; at once;

proximus, proxima, proximum *adj* nearest, closest, next; most recent, immediately preceding, last; most, very like;

pubes, (gen.), puberis *adj* adult, grown-up; full of sap;

puella, puellae *n* (1st) *f* girl, (female) child, daughter; maiden; young woman, wife; sweetheart; slavegirl;

puer, pueri *n* (2nd) *m* boy, lad, young man; servant; (male) child;

pugno, pugnare, pugnavi, pugnatus *v* (1st) fight; dispute;

pulcher, pulchra -um, pulchrior -or -us, pulcherrimus -a -um *adj* pretty; beautiful; handsome; noble, illustrious;

pulso, pulsare, pulsavi, pulsatus *v* (1st) beat; pulsate;

puppis, puppis *n* (3rd) *f* stern, aft (of ship); poop; ship; back;

purpureus, purpurea, purpureum *adj* purple, dark red;

purus, pura -um, purior -or -us, purissimus -a -um *adj* pure, clean, unsoiled; free from defilement, taboo, stain; blameless, innocent; chaste, unpolluted by sex; plain, unadulterated; genuine; absolute; refined; clear, limpid, free of mist, cloud; ringing (voice); open (land); net; simple;

puto, putare, putavi, putatus *v* (1st) *trans* think, believe, suppose, hold; reckon, estimate, value; clear up, settle;

pyra, pyrae *n* (1st) *f* funeral pile, pyre;

qua *adv* where; by which route;

quadrigarius, quadrigaria, quadrigarium *adj* of a racing charioteer;

quaero, quaerere, quaesivi, quaesitus *v* (3rd) search for, seek, strive for; obtain; ask, inquire, demand;

quaesitus, quaesita -um, quaesitior -or -us, quaesitissimus -a -um *adj* special, sought out, looked for; select; artificial, studied, affected;

qualis, qualis, quale *adj* what kind, sort, condition (of); what is (he, it) like; what, how excellent a ...;

quam *adv* how, how much; as, than; [quam + superlative => as ... as possible];

quam *conj* how, than;

quamquam *conj* though, although; yet; nevertheless;

quando *adv* when (interog), at what time; at any time (indef adv);

quando *conj* when, since, because;

quantus, quanta, quantum *adj* how great; how much, many; of what size, amount, degree, number, worth, price;

quasso, quassare, quassavi, quassatus *v* (1st) shake repeatedly; wave, flourish; batter; weaken;

quatio, quatere, -, quassus *v* (3rd) shake;

quattuor, quartus -a -um, quaterni -ae -a, – *num* four;

queo, quire, quivi(ii), quitus *v* be able;

quercus, quercus *n* (4th) *f* oak, oak-tree; oak wood, timber, object; oak leaf garland (honour); sea-oak;

qui *adv* how?; how so; in what way; by what, which means; whereby; at whatever price;

qui, quae, qua *pron* any; some; someone (preceded by si, nisi, numquid, ne), something, anyone;

qui, quae, quod *pron* who, which; (relative pronoun);

quies, quietis *n* (3rd) *f* quiet, calm, rest, peace; sleep;

quiesco, quiescere, quievi, quietus *v* (3rd) rest, keep quiet, calm, be at peace, rest; be inactive, neutral; permit; sleep;

quin *conj* so that not, without; that not; but that; that; [quin etiam => moreover];

quinquaginta, quinquagesimus -a -um, quinquageni -ae -a, quinquagie(n)s *num* fifty;

quis, quis, quid *pron* anyone, anybody, anything; someone, something; one or another;

quis, quis, quid *pron* who?, which one?, what man?, what thing? (type, nature); what kind of; what?;

quisquam, quaequam, quidquam *pack adiect* (w, -quam) any; anyone, anybody;

quisque, quaeque, quodque *pack* (w, -que) each, each one; every, everybody, everything (more than 2); whatever;

quisquis *pron* 1 2 *nom* **S** *c* whoever; every one who; whoever it be; everyone; each;

quondam *adv* formerly, once, at one time; some day, hereafter;

quot, undeclined *adj* how many; of what number; as many;

quotannis *adv* every year, yearly;

rabidus, rabida, rabidum *adj* mad, raging, frenzied, wild;

rabies, rabiei *n* **(5th)** *f* madness;

radius, radi(i) *n* **(2nd)** *m* ray; rod;

ramus, rami *n* **(2nd)** *m* branch, bough;

rapidus, rapida -um, rapidior -or -us, rapidissimus -a -um *adj* rapid, swift;

rapio, rapere, rapui, raptus *v* **(3rd)** drag off; snatch; destroy; seize, carry off; pillage; hurry;

ratio, rationis *n* **(3rd)** *f* account, reckoning, invoice; plan; prudence; method; reasoning; rule; regard;

ratis, ratis *n* **(3rd)** *f* raft; ship, boat;

raucus, rauca, raucum *adj* hoarse; husky; raucous;

rebellis, rebellis *n* **(3rd)** *m* insurgent, rebel;

rebello, rebellare, rebellavi, rebellatus *v* **(1st)** rebel, revolt;

recens, (gen.), recentis *adj* fresh, recent;

rested;

recenseo, recensere, recensui, recensitus *v* **(2nd)** *trans* review, examine, survey, muster; enumerate, count, make census, roll; pass in review;

recipio, recipere, recepi, receptus *v* **(3rd)** keep back; recover; undertake; guarantee; accept, take in; take back;

recolo, recolere, recolui, recultus *v* **(3rd)** cultivate afresh; go over in one's mind;

rectus, recta -um, rectior -or -us, rectissimus -a -um *adj* right, proper; straight; honest;

recubo, recubare, recubui, recubitus *v* **(1st)** lie down, back, recline, lie on the back;

reddo, reddere, reddidi, redditus *v* **(3rd)** return; restore; deliver; hand over, pay back, render, give back; translate;

redeo, redire, redivi(ii), reditus *v* return, go back, give back; fall back on, revert to; respond, pay back;

redimo, redimere, redemi, redemptus *v* **(3rd)** *trans* buy back, recover, replace by purchase; buy up; make good, fulfill (promise); redeem; atone for; ransom; rescue, save; contract for; buy, purchase; buy off;

refero, referre, rettuli, relatus *v* bring, carry back, again, home; move, draw, force back, withdraw; go back, return; report (on), bring back news; record, enter; propose, open debate; assign, count; give, pay back, render, tender; restore; redirect; revive, repeat; recall;

refigo, refigere, refixi, refixus *v* **(3rd)** unfix, unfasten, detach; pull out, take off, tear down;

refringo, refringere, refregi, refractus *v* **(3rd)** break open;

refugus, refuga, refugum *adj* fleeing, receding;

refulgeo, refulgere, refulsi, - *v* **(2nd)** flash back, reflect light; shine brightly;

gleam, glitter, glisten;

refundo, refundere, refudi, refusus *v* **(3rd)** pour back;

regina, reginae *n* (1st) *f* queen;

regio, regionis *n* **(3rd)** *f* area, region; neighbourhood; district, country; direction;

regno, regnare, regnavi, regnatus *v* (1st) reign, rule; be king; play the lord, be master;

regnum, regni *n* **(2nd)** *n* royal power; power; control; kingdom;

rego, regere, rexi, rectus *v* **(3rd)** rule, guide; manage, direct;

relictus, relicta -um, relictior -or -us, relictissimus -a -um *adj* forsaken, abandoned, derelict; left untouched;

relinquo, relinquere, reliqui, relictus *v* **(3rd)** leave behind, abandon; (pass.) be left, remain; bequeath;

remigium, remigi(i) *n* **(2nd)** *n* rowing, oarage;

remugio, remugire, -, – *v* **(4th)** bellow back, moo in reply; resound;

reno, renonis *n* **(3rd)** *m* reindeer-skin; deerskin garment; fur cloak;

reor, reri, ratus sum *v* **(2nd)** *dep* think, regard; deem; suppose, believe, reckon;

reperio, reperire, repperi, repertus *v* **(4th)** *trans* discover, learn; light on; find, obtain, get; find out, to be, get to know; invent;

repono, reponere, reposui, repositus *v* **(3rd)** put back; restore; store; repeat;

reposco, reposcere, -, – *v* **(3rd)** demand back; claim as one's due;

requies, requietis *n* **(3rd)** *f* rest (from labour), respite; intermission, pause, break; amusement, hobby;

requiro, requirere, requisivi, requisitus *v* **(3rd)** require, seek, ask for; need; miss, pine for;

res, rei *n* **(5th)** *f* thing; event, affair, business; fact; cause; property; [~ familiaris => property];

rescindo, rescindere, rescidi, rescissus *v* **(3rd)** cut out; cut down, destroy; annul; rescind;

resideo, residere, resedi, resessus *v* **(2nd)** sit down, on, in; settle; be perched; remain seated, idle, fixed, in place; squat; abate, subside; be left over, retained, persist, stay; fall back; W:be encamped;

resido, residere, residi, – *v* **(3rd)** sit down; settle; abate; subside, quieten down;

resolvo, resolvere, resolvi, resolutus *v* **(3rd)** loosen, release, disperse, melt; relax; pay; enervate, pay back; break up;

respicio, respicere, respexi, respectus *v* **(3rd)** look back at; gaze at; consider; respect; care for, provide for;

respondeo, respondere, respondi, responsus *v* **(2nd)** answer;

responsum, responsi *n* **(2nd)** *n* answer, response;

restituo, restituere, restitui, restitutus *v* **(3rd)** restore; revive; bring back; make good;

revello, revellere, revelli, revulsus *v* **(3rd)** *trans* tear, pull away, loose, out, from, down, up; wrench off; remove (person); raise, pull up (skin); pluck away, loose; open (vein); violate, disturb;

reverto, revertere, reverti, – *v* **(3rd)** turn back, go back, return; recur (usually DEP);

reviso, revisere, -, – *v* **(3rd)** revisit, go back and see;

revoco, revocare, revocavi, revocatus *v* **(1st)** call back, recall; revive; regain;

revolvo, revolvere, revolvi, revolutus *v* **(3rd)** throw back, roll back;

rex, regis *n* **(3rd)** *m* king;

rigo, rigare, rigavi, rigatus *v* **(1st)**

Aeneid VI

moisten, wet, water, irrigate;

rimosus, rimosa, rimosum *adj* full of cracks or fissures;

ripa, ripae *n* (1st) *f* bank;

rite *adv* duly, according to religious usage, with due observance; solemnly; well;

robur, roboris *n* (3rd) *n* oak (tree, timber, trunk, club, post, cell); tough core; resolve, purpose; strength, firmness, solidity; vigour, robustness; potency, force, effectiveness; military strength, might, power; heart, main strength, strongest element; mainstay, bulwark, source of strength; stronghold, position of strength;

rogus, rogi *n* (2nd) *m* funeral pyre;

rostrum, rostri *n* (2nd) *n* beak, curved bow (of a ship); speaker's platform (in Rome's Forum) (pl.);

rota, rotae *n* (1st) *f* wheel (rotate);

rumpo, rumpere, rupi, ruptus *v* (3rd) break; destroy;

ruo, ruere, rui, rutus *v* (3rd) destroy, ruin, overthrow; rush on, run; fall; charge (in + acc); be ruined;

rupes, rupis *n* (3rd) *f* cliff; rock;

rursus *adv* turned back, backward; on the contrary, other hand, in return, in turn, again;

sacer, sacra, sacrum *adj* sacred, holy, consecrated; accursed, horrible, detestable;

sacerdos, sacerdotis *n* (3rd) *c* priest, priestess;

sacro, sacrare, sacravi, sacratus *v* (1st) consecrate, make sacred, dedicate;

sacrum, sacri *n* (2nd) *n* sacrifice; sacred vessel; religious rites (pl.);

saeculum, saeculi *n* (2nd) *n* age; generation, people born at a time; breed; race; present time, age; century;

saeps, saepis *n* (3rd) *f* hedge; fence; anything planted, erected to form surrounding barrier;

saevus, saeva -um, saevior -or -us, saevissimus -a -um *adj* savage; fierce, ferocious; violent, wild, raging; cruel, harsh, severe; vehement;

saevus, saeva -um, saevior -or -us, saevissimus -a -um *adj* savage; fierce, ferocious; violent, wild, raging; cruel, harsh, severe; vehement;

saltem *adv* at least, anyhow, in all events; (on to more practical idea); even, so much as;

salus, salutis *n* (3rd) *f* health; prosperity; good wish; greeting; salvation, safety;

sancio, sancire, sanxi, sanctus *v* (4th) *trans* confirm, ratify; sanction; fulfill (prophesy); enact (law); ordain; dedicate;

sanctus, sancta -um, sanctior -or -us, sanctissimus -a -um *adj* consecrated, sacred, inviolable; venerable, august, divine, holy, pious, just;

sanguis, sanguinis *n* (3rd) *m* blood; family;

satis, undeclined *adj* enough, adequate, sufficient; satisfactory;

satus, sata, satum *adj* sprung (from); native;

saxum, saxi *n* (2nd) *n* stone;

scelestus, scelesta, scelestum *adj* infamous, wicked; accursed;

scelus, sceleris *n* (3rd) *n* crime; calamity; wickedness, sin, evil deed;

scilicet *adv* one may know, certainly; of course;

scindo, scindere, scicidi, scisus *v* (3rd) *trans* tear, rend, cut to pieces; tear (clothes, hair) in rage, grief, despair;

scrupeus, scrupea, scrupeum *adj* composed of sharp rocks;

seclusus, seclusa, seclusum *adj* remote;

199

seco, secare, secavi, secatus *v* **(1st)** *trans* cut, sever; decide; divide in two, halve, split; slice, chop, cut up, carve; detach;

secretum, secreti *n* **(2nd)** *n* secret, mystic rite, haunt;

securis, securis *n* **(3rd)** *f* ax (battle, headsman's), hatchet, chopper; (death) blow; vine-dresser's blade; ax (bundled in fasces); sovereignty (usu. pl.), authority, domain, supremacy;

securus, secura, securum *adj* secure, safe, untroubled, free from care;

sed *conj* but, but also; yet; however, but in fact, truth; not to mention; yes but;

sedeo, sedere, sedi, sessus *v* **(2nd)** sit, remain; settle; encamp;

sedes, sedis *n* **(3rd)** *f* seat; home, residence; settlement, habitation; chair;

semen, seminis *n* **(3rd)** *n* seed;

semper *adv* always;

senectus, senectutis *n* **(3rd)** *f* old age; extreme age; senility; old men; gray hairs; shed snake skin;

senex, senis (gen.), senior -or -us, - *adj* aged, old;

senior, senioris *n* **(3rd)** *m* older, elderly man, senior; (in Rome a man over 45);

sensus, sensus *n* **(4th)** *m* feeling, sense;

sepelio, sepelire, sepelivi, sepultus *v* **(4th)** *trans* bury, inter; (Romans cremate + inter ashes); submerge, overcome; suppress; ruin;

septem, septimus -a -um, septeni -ae -a, septie(n)s *num* seven;

septemgeminus, septemgemina, septemgeminum *adj* sevenfold;

septentrionalis, septentrionalis, septentrionale *adj* northern, north;

sepulcrum, sepulcri *n* **(2nd)** *n* grave, tomb;

sepultus, sepulti *n* **(2nd)** *m* grave; burial;

sequentia, sequentiae *n* **(1st)** *f* sequence;

sequor, sequi, secutus sum *v* **(3rd)** *dep* follow; escort, attend, accompany; aim at, reach after, strive for, make for, seek; support, back, side with; obey, observe; pursue, chase; range, spread over; attain;

serenus, serena, serenum *adj* clear, fair, bright; serene, tranquil; cheerful, glad;

sermo, sermonis *n* **(3rd)** *m* conversation, discussion; rumor; diction; speech; talk; the word;

serus, sera -um, serior -or -us, serissimus -a -um *adj* late; too late; slow, tardy; after the expected, proper time; at a late hour;

servo, servare, additional, forms *v* watch over; protect, store, keep, guard, preserve, save;

seu *conj* or if; or; [sive ... sive => whether ... or, either ... or];

si *conj* if, if only; whether; [quod si, si quis or quid => but if, if anyone or anything];

sic *adv* thus, so; as follows; in another way; in such a way;

siccus, sicca, siccum *adj* dry;

sidus, sideris *n* **(3rd)** *n* star; constellation;

signum, signi *n* **(2nd)** *n* battle standard; indication; seal; sign, proof; signal; image, statue;

sileo, silere, silui, – *v* **(2nd)** be silent, not to speak (about); be quiet; not to function;

silex, silicis *n* **(3rd)** *c* pebble, stone, flint; boulder, stone;

silva, silvae *n* **(1st)** *f* wood, forest (sylvan);

similis, simile, similior -or -us, simillimus -a -um *adj* like, similar, resembling;

simplex, simplicis *adj* single; simple, unaffected; plain;

simul *adv* at the same time; likewise; also; simultaneously; at once;

simulans, (gen.), simulantis *adj* imitating;

simulo, simulare, simulavi, simulatus *v* **(1st)** imitate, copy; pretend (to have, be); look like; simulate; counterfeit; feint;

sine *prep abl* without; (sometimes after object); lack;

singulus, singula, singulum *adj* apiece (pl.); every; one each, at a time; individual, separate, single; several;

sinister, sinistera -um, sinisterior -or - us, sinistimus -a -um *adj* left, improper, adverse; inauspicious;

sinistra, sinistrae *n* **(1st)** *f* left hand;

sino, sinere, sivi, situs *v* **(3rd)** allow, permit;

sinus, sinus *n* **(4th)** *m* curved or bent surface; bending, curve, fold; bosom, lap; bay;

sisto, sistere, stiti, status *v* **(3rd)** stop, check; cause to stand; set up;

situs, situs *n* **(4th)** *m* situation, position, site; structure; neglect, disuse, stagnation; mold;

sive *conj* or if; or;

socer, soceri *n* **(2nd)** *m* father in law;

socius, soci(i) *n* **(2nd)** *m* associate, companion; ally;

sol, solis *n* **(3rd)** *m* sun;

solacium, solaci(i) *n* **(2nd)** *n* comfort, solace; relief in sorrow, misfortune; source of comfort, consolation; consolation for disappointment, deprivation; compensation, indemnification;

soleo, solere, solitus sum *v* **(2nd)** *semidep* be in the habit of; become accustomed to;

solidus, solida -um, solidior -or -us, solidissimus -a -um *adj* solid; same material throughout, unalloyed; not hollow; dense; unbroken, whole; three dimensional; retaining form, rigidity,

firm; real, lasting; perfect; full;

sollemnis, sollemne, sollemnior -or -us, sollemnissimus -a -um *adj* solemn, ceremonial, sacred, in accordance w, religion, law; traditional, customary;

solvo, solvere, solvi, solutus *v* **(3rd)** loosen, release, unbind, untie, free; open; set sail; scatter; pay off, back;

somnium, somni(i) *n* **(2nd)** *n* dream, vision; fantasy, day-dream;

somnus, somni *n* **(2nd)** *m* sleep;

sonitus, sonitus *n* **(4th)** *m* noise, loud sound;

sono, sonare, sonavi, sonatus *v* **(1st)** make a noise, sound; speak, utter, emit sound; be spoken of (as); express, denote; echo, resound; be heard, sound; be spoken of (as); celebrate in speech;

sopor, soporis *n* **(3rd)** *m* deep sleep;

soporo, soporare, soporavi, soporatus *v* **(1st)** rend to sleep, render unconscious, stupefy;

sordidus, sordida -um, sordidior -or - us, sordidissimus -a -um *adj* dirty, unclean, foul, filthy; vulgar, sordid; low, base, mean, paltry; vile;

soror, sororis *n* **(3rd)** *f* sister; (applied also to half sister, sister-in-law, and mistress!);

sors, sortis *n* **(3rd)** *f* lot, fate; oracular response;

spargo, spargere, sparsi, sparsus *v* **(3rd)** scatter, strew, sprinkle; spot;

spatium, spati(i) *n* **(2nd)** *n* space; area, expanse, room (for); intervening space, gap, interval; length, width; race course, lap, circuit; closed way, walk, turn; track (planet); act of play; interval, time, extent, period, term; duration; distance; area; size; bulk;

species, speciei *n* **(5th)** *f* sight, appearance, show; splendor, beauty; kind, type;

spectaculum, spectaculi *n* **(2nd)** *n* show, spectacle; spectators' seats (pl.);

spelunca, speluncae *n* **(1st)** *f* cave;

spero, sperare, speravi, speratus *v* **(1st)** hope for; trust; look forward to; hope;

spes, spei *n* **(5th)** *f* hope, anticipation, expectation; prospect, hope, promise; (inheriting, succeeding); object, embodiment of hope; [optio ad ~ => junior hoping to make centurion]; spes, goddess of hope; hope personified;

spiritus, spiritus *n* **(4th)** *m* breath, breathing, air, soul, life;

spolio, spoliare, spoliavi, spoliatus *v* **(1st)** rob, strip; despoil, plunder; deprive (with abl.);

spolium, spoli(i) *n* **(2nd)** *n* spoils, booty; skin, hide;

sponte *adv* of one's own will; voluntarily; for one's own sake;

spumo, spumare, spumavi, spumatus *v* **(1st)** foam, froth; be covered in foam; cover with foam;

spumosus, spumosa, spumosum *adj* foaming, frothy;

squalor, squaloris *n* **(3rd)** *m* squalor, filth;

stabulum, stabuli *n* **(2nd)** *n* stall, stable, enclosure, fold; lair, den; herd; garage; inn, tavern; brothel; dwelling, hut;

stagnum, stagni *n* **(2nd)** *n* pool, lake, lagoon, expanse of water; bath, swimming pool;

stella, stellae *n* **(1st)** *f* star; planet, heavenly body; point of light in jewel; constellation; star shape;

sterilis, sterilis, sterile *adj* barren, sterile; fruitless; unprofitable, futile;

sterno, sternere, stravi, stratus *v* **(3rd)** spread, strew, scatter; lay out;

stimulus, stimuli *n* **(2nd)** *m* spur, goad; trap, spike in earth; prick, sting, cause of

torment, torture instrument;

stirps, stirpis *n* **(3rd)** *f* race;

sto, stare, steti, status *v* **(1st)** stand, stand still, stand firm; remain, rest;

strages, stragis *n* **(3rd)** *f* overthrow; massacre, slaughter, cutting down; havoc; confused heap;

strepitus, strepitus *n* **(4th)** *m* noise, racket; sound; din, crash, uproar;

strideo, stridere, stridi, - *v* **(2nd)** *intrans* creak, squeak, grate, shriek, whistle; (make shrill sound); hiss; gnash;

stridor, stridoris *n* **(3rd)** *m* hissing, buzzing, rattling, whistling; high-pitched sound;

stringo, stringere, strinxi, strictus *v* **(3rd)** draw tight; draw; graze; strip off;

struo, struere, struxi, structus *v* **(3rd)** build, construct;

studium, studi(i) *n* **(2nd)** *n* eagerness, enthusiasm, zeal, spirit; devotion, pursuit, study;

sub *prep abl* under, beneath, behind, at the foot of (rest); within; during, about (time);

subduco, subducere, subduxi, subductus *v* **(3rd)** lead up, carry off; transfer; haul;

subeo, subire, subivi(ii), subitus *v* *intrans* go, move, pass, sink, extend underneath, into; climb, come, go up, ascend; steal in on; lace, be placed under, in support; come up w, aid; assume a form; undergo, endure

subiectus, subiecta -um, subiectior -or - us, subiectissimus -a -um *adj* lying near, humble; adjacent;

subigo, subigere, subegi, subactus *v* **(3rd)** conquer, subjugate; compel;

subito *adv* suddenly, unexpectedly; at once, at short notice, quickly; in no time at all;

sublimis, sublime, sublimior -or -us,

sublimissimus -a -um *adj* high, lofty; eminent, exalted, elevated; raised on high; in high position;

submoveo, submovere, submovi, submotus *v* **(2nd)** remove; drive off, dislodge; expel; ward off; keep at a distance; bar, debar;

subtraho, subtrahere, subtraxi, subtractus *v* **(3rd)** carry off; take away; subtract;

subvecto, subvectare, subvectavi, subvectatus *v* **(1st)** convey (often or laboriously) upwards;

succingo, succingere, succinxi, succinctus *v* **(3rd)** gather up with a belt or girdle; prepare for action; surround;

suesco, suescere, suevi, suetus *v* **(3rd)** become accustomed (to);

sui (gen) *pron* **reflex.** him, her, it, oneself; him, her, it; them (selves) (pl.); each other, one another;

summum, summi *n* **(2nd)** *n* top; summit, end, last; highest place; top surface; (voice) highest, loudest;

sumo, sumere, sumpsi, sumptus *v* **(3rd)** take up; begin; suppose, assume; select; purchase; exact (punishment); obtain;

super *adv* above, on top, over; upwards; moreover, in addition, besides;

super *prep abl* over (space), above, upon, in addition to; during (time); concerning; beyond;

super *prep acc* upon, on; over, above, about; besides (space); during (time); beyond (degree);

superbus, superba, superbum *adj* arrogant, overbearing, haughty, proud;

superemineo, supereminere, -, – *v* **(2nd)** overtop, stand out above the level of;

superus, supera -um, superior -or -us, supremus -a -um *adj* above, high; higher, upper, of this world; greatest, last, highest;

supplex, supplicis *n* **(3rd)** *m* suppliant;

supplicium, supplici(i) *n* **(2nd)** *n* punishment, suffering; supplication; torture;

supremum, supremi *n* **(2nd)** *n* funeral rites (pl.) or offerings;

surgo, surgere, surrexi, surrectus *v* **(3rd)** rise, lift; grow;

suscipio, suscipere, suscepi, susceptus *v* **(3rd)** undertake; support; accept, receive, take up;

suspendo, suspendere, suspendi, suspensus *v* **(3rd)** hang up, suspend;

suspicio, suspicere, suspexi, suspectus *v* **(3rd)** look up to; admire;

sutilis, sutilis, sutile *adj* made by sewing, consisting of things stitched together;

suus, sua, suum *adj* his, one's (own), her (own), hers, its (own); (pl.) their (own), theirs;

taceo, tacere, tacui, tacitus *v* **(2nd)** be silent; pass over in silence; leave unmentioned, be silent about something;

tacitus, tacita, tacitum *adj* silent, secret;

taedet, taedere, taeduit, taesus est *v* **(2nd)** *impers* be tired, weary, sick (of) (w, gen or inf+acc of person); be disgusted, offended;

talis, talis, tale *adj* such; so great; so excellent; of such kind;

tam *adv* so, so much (as); to such an extent, degree; nevertheless, all the same;

tamen *adv* yet, nevertheless, still;

tandem *adv* finally; at last, in the end; after some time, eventually; at length;

tantus, tanta, tantum *adj* of such size; so great, so much;

tardus, tarda -um, tardior -or -us, tardissimus -a -um *adj* slow, limping; deliberate; late;

taurus, tauri *n* **(2nd)** *m* bull;

taurus, tauri *n* **(2nd)** *m* bull;

tego, tegere, texi, tectus *v* **(3rd)** cover, protect; defend; hide;

tellus, telluris *n* **(3rd)** *f* earth, ground; the earth; land, country;

telum, teli *n* **(2nd)** *n* dart, spear; weapon, javelin; bullet (gun);

temno, temnere, -, - *v* **(3rd)** scorn, despise;

templum, templi *n* **(2nd)** *n* temple, church; shrine; holy place;

tempus, tempi *n* **(2nd)** *m* weather;

tenax, tenacis (gen.), tenacior -or -us, tenacissimus -a -um *adj* holding fast, clinging; tenacious; retentive; close-fisted, tight, niggardly; restraining; (fetters, embrace); steadfast, persistent; obstinate, stubborn;

tendo, tendere, tetendi, tensus *v* **(3rd)** stretch, spread, extend; distend; aim, direct weapon, glance, steps, course; strive; itch tent, encamp; pull tight; draw (bow); press on, insist; exert oneself;

tenebrasco, tenebrascere, -, - *v* **(3rd)** *intrans* grow dark; become dark;

tenebrosus, tenebrosa, tenebrosum *adj* dark, gloomy;

teneo, tenere, tenui, tentus *v* **(2nd)** hold, keep; comprehend; possess; master; preserve;]; represent; support;

tenus *prep abl* as far as, to the extent of, up to, down to;

tepidus, tepida, tepidum *adj* warm, tepid;

ter *adv* three times; on three occasions;

tergum, tergi *n* **(2nd)** *n* back, rear; reverse, far side; outer covering, surface;

terra, terrae *n* **(1st)** *f* earth, land, ground; country, region;

terrenus, terrena, terrenum *adj* of earth, earthly; earthy; terrestrial;

terribilis, terribilis, terribile *adj* frightful, terrible;

testor, testari, testatus sum *v* **(1st)** *dep* give as evidence; bear witness; make a will; swear; testify;

thalamus, thalami *n* **(2nd)** *m* bedroom; marriage;

tigris, tigridos/is *n m* tiger;

timor, timoris *n* **(3rd)** *m* fear; dread;

tollo, tollere, sustuli, sublatus *v* **(3rd)** *trans* lift, raise; destroy; remove, steal; take, lift up, away;

torqueo, torquere, torsi, tortus *v* **(2nd)** turn, twist; hurl; torture; torment; bend, distort; spin, whirl; wind (round);

torreo, torrere, torrui, tostus *v* **(2nd)** *trans* parch, roast, scorch, bake, burn; dry up; begin to burn; harden by charring;

torus, tori *n* **(2nd)** *m* swelling, protuberance; mussel, brawn; bed, couch, stuffed bolster, cushion;

torvus, torva, torvum *adj* pitiless, grim; fierce, stern, harsh, savage, dreadful; staring, piercing, wild (eye);

tot *num* as, so often, so many times, such a great number of times; that number of times;

totidem, undeclined *adj* as many; just so, as many; the equivalent number of, same (as specified before);

totus, tota, totum (gen -ius) *adj* whole, all, entire, total, complete; every part; all together, at once;

trabs, trabis *n* **(3rd)** *f* tree trunk; log, club, spear; beam, timber, rafter; ship, vessel; roof, house;

traho, trahere, traxi, tractus *v* **(3rd)** draw, drag, haul; derive, get;

trans *prep acc* across, over; beyond; on the other side; (only local relations);

transmitto, transmittere, transmisi, transmissus *v* **(3rd)** send across; go across; transmit;

transporto, transportare, transportavi,

transportatus *v* **(1st)** carry across, transport;

tremefacio, tremefacere, tremefeci, tremefactus *v* **(3rd)** *trans* cause to tremble;

tremor, tremoris *n* **(3rd)** *m* trembling, shuddering; quivering, quaking;

trepidus, trepida, trepidum *adj* nervous, jumpy, agitated; perilous, alarming, frightened; boiling, foaming;

tres -es -ia, tertius -a -um, terni -ae -a, ter *num* three;

tricorpor, (gen.), tricorporis *adj* having three bodies;

trifaux, (gen.), trifaucis *adj* triple-throated;

triplex, (gen.), triplicis *adj* threefold, triple; three;

tristis, tristis, triste *adj* sad, sorrowful; gloomy;

triumpho, triumphare, triumphavi, triumphatus *v* **(1st)** triumph over; celebrate a triumph; conquer completely, triumph;

truncus, trunci *n* **(2nd)** *m* trunk (of a tree);

tu, tui *pron pers* you, thee;

tuba, tubae *n* **(1st)** *f* trumpet (straight tube); (military signals, religious rites); hydraulic ram pipe;

tueor, tueri, tuitus sum *v* **(2nd)** *dep* see, look at; protect, watch; uphold;

tum *adv* then, next; besides; at that time; [cum...tum => not only...but also];

tumultus, tumultus *n* **(4th)** *m* commotion, confusion, uproar; rebellion, uprising, disturbance;

tumulus, tumuli *n* **(2nd)** *m* mound, hillock; mound, tomb;

tunc *adv* then, thereupon, at that time;

turba, turbae *n* **(1st)** *f* commotion, uproar, turmoil, tumult, disturbance; crowd, mob, multitude;

turbidus, turbida, turbidum *adj* wild, stormy; muddy, turbid; murky, foggy, clouded, opaque; gloomy, frowning; confused, disordered; impatient, troubled, dazed, frantic; unruly, mutinous;

turbo, turbare, turbavi, turbatus *v* **(1st)** disturb, agitate, throw into confusion;

tureus, turea, tureum *adj* of or connected with incense;

turpis, turpe, turpior -or -us, turpissimus -a -um *adj* ugly; nasty; disgraceful; indecent; base, shameful, disgusting, repulsive;

turris, turris *n* **(3rd)** *f* tower; high building, palace, citadel; dove tower, dove cot;

tuus, tua, tuum *adj* your (*sing.*);

uber, uberis (gen.), uberior -or -us, uberrimus -a -um *adj* fertile, rich, abundant, abounding, fruitful, plentiful, copious, productive;

ubi *adv* where; in what place; (time) when, whenever; as soon as; in which; with whom;

ulciscor, ulcisci, ultus sum *v* **(3rd)** *dep* avenge; punish;

ullus, ulla, ullum (gen -ius) *adj* any;

ulmus, ulmi *n* **(2nd)** *f* elm tree;

ulterior -or -us, ultimus -a -um *adj* far; farther; farthest; latest; last; highest, greatest;

ultimum *adv* extremely, to the last degree, utterly; finally, at last;

ultor, ultoris *n* **(3rd)** *m* avenger, revenger;

ultra *prep acc* beyond, on the other side, on that side; more than, besides;

ultra, ulterius, ultimum *adv* beyond, further; on the other side; more, more than, in addition, besides;

ultrix, (gen.), ultricis *adj* avenging, vengeful;

ultro *adv* besides, beyond; to, on the further, other side; voluntarily, unaided; wantonly;

ululo, ululare, ululavi, ululatus *v* (1st) howl, yell, shriek; celebrate or proclaim with howling;

umbra, umbrae *n* (1st) *f* shade; ghost; shadow;

umbrifer, umbrifera, umbriferum *adj* providing shade, shady;

umbro, umbrare, umbravi, umbratus *v* (1st) cast a shadow on, shade;

umerus, umeri *n* (2nd) *m* upper arm, shoulder;

umquam *adv* ever, at any time;

uncus, unci *n* (2nd) *m* hook, barb, clamp; hook in neck used to drag condemned, executed criminals;

unda, undae *n* (1st) *f* wave;

unde *adv* from where, whence, from what or which place; from which; from whom;

undo, undare, undavi, undatus *v* (1st) *intrans* surge, flood, rise in waves; gush, well up; run, stream; billow; undulate; waver;

unus -a -um, primus -a -um, singuli -ae -a, semel *num* one;

unus, una, unum (gen -ius) *adj* alone, a single, sole; some, some one; only (pl.); one set of (denoting entity);

urbs, urbis *n* (3rd) *f* city; City of Rome;

urgeo, urgere, ursi, – *v* (2nd) press, squeeze, bear hard, down; tread, traverse continually; push, shove, thrust; spur on, urge; press hard in attack, pursuit, beset, follow hard on heels of; hem in; threaten by proximity; press verbally, argument, point; follow up;

urna, urnae *n* (1st) *f* pot; cinerary urn; urn used for drawing lots; voting urn;

water jar;

usquam *adv* anywhere, in any place; to any place;

usque *adv* all the way, right on; all the time, continuously, at every point, always;

usque *prep acc* up to (name of town or locality);

ut *conj* to (+ subjunctive), in order that, to; how, as, when, while; even if;

utcumque *adv* whatever, as far as; in whatever manner, degree. no matter how, to what extent;

uterus, uteri *n* (2nd) *m* womb; belly, abdomen;

utor, uti, usus sum *v* (3rd) *dep* use, make use of, enjoy; enjoy the friendship of (with *abl*);

vacca, vaccae *n* (1st) *f* cow;

vacuus, vacua, vacuum *adj* empty, vacant, unoccupied; devoid of, free of;

vado, vadare, -, – *v* (1st) ford;

vagina, vaginae *n* (1st) *f* sheath, scabbard;

vagitus, vagitus *n* (4th) *m* crying;

vagor, vagari, vagatus sum *v* (1st) *dep* wander, roam;

valeo, valere, valui, valitus *v* (2nd) be strong, powerful, influential, healthy; prevail; bid farewell;

validus, valida, validum *adj* strong, powerful; valid;

vallis, vallis *n* (3rd) *f* valley, vale, hollow;

vanus, vana, vanum *adj* empty, vain; false, untrustworthy;

varius, varia, varium *adj* different; various, diverse; changing; coloured; party coloured, variegated;

vastus, vasta -um, vastior -or -us, vastissimus -a -um *adj* huge, vast; monstrous;

vates, vatis *n* **(3rd)** *m* prophet, seer, mouthpiece of deity; oracle, soothsayer; poet (divinely inspired);

vecto, vectare, vectavi, vectatus *v* **(1st)** *trans* transport, carry; (of habitual agent, means); (*passive*) ride, be conveyed, travel;

veho, vehere, vexi, vectus *v* **(3rd)** bear, carry, convey; pass, ride, sail;

vel *adv* even, actually; or even, in deed; or;

vel *conj* or; [vel ... vel => either ... or];

velamen, velaminis *n* **(3rd)** *n* veil; covering (esp. clothing for body, parts);

velut *adv* just as, as if;

veluti *adv* just as, as if;

vendo, vendere, vendidi, venditus *v* **(3rd)** sell;

venerabilis, venerabilis, venerabile *adj* venerable, august;

venio, venire, veni, ventus *v* **(4th)** come;

ventosus, ventosa, ventosum *adj* windy; swift (as the wind); fickle, changeable; vain, puffed up;

verbum, verbi *n* **(2nd)** *n* word; proverb; [verba dare alicui => cheat, deceive someone];

vereor, vereri, veritus sum *v* **(2nd)** *dep* revere, respect; fear; dread;

vertex, verticis *n* **(3rd)** *m* whirlpool, eddy, vortex; crown of the head; peak, top, summit; the pole;

verto, vertere, verti, versus *v* **(3rd)** turn, turn around; change, alter; overthrow, destroy;

verus, vera -um, verior -or -us, verissimus -a -um *adj* true, real, genuine, actual; properly named; well founded; right, fair, proper;

vescor, vesci, – *v* **(3rd)** *dep* feed on, eat, enjoy (with *abl*);

vester, vestra, vestrum *adj* your (pl.), of, belonging to, associated with you;

vestibulum, vestibuli *n* **(2nd)** *n* entrance, court;

vestigium, vestigi(i) *n* **(2nd)** *n* step, track; trace; footstep;

vestigo, vestigare, vestigavi, vestigatus *v* **(1st)** track down, search for; search out; try to find out by searching; investigate;

vestio, vestire, vestivi, vestitus *v* **(4th)** clothe;

vestis, vestis *n* **(3rd)** *f* garment, clothing, blanket; clothes; robe;

veto, vetare, vetavi, vetatus *v* **(1st)** *trans* forbid, prohibit; reject, veto; be an obstacle to; prevent;

via, viae *n* **(1st)** *f* way, road, street; journey;

vicissim *adv* in turn, again;

victor, victoris *n* **(3rd)** *m* conqueror; victor;

video, videre, vidi, visus *v* **(2nd)** see, look at; consider; (*passive*) seem, seem good, appear, be seen;

vigor, vigoris *n* **(3rd)** *m* vigour, liveliness;

vinco, vincere, vici, victus *v* **(3rd)** conquer, defeat, excel; outlast; succeed;

vinculum, vinculi *n* **(2nd)** *n* chain, bond, fetter; imprisonment (pl.);

vinum, vini *n* **(2nd)** *n* wine;

violentus, violenta, violentum *adj* violent, vehement, impetuous, boisterous;

vipereus, viperea, vipereum *adj* of a viper, snake; of vipers;

vir, viri *n* **(2nd)** *m* man; husband; hero; person of courage, honour, and nobility;

virectum, virecti *n* **(2nd)** *n* area of greenery;

vireo, virere, virui, – *v* **(2nd)** be green or verdant; be lively or vigourous; be full of youthful vigour;

virga, virgae *n* (1st) *f* twig, sprout, stalk; switch, rod; staff, wand; stripe, streak; scepter;

virgo, virginis *n* (3rd) *f* maiden, young woman, girl of marriageable age; virgin, woman sexually intact;

virgultum, virgulti *n* (2nd) *n* brushwood;

viridis, viridis, viride *adj* fresh, green; blooming,youthful;

virtus, virtutis *n* (3rd) *f* strength, power; courage, bravery; worth, manliness, virtue, character, excellence; army; host; mighty works (pl.);

virus, viri *n* (2nd) *n* venom (sg.), poisonous secretion of snakes, creatures, plants; acrid element;

vis, viris *n* (3rd) *f* strength (bodily) (pl.), force, power, might, violence; resources; large body;

viscus, visceris *n* (3rd) *n* soft fleshy body parts (usu. pl.), internal organs; entrails, flesh; offspring;

viscus, visci *n* (2nd) *m* mistletoe; bird-lime (made from mistletoe berries);

visum, visi *n* (2nd) *n* vision; that which is seen, appearance, sight; visual, mental image;

vita, vitae *n* (1st) *f* life, career, livelihood; mode of life;

vitta, vittae *n* (1st) *f* band, ribbon; fillet;

vivus, viva, vivum *adj* alive, fresh; living;

vix *adv* hardly, scarcely, barely, only just; with difficulty, not easily; reluctantly;

voco, vocare, vocavi, vocatus *v* (1st) call, summon; name; call upon;

volito, volitare, volitavi, volitatus *v* (1st) fly about, hover over;

volo, velle, volui, – *v* wish, want, prefer; be willing, will;

volo, volare, volavi, volatus *v* (1st) fly;

volucer, voluceris, volucere *adj* winged; able to fly; flying; in rapid motion, fleet, swift; transient, fleeting;

voluntas, voluntatis *n* (3rd) *f* will, desire; purpose; good will; wish, favour, consent;

voluto, volutare, volutavi, volutatus *v* (1st) roll, wallow, turn over in one's mind, think or talk over;

volvo, volvere, volvi, volutus *v* (3rd) *trans* roll, cause to roll; travel in circle, circuit; bring around, about; revolve; envelop, wrap up; unroll (scroll); recite, reel off; turn over (in mind); roll along, forward; (*passive*) move sinuously (snake); grovel, roll on ground;

votum, voti *n* (2nd) *n* vow, pledge, religious undertaking, promise; prayer, wish; votive offering; vote;

vox, vocis *n* (3rd) *f* voice, tone, expression;

vulgus, vulgi *n* (2nd) *n* common people, general public, multitude, common herd, rabble, crowd, mob; flock;

vulnus, vulneris *n* (3rd) *n* wound; mental, emotional hurt; injury to one's interests; wound of love;

vultus, vultus *n* (4th) *m* face, expression; looks;

40397556R00129

Printed in Poland
by Amazon Fulfillment
Poland Sp. z o.o., Wrocław